R O W A N

KNITTING & CROCHET
Magazine Number 65

INCLUDES 42 DESIGNS

STORIES

FEATURES

REGULAR FEATURES

THE
DESIGNERS

ROWAN

Lisa Richardson

Martin Storey

Sarah Hatton

Kaffe Fassett

ARNE & CARLOS

Vibe Ulrik

Galina Caroll

Sasha Kagan

Sharon Miller

Grace Jones

Emma Wright

Annika Andrea Wolke

Dee Hardwicke

quail studio

Quail Studio

ROWAN
EST 1978

. . . .

MODERN
HERITAGE

*A collection of 12 designs taking inspiration from heritage
knitting techniques of the British Isles and Ireland.*

. . . .

ROWAN

KIRKIN
Summerlite 4ply & Kidsilk Haze
Sasha Kagan
125

AESTER
Cotton Cashmere
ARNE & CARLOS
140

OWRE
Summerlite DK
Vibe Ulrik
139

YATLEN
Kidsilk Haze
Grace Jones
116

RAKKI
Kidsilk Haze & Fine Lace
Martin Storey
134

WITTER
Softyak DK
Martin Storey
160

18

PENGA
Creative Linen
Emma Wright
150

TOORIE
Felted Tweed
Martin Storey
154

TOORIE
Felted Tweed
Martin Storey
154

MAREEL
Cotton Cashmere
Sarah Hatton
130

CUGGLE
Creative Linen
Lisa Richardson
152

GENNER
Cotton Cashmere
ARNE & CARLOS
129

BISMAR
Summerlite 4ply
Annika Andrea Wolke
146

Photographer: Craig Fordham. **Styling & Art Direction:** Lisa Richardson. **Hair & Make Up:** Michaela Taylor
Model: Tegan Dermek (Nevs Models) **Location:** Edale in Derbyshire.

THE ARNE & CARLOS CUSHION COLLECTION

ARNE & CARLOS have created a striking set of cushions
to enliven any living room

Words by Rosee Woodland

. . . .

ROWAN

Built on a foundation of Norwegian folk art and a playful love for colour, the new cushion collection from ARNE & CARLOS features an array of designs that can be mixed and matched to the maker's desire.

There are four floral patterns and four geometric patterns, which can either be used with a plain cushion back, or paired front and back to spectacular effect.

Much of the work of ARNE & CARLOS is influenced by Norway's rich textile heritage, which they reimagine using both classic and contemporary colourways.

The larger motifs in these new cushions echo both the designs found in rosemaling – a form of Norwegian floral painting, and those seen in Norwegian embroidery, while the smaller repeating patterns offer a new twist on Scandinavian colourwork, tapestry and cross stitch.

The designs all have been worked up in Softyak DK. It's a cotton and yak fibre mix chainette yarn with a rich colour palette and a luxurious feel. Helpfully, it's machine washable too, making it perfect for homewares.

Whether you choose to work the small or large motifs – or indeed combine them – this set of new cushion designs from ARNE & CARLOS is sure to find a happy place in your home.

The ARNE & CARLOS Cushion Collection is available to download now from knitrowan.com

01. Geometric Cushions Britta (version B), Greta (version B), Kerstin (version B) & Agda (version B).
02. Kerstin Floral (version A).
03. Kerstin Geometric (version B) & Greta Floral (version A).
04. Greta Geometric & Floral versions.
05. Geometric Cushions Kerstin (version B), Britta (version B), Greta (version B), & Agda (version B).
06. Agda Geometric (version B) & Floral (version A).

02

05

06

07 & 12. The full collection of Geometric (version B) & Floral (version A).

08 & 09. Britta Geometric (version B) & Floral (version A).

10. Floral (versions A), Britta, Greta, Agda & Kerstin.   **11.** Greta Floral (version A).

13. Agda Floral (version A), Kerstin Geometric (version B), Britta Floral (version A), Britta Plain back (version B) & Greta Floral (version A).

Photographer: Hannah Webster. **Art Direction:** Lisa Richardson. **Location:** Brook House Farm.

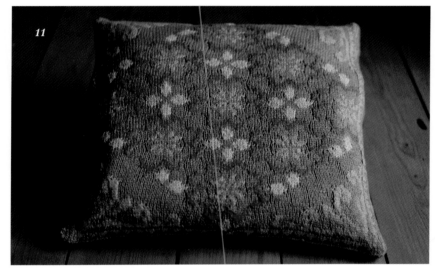

PLAIN & SIMPLE

A collection of 10 essential pieces, designed to compliment your wardrobe classics.

ROWAN

ELEMENTARY
Softyak DK
Martin Storey
148

ESSENTIAL
Fine Lace
Lisa Richardson
156

42

MINIMAL
Cotton Glacé
Martin Storey
122

RESTORE
Cotton Glacé & Kidsilk Haze
Lisa Richardson
136

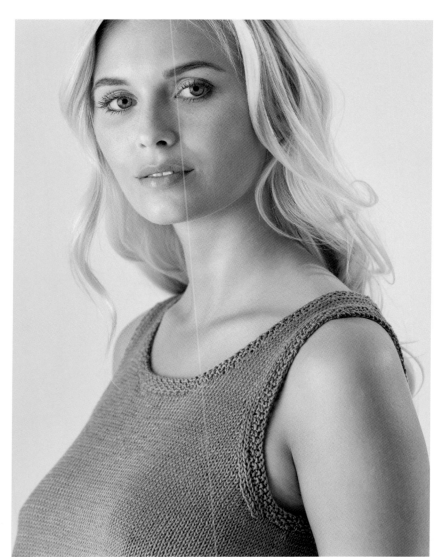

RECLAIM
Softyak DK
Martin Storey
109

48

INTRINSIC
Creative Linen
Lisa Richardson
127

50

PURPOSE
Creative Linen
Lisa Richardson
118

REGAIN
Kidsilk Haze
Martin Storey
161

VITAL
Fine Lace
Lisa Richardson
110

56

SIMPLE
Kidsilk Haze & Fine Lace
Martin Storey
121

Photographer: Jesse Wild. **Styling & Art Direction:** Georgina Brant.
Hair & Make Up: Lauren Palmer. **Model:** Elvira B (BMA Models).

TRAVEL WARDROBE

Words by Annika Andrea Wolke

ROWAN

Spring and summer time is also travel time, and while you might not consider your knitted creations suitable for your travel wardrobe, at Rowan we think there is no better time to show off your handknit creations. Which is why we have put together a few of our favourite garments from this magazine to inspire your travel wardrobe. As well as a few useful tips for packing a minimal yet stylish travel wardrobe this summer.

We all know how stressful holiday packing can be, especially when you are only taking carry-on luggage. However, one of the best rules for putting together your travel wardrobe is really straightforward. Simply select pieces that are versatile and that you will get a lot of wear out of during your stay.

Always consider the weather wherever you are going. Packing your favourite woolly cable jumper makes little sense if you are going to a hot climate, but if you are going to Iceland, even in summertime, it might be worth considering. And don't forget to consider the activities you are planning to do. For a relaxed time at the beach you might need fewer knitted garments, whereas on a city break you could require a variety of pieces appropriate for churches, museums and restaurants.

Before you start pulling items together settle on a colour scheme. Pick up to three colours that go well together. For our selection of knitted pieces, we stuck to white, blue and green as our basics and added a little pop of colour with a purple vest top. Limiting your colour scheme

61

ensures that all of your pieces will work well together.

To achieve a travel wardrobe that allows you to mix and match, you will need about four tops. Depending on the weather, these can be a combination of sleeveless, short and/or long sleeve. You will also need three bottoms, such as a pair of jeans or linen trousers, as well as two dresses or skirts. Consider making one of these pieces something that you can wear on an evening. It is also advisable to take at least one cardigan and/or jumper for colder mornings and evenings, or a shawl if you feel that this is a more versatile option for your chosen garments.

With all the basics of packing a versatile travel wardrobe covered, let's look in more detail at the pieces we chose and tell you why we think

they make the perfect travel companions.

Essential, Restore and Paloma by Lisa Richardson, have all been designed in solid colours, which make them easy to combine with other items. However, each garment features little details that make them unique. Essential, knitted in Fine Lace, is the perfect, delicate summer vest top and features a beautiful picot and lace detail hem. Restore is our real pop of colour in this selection. It is knitted in Cotton Glace and uses Kidsilk Haze for the inside of a back pleat. This is a lovely little detail that works well with trousers and skirts. The last top we selected is another piece knitted in Fine Lace. Paloma features a beautiful lace panel on the body, as well as on the sleeve hems. It would look beautiful with a skirt or dress, perfect for a night out!

63

For when you are in need of an extra layer we have selected Witter by Martin Storey, a patterned and textured jumper that's easy to mix and match. It is knitted in Softyak DK, which makes this garment exceptionally lightweight. For the perfect travel cardigan, we have selected Bismar, knitted in Summerlite 4ply and featuring an all-over lace pattern. This light cardigan, by Annika Andrea Wolke, works well with all the tops selected and can easily be worn with trousers and dresses.

The last piece we selected is Fontana. This patterned shawl by ARNE & CARLOS is an eye-catching accessory, perfectly suited as an extra layer if a cardigan or jumper is too warm or as a comforting wrap when faced with freezing air conditioning on the plane. It is knitted in Cotton Cashmere, which makes this a cosy, yet lightweight accessory.

Although not an obvious choice, we hope that we've inspired you to incorporate your lovely handknits into your travel wardrobe and take delight in discovering new designs in this magazine. Now you are ready to pack stress-free, sit back and relax wherever your travels may take you, enjoying your knitwear all year round, whatever the climate. Bon voyage!

Photographer: Moy Williams. **Art Direction & Styling:** Grace Jones. **Hair & Make-up:** Liz Rochford (Boss models). **Model:** Eleanor Davis (Boss Models).

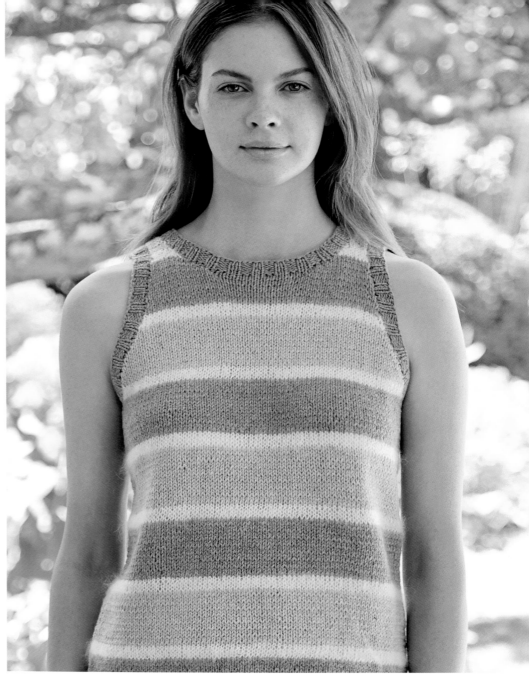

REFLECTIONS

*A collection of 20 designs using 9 combinations of ecru,
charcoals and muted shades to give a monochrome feel*

R O W A N

PIA
Cotton Cashmere
Martin Storey
132

RIVERA
Cotton Cashmere
Quail Studio
138

FRITZIA
Cotton Cashmere
Martin Storey
143

73

TOREY
Cotton Cashmere & Kidsilk Haze
Martin Storey
163

DALI
Cotton Cashmere
Lisa Richardson
153

DADA
Cotton Cashmere & Kidsilk Haze
Lisa Richardson
142

KINETIC
Cotton Cashmere & Kidsilk Haze
Lisa Richardson
126

BERENICE
Cotton Cashmere
ARNE & CARLOS
144

JONI
Cotton Cashmere
Dee Hardwicke
157

SHEELER
Cotton Cashmere & Fine Lace
Emma Wright
112

ROTHKO
Kidsilk Haze
Kaffe Fassett
147

FONTANA
Cotton Cashmere
ARNE & CARLOS
159

MONDRIAN
Fine Lace
Annika Andrea Wolke
119

92

MUCHA
Cotton Cashmere
Galina Caroll
115

94

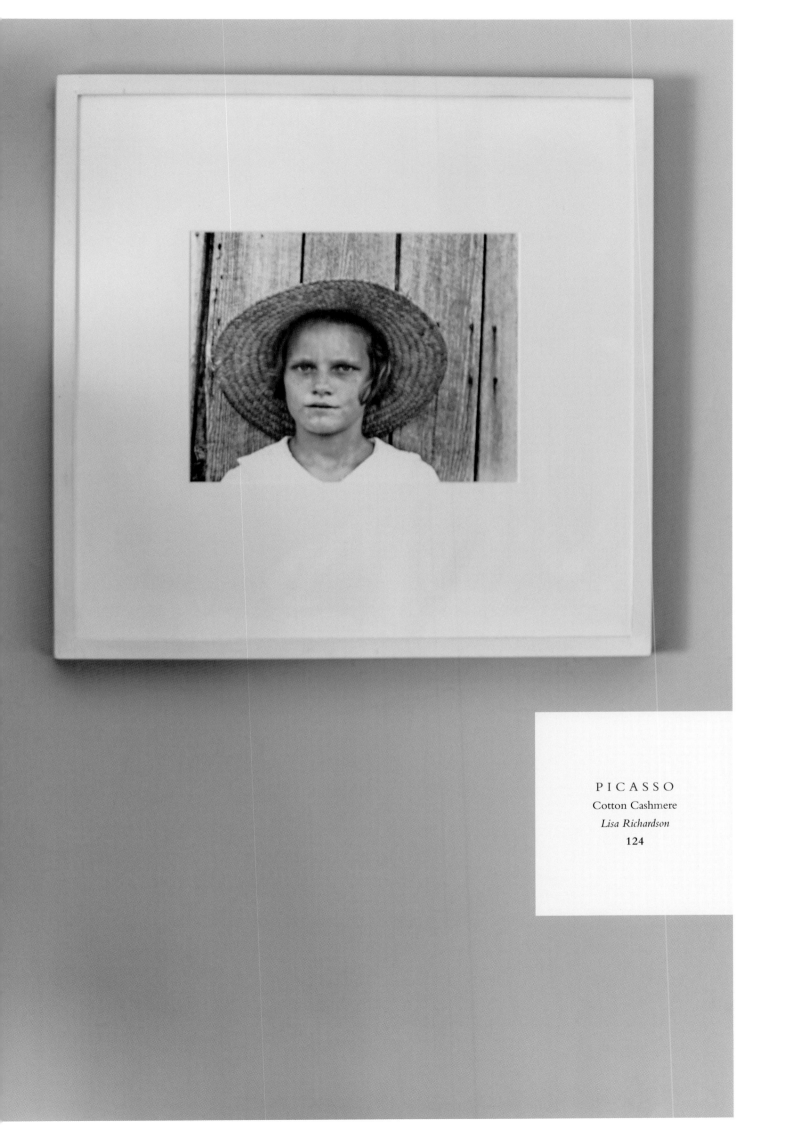

PICASSO
Cotton Cashmere
Lisa Richardson
124

MARISOL
Cotton Cashmere
Lisa Richardson
128

PALOMA
Fine Lace
Lisa Richardson
108

Photography: Moy Williams. Art Direction & Styling: Lisa Richardson. Hair & Make Up: Michaela Taylor (Boss Models).
Models: Catriona (First Model Management) & Sophia Goslitski (Nevs Models). Location: The Old Vicarage (Carol Hayes Management).

YOKO
Fine Lace
Sharon Miller
113

ROWAN
SUBSCRIPTION

Inspiration

all year round

Subscription includes...

Rowan's Knitting & Crochet Magazine

twice a year (RRP £25)

Newsletter twice a year

Subscribers pattern brochure

Welcome or renewal gift of yarn (RRP £20)

Subscribe for £25.00

Postage charges: UK £5 • Europe £10 • North America £10 • Rest of World £20

To join or renew ...

www.knitrowan.com | ☎ *0333 200 6466*

WHAT'S NEW

Rowan brochures are available from Rowan stockists.

View the collections online: *www.knitrowan.com*

....

R O W A N

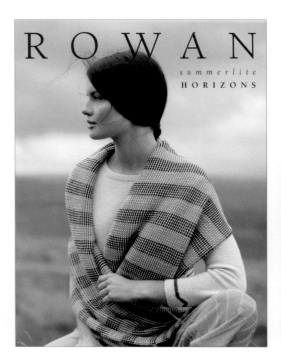

SUMMERLITE HORIZONS

Summerlite Horizons ...a collection of 15 designs incorporating stripes of all types – bold and subtle, vertical and horizontal, bright and neutral. A stripe garment for all from some of our favourite Rowan designers.

ZB248
Spring Summer 2019

OCEAN BLUE

Ocean Blue ..."Sun, sand and a gentle sea breeze". A collection of 14 men's & women's beach inspired knits. The perfect knits for a holiday by the seashore. All knitted in Rowan's new & exciting recycled denim yarn.

ZB249
Spring Summer 2019

PRECIOUS KNITS

Precious Knits ...is a collection of 14 designs for children aged 0-3 years by Grace Jones. Classic styles with adorable details and a trio of cute toys.

ZB247
Spring Summer 2019

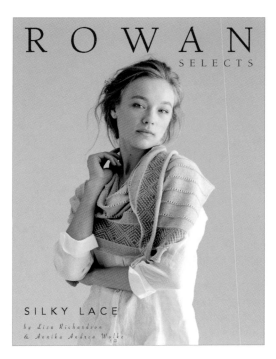

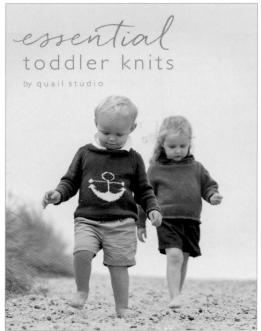

ROWAN SELECTS
SILKY LACE

7 designs by Lisa Richardson and
Annika Andrea Wolke showcasing
the new Selects yarn Silky Lace.
Accessories and garments with
modern lace work and textures are
complimented perfectly using the
neutral and vibrant shades.

ZB250
Spring Summer 2019

ESSENTIAL
KNITS
TODDLERS

10 essential knitted garments by
Quail Studio for your little one using
Summerlite DK, Summerlite 4ply
and Handknit Cotton

978-0-9935908-7-0
Spring Summer 2019

MOORDALE

14 designs by Martin Storey using
Rowan's new yarn Moordale.

A collection of timeless knits for both
men & women, featuring Martin's
signature cabled and textured detail
designs.

Whether going for a late autumn
weekend break, relaxing in your cosy
holiday cottage or a brisk winter
walk, this collection of wide-ranging
knits is perfect for weekend wear.

ZB246
Spring Summer 2019

PALOMA

Lisa Richardson

Main image page **80, 100, 101**

● ● ●

SIZE

To fit bust

81–86 91–97 102–107 112–117 122–127cm

32–34 36–38 40–42 44–46 48–50 in

Actual bust measurement of garment, below cap sleeves

111.5	121.5	132.5	142	151.5	cm
44	47¾	52¼	56	59¾	in

YARN

Fine Lace

3	3	3	4	4	x 50gm

(photographed in White 944)

NEEDLES

1 pair 3mm (no 11) (US 2/3) needles
3mm (no 11) (US 2/3) circular needle no more than 50 cm long

TENSION

29 sts and 41 rows to 10 cm measured over rev st st using 3mm (US 2/3) needles.

BACK

Using 3mm (US 2/3) needles cast on 162 [176: 192: 206: 220] sts.
Beg with a P row, now work in rev st st throughout as folls:
Work 58 rows, ending with RS facing for next row. (Back should meas approx 14 cm.)

Shape for sleeves

Inc 1 st at each end of next and foll 4th row, then on foll 3 alt rows, then on foll 9 rows, taking inc sts into rev st st and ending with RS facing for next row. 190 [204: 220: 234: 248] sts.
Cast on 15 sts at beg of next 2 rows, ending with RS facing for next row.
220 [234: 250: 264: 278] sts.
Place markers at both ends of last row (to denote base of armhole openings).
Now work patt along armhole edge sts as folls:

Row 1 (RS): K2, K2tog, K4, yfwd, K2, P2, yon, K2tog, P to last 14 sts, yon, K2tog, P2, K2, yfwd, K4, sl 1, K1, psso, K2.
Row 2 and every foll alt row: K1, P9, K2, P2, K to last 14 sts, P2, K2, P9, K1.
Row 3: K1, K2tog, K4, yfwd, K3, P2, K2tog, yfrn, P to last 14 sts, K2tog, yfrn, P2, K3, yfwd, K4, sl 1, K1, psso, K1.
Row 5: K4, K2tog, K4, yfrn, P2, yon, K2tog, P to last 14 sts, yon, K2tog, P2, yon, K4, sl 1, K1, psso, K4.
Row 7: K3, K2tog, K4, yfwd, K1, P2, K2tog, yfrn, P to last 14 sts, K2tog, yfrn, P2, K1, yfwd, K4, sl 1, K1, psso, K3.
Row 8: As row 2.
These 8 rows form patt.
Cont in patt until armhole meas 23 [24.5: 26: 27.5: 29] cm from markers, ending with RS facing for next row.

Shape shoulders

Keeping patt correct, cast off 4 [5: 5: 6: 6] sts at beg of next 2 [18: 6: 20: 10] rows, then 5 [6: 6: –: 7] sts at beg of foll 18 [2: 14: –: 10] rows.
122 [132: 136: 144: 148] sts.

Shape back neck

Next row (RS): Cast off 5 [6: 6: 6: 7] sts, P until there are 26 [30: 30: 34: 34] sts on right needle and turn, leaving rem sts on a holder.
Work each side of neck separately.
Dec 1 st at neck edge of next 6 rows **and at same time** cast off 5 [6: 6: 7: 7] sts at beg of 2nd and foll 2 alt rows.
Work 1 row.
Cast off rem 5 [6: 6: 7: 7] sts.
With RS facing, slip centre 60 [60: 64: 64: 66] sts onto a holder (for neckband), rejoin yarn and patt to end.
Complete to match first side, reversing shapings.

FRONT

Using 3mm (US 2/3) needles cast on 162 [176: 192: 206: 220] sts.
Work in patt as folls:
Row 1 (RS): P69 [76: 84: 91: 98], K3, K2tog, K4, yfrn, P2, yon, K2tog, P2, yon, K4, sl 1, K1, psso, K3, P69 [76: 84: 91: 98].
Row 2 and every foll alt row: K69 [76: 84: 91: 98], P9, K2, P2, K2, P9, K69 [76: 84: 91: 98].
Row 3: P69 [76: 84: 91: 98], K2, K2tog, K4, yfwd, K1, P2, K2tog, yfrn, P2, K1, yfwd, K4, sl 1, K1, psso, K2, P69 [76: 84: 91: 98].
Row 5: P69 [76: 84: 91: 98], K1, K2tog, K4, yfwd, K2, P2, yon, K2tog, P2, K2, yfwd, K4, sl 1, K1, psso, K1, P69 [76: 84: 91: 98].
Row 7: P69 [76: 84: 91: 98], K2tog, K4, yfwd, K3, P2, K2tog, yfrn, P2, K3, yfwd, K4, sl 1, K1, psso, P69 [76: 84: 91: 98].
Row 8: As row 2.
These 8 rows form patt.
Cont in patt for a further 50 rows, ending after patt row 2 and with RS facing for next row.
Keeping patt correct, now work as given for back from beg of sleeve shaping until 8 [8: 12: 12: 16] rows less have been worked than on back to beg of shoulder shaping, ending with RS facing for next row.

Shape front neck

Next row (RS): Patt 90 [97: 104: 111: 118] sts and turn, leaving rem sts on a holder.
Work each side of neck separately.
Keeping patt correct, dec 1 st at neck edge of next 7 [7: 10: 10: 10] rows, then on foll 0 [0: 0: 0: 2] alt rows. 83 [90: 94: 101: 106] sts.
Work 0 [0: 1: 1: 1] row, ending with RS facing for next row.

Shape shoulder

Cast off 4 [5: 5: 6: 6] sts at beg of next and foll 0 [8: 2: 10: 4] alt rows, then 5 [6: 6: 7: 7] sts at beg of foll 13 [5: 11: 3: 9] alt rows **and at same time** dec 1 st at neck edge of next 3 [3: 1: 1: 1] rows, then on foll 3 [3: 2: 2: 0] alt rows, then on 3 [3: 4: 4: 5] foll 4th rows.
Work 1 row.
Cast off rem 5 [6: 6: 7: 7] sts.
With RS facing, slip centre 40 [40: 42: 42: 42] sts onto a holder (for neckband), rejoin yarn and patt to end.
Complete to match first side, reversing shapings.

MAKING UP

Press as described on the information page.
Join both shoulder seams using back stitch, or mattress stitch if preferred.

Neckband

With RS facing and using 3mm (US 2/3) circular needle, pick up and knit 30 [30: 33: 33: 36] sts down left side of front neck, K across 40 [40: 42: 42: 42] sts on front holder, pick up and knit 30 [30: 33: 33: 36] sts up right side of front neck, and 7 sts down right side of back

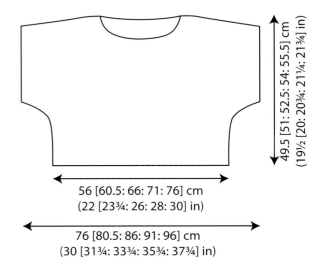

56 [60.5: 66: 71: 76] cm
(22 [23¾: 26: 28: 30] in)

76 [80.5: 86: 91: 96] cm
(30 [31¾: 33¾: 35¾: 37¾] in)

49.5 [51: 52.5: 54: 55.5] cm
(19½ [20: 20¾: 21¼: 21¾] in)

neck, K across 60 [60: 64: 64: 66] sts on back holder, then pick up and knit 7 sts up left side of back neck. 174 [174: 186: 186: 194] sts.

Next round (RS): Knit.
Rep this round 4 times more.
Cast off.

See information page for finishing instructions, joining side seams below markers.

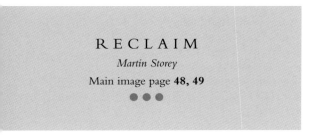

RECLAIM
Martin Storey
Main image page **48, 49**
● ● ●

SIZE
To fit bust
81-86 91-97 102-107 112-117 122-127cm

32-34 36-38 40-42 44-46 48-50 in
Actual bust measurement of garment

| 117.5 | 128 | 137.5 | 148 | 157.5 | cm |
| 46¼ | 50½ | 54¼ | 58¼ | 62 | in |

YARN
Softyak DK

| 16 | 17 | 19 | 20 | 22 | x 50gm |

(photographed in Driftwood 244)

NEEDLES
1 pair 3¼mm (no 10) (US 3) needles
1 pair 4mm (no 8) (US 6) needles
Cable needle

TENSION
22 sts and 30 rows to 10 cm measured over st st using 4mm (US 6) needles. Cable panel (28 sts) measures 7.5 cm.

SPECIAL ABBREVIATIONS
C8B = slip next 4 sts onto cable needle and leave at back of work, K4, then K4 from cable needle; **C8F** = slip next 4 sts onto cable needle and leave at front of work, K4, then K4 from cable needle.

BACK
Using 3¼mm (US 3) needles cast on 185 [205: 217: 237: 249] sts.
Row 1 (RS): *P2, K2, rep from * to last st, P1.
Row 2: *K2, P2, rep from * to last st, K1.
These 2 rows form fancy rib.
Cont in fancy rib for a further 19 rows, ending with **WS** facing for next row.
Row 22 (WS): Rib 9 [7: 10: 8: 11], work 2 tog, (rib 1, work 2 tog) 55 [63: 65: 73: 75] times, rib 9 [7: 10: 8: 11]. 129 [141: 151: 163: 173] sts.
Change to 4mm (US 6) needles.
Beg with a K row, now work in st st throughout as folls:
Cont straight until back meas 84 [86: 88: 90: 92] cm, ending with RS facing for next row.
Shape shoulders and back neck
Cast off 11 [12: 13: 15: 16] sts at beg of next 2 rows. 107 [117: 125: 133: 141] sts.
Next row (RS): Cast off 11 [13: 14: 15: 16] sts, K until there are 26 [29: 31: 34: 36] sts on right needle and turn.
Work each side of neck separately.
Dec 1 st at neck edge of next 3 rows, ending with RS facing for next row, **and at same time** cast off 11 [13: 14: 15: 16] sts at beg of 2nd row.
Cast off rem 12 [13: 14: 16: 17] sts.
With RS facing, slip centre 33 [33: 35: 35: 37] sts onto a holder (for neckband), rejoin yarn and K to end.
Complete to match first side, reversing shapings.

LEFT FRONT
Using 3¼mm (US 3) needles cast on 93 [101: 109: 117: 125] sts.
Work in fancy rib as given for back for 21 rows, ending with **WS** facing for next row.
Row 22 (WS): Rib 3 [4: 4: 5: 4], work 2 tog,

(rib 1, work 2 tog) 28 [30: 33: 35: 38] times, rib 4 [5: 4: 5: 5]. 64 [70: 75: 81: 86] sts.
Change to 4mm (US 6) needles.
Next row (RS): K to last 17 sts, inc purlwise in next st, inc knitwise in next st, K1, inc knitwise in each of next 2 sts, (K1, inc knitwise in next st) 3 times, K1, inc knitwise in each of next 2 sts, K1, inc knitwise in next st, inc purlwise in last st. 75 [81: 86: 92: 97] sts.
Now work in patt as folls:
Row 1 and every foll alt row (WS): K2, P24, K2, P to end.
Row 2: K to last 28 sts, P2, K24, P2.
Row 4: K to last 28 sts, P2, (C8B) 3 times, P2.
Row 6: As row 2.
Row 8: As row 2.
Row 10: K to last 28 sts, P2, K4, (C8F) twice, K4, P2.
Row 12: As row 2.
These 12 rows form patt.
Cont in patt until 18 [18: 20: 20: 22] rows less have been worked than on back to beg of shoulder shaping, ending with RS facing for next row.
Shape front neck
Next row (RS): Patt 58 [64: 69: 75: 80] sts and turn, leaving rem 17 sts on a holder (for neckband).
Keeping patt correct, dec 1 st at neck edge of next 10 rows, then on foll 3 [3: 4: 4: 5] alt rows. 45 [51: 55: 61: 65] sts.
Work 1 row, ending with RS facing for next row.
Shape shoulder
Cast off 11 [12: 13: 15: 16] sts at beg of next row, then 11 [13: 14: 15: 16] sts at beg of foll 2 alt rows.
Work 1 row.
Cast off rem 12 [13: 14: 16: 17] sts.

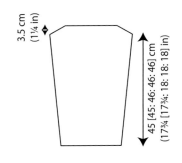

3.5 cm (1¼ in)

45 [45: 46: 46: 46] cm (17¾ [17¾: 18: 18: 18] in)

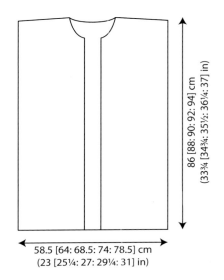

86 [88: 90: 92: 94] cm (33¾ [34¾: 35½: 36¼: 37] in)

58.5 [64: 68.5: 74: 78.5] cm (23 [25¼: 27: 29¼: 31] in)

RIGHT FRONT

Using 3¼mm (US 3) needles cast on 93 [101: 109: 117: 125] sts.

Work in fancy rib as given for back for 21 rows, ending with **WS** facing for next row.

Row 22 (WS): Rib 4 [5: 4: 5: 5], work 2 tog, (rib 1, work 2 tog) 28 [30: 33: 35: 38] times, rib 3 [4: 4: 5: 4]. 64 [70: 75: 81: 86] sts.

Change to 4mm (US 6) needles.

Next row (RS): Inc purlwise in first st, inc knitwise in next st, K1, inc knitwise in each of next 2 sts, (K1, inc knitwise in next st) 3 times, K1, inc knitwise in each of next 2 sts, K1, inc knitwise in next st, inc purlwise in next st, K to end. 75 [81: 86: 92: 97] sts.

Now work in patt as folls:

Row 1 and every foll alt row (WS): P to last 28 sts, K2, P24, K2.

Row 2: P2, K24, P2, K to end.

Row 4: P2, (C8F) 3 times, P2, K to end.

Row 6: As row 2.

Row 8: As row 2.

Row 10: P2, K4, (C8B) twice, K4, P2, K to end.

Row 12: As row 2.

These 12 rows form patt.

Cont in patt until 18 [18: 20: 20: 22] rows less have been worked than on back to beg of shoulder shaping, ending with RS facing for next row.

Shape front neck

Next row (RS): Patt 17 sts and slip these sts onto a holder (for neckband), patt to end.
58 [64: 69: 75: 80] sts.

Complete to match left front, reversing shapings.

SLEEVES

Using 3¼mm (US 3) needles cast on 89 [93: 97: 97: 101] sts.

Work in fancy rib as given for back for 21 rows, ending with **WS** facing for next row.

Row 22 (WS): Rib 6 [8: 7: 7: 6], work 2 tog, (rib 1, work 2 tog) 25 [25: 27: 27: 29] times, rib 6 [8: 7: 7: 6]. 63 [67: 69: 69: 71] sts.

Change to 4mm (US 6) needles.

Beg with a K row, now work in st st throughout as folls:

Inc 1 st at each end of 3rd and every foll 4th row to 69 [73: 83: 107: 121] sts, then on every foll 6th row until there are 99 [103: 109: 117: 123] sts.

Cont straight until sleeve meas 45 [45: 46: 46: 46] cm, ending with RS facing for next row.

Shape top

Cast off 6 [6: 7: 7: 8] sts at beg of next 4 [2: 8: 2: 8] rows, then 7 [7: 8: 8: 9] sts at beg of foll 6 [8: 2: 8: 2] rows.

Cast off rem 33 [35: 37: 39: 41] sts.

MAKING UP

Press as described on the information page.

Join both shoulder seams using back stitch, or mattress stitch if preferred.

Neckband

With RS facing and using 3¼mm (US 3) needles, slip 17 sts on right front holder onto right needle, rejoin yarn with RS facing and pick up and knit 24 [24: 25: 25: 28] sts up right side

of front neck, and 3 sts down right side of back neck, K across 33 [33: 35: 35: 37] sts on back holder inc 4 sts evenly, pick up and knit 3 sts up left side of back neck, and 24 [24: 25: 25: 28] sts down left side of front neck, then patt across 17 sts on left front holder.
125 [125: 129: 129: 137] sts.

Beg with row 2, work in fancy rib as given for back for 11 rows, ending with RS facing for next row.

Cast off in rib.

Front bands (both alike)

With RS facing and using 3¼mm (US 3) needles, pick up and knit 259 [263: 267: 275: 279] sts evenly along front opening edge, between cast-on edge and top of neckband.

Row 1 (WS): K1, P1, *K2, P2, rep from * to last st, K1.

Row 2: K2, *P2, K2, rep from * to last st, K1.

These 2 rows form fancy rib.

Work in fancy rib for a further 21 rows, ending with RS facing for next row.

Cast off in rib.

Mark points along side seam edges 23 [24.5: 26: 27.5: 29] cm either side of shoulder seams (to denote base of armhole openings). See information page for finishing instructions, setting in sleeves using the straight cast-off method.

VITAL

Lisa Richardson

Main image page **56, 57**

● ●

SIZE
To fit bust
81-86 91-97 102-107 112-117 122-127cm
32-34 36-38 40-42 44-46 48-50 in
Actual bust measurement of garment
94.5 104 114 123.5 134.5 cm
37¼ 41 45 48½ 53 in

YARN
Fine Lace
3 3 3 4 4 x 50gm
(photographed in Cobweb 922)

NEEDLES
1 pair 3mm (no 11) (US 2/3) needles

BUTTONS – 6 x BN1150 (13mm) from Bedecked. Please see information page for contact details.

TENSION
29 sts and 41 rows to 10 cm measured over st st using 3mm (US 2/3) needles.

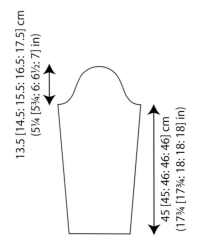

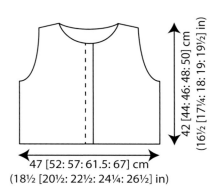

BACK

Using 3mm (US 2/3) needles cast on as folls: cast on 5 sts, *cast off 2 sts, slip st on right needle back onto left needle**, cast on 3 sts, rep from * until there are 73 [80: 87: 94: 102] sts on left needle (ending last rep at **), cast on 1 st.
74 [81: 88: 95: 103] sts.
Row 1 (RS): K2, *yfwd, K1, rep from * to last st, K1. 145 [159: 173: 187: 203] sts.
Beg with a P row, now work in st st throughout as folls:
Work 15 rows, ending with RS facing for next row.
Dec 1 st at each end of next and 3 foll 16th rows.
137 [151: 165: 179: 195] sts.
Cont straight until back meas 20 [20.5: 21: 21.5: 22] cm, ending with RS facing for next row.
Shape armholes
Cast off 6 [7: 8: 9: 10] sts at beg of next 2 rows.
125 [137: 149: 161: 175] sts.
Next row (RS): K2, sl 1, K1, psso, K to last 4 sts, K2tog, K2.
Next row: P2, P2tog, P to last 4 sts, P2tog tbl, P2.
Working all armhole decreases as set by last 2 rows, dec 1 st at each end of next 5 [5: 7: 7: 9] rows, then on foll 6 [9: 9: 11: 11] alt rows.
99 [105: 113: 121: 131] sts.
Cont straight until armhole meas 20 [21.5: 23: 24.5: 26] cm, ending with RS facing for next row.
Shape shoulders and back neck
Next row (RS): Cast off 4 [5: 5: 6: 7] sts, K until there are 25 [27: 30: 33: 36] sts on right needle and turn.
Work each side of neck separately.
Working all neck decreases in same way as armhole decreases, dec 1 st at neck edge of next 6 rows **and at same time** cast off 4 [5: 6: 6: 7] sts at beg of 2nd and foll 0 [2: 2: 0: 1] alt rows, then 5 [-: -: 7: 8] sts at beg of foll 2 [-: -: 2: 1] alt rows.
Work 1 row.
Cast off rem 5 [6: 6: 7: 8] sts.
With RS facing, slip centre 41 [41: 43: 43: 45] sts onto a holder (for neckband), rejoin yarn and K to end.
Complete to match first side, reversing shapings.

LEFT FRONT

Using 3mm (US 2/3) needles cast on as folls: cast on 5 sts, *cast off 2 sts, slip st on right needle back onto left needle**, cast on 3 sts, rep from * until there are 38 [42: 45: 49: 53] sts on left needle (ending last rep at **), cast on 1 st.
39 [43: 46: 50: 54] sts.
Row 1 (RS): K2, *yfwd, K1, rep from * to last 1 [2: 1: 2: 2] sts, K1 [2: 1: 2: 2].
75 [82: 89: 96: 104] sts.
Row 2: Cast on and P 6 sts, P to end.
81 [88: 95: 102: 110] sts.
Beg with a K row, now work in st st throughout as folls:
Work 14 rows, ending with RS facing for next row.
Dec 1 st at beg of next and 3 foll 16th rows.
77 [84: 91: 98: 106] sts.

Cont straight until left front matches back to beg of armhole shaping, ending with RS facing for next row.
Shape armhole
Cast off 6 [7: 8: 9: 10] sts at beg of next row.
71 [77: 83: 89: 96] sts.
Work 1 row.
Working all armhole decreases as set by back, dec 1 st at armhole edge of next 7 [7: 9: 9: 11] rows, then on foll 6 [9: 9: 11: 11] alt rows.
58 [61: 65: 69: 74] sts.
Cont straight until 20 [20: 24: 24: 28] rows less have been worked than on back to beg of shoulder shaping, ending with RS facing for next row.
Shape front neck
Next row (RS): K36 [39: 43: 47: 52] and turn, leaving rem 22 sts on a holder (for neckband).
Working all neck decreases in same way as armhole decreases, dec 1 st at neck edge of next 8 rows, then on foll 5 alt rows, then on 0 [0: 1: 1: 2] foll 4th rows. 23 [26: 29: 33: 37] sts.
Work 1 row, ending with RS facing for next row.
Shape shoulder
Cast off 4 [5: 5: 6: 7] sts at beg of next and foll 1 [3: 0: 1: 2] alt rows, then 5 [-: 6: 7: 8] sts at beg of foll 2 [-: 3: 2: 1] alt rows.
Work 1 row.
Cast off rem 5 [6: 6: 7: 8] sts.
Mark positions for 6 buttons along left front opening edge – first button to come level with row 7, last button to come just below neck shaping, and rem 4 buttons evenly spaced between.

RIGHT FRONT

Using 3mm (US 2/3) needles cast on as folls: cast on 5 sts, *cast off 2 sts, slip st on right needle back onto left needle**, cast on 3 sts, rep from * until there are 38 [42: 45: 49: 53] sts on left needle (ending last rep at **), cast on 1 st.
39 [43: 46: 50: 54] sts.
Row 1 (RS): K2 [3: 2: 3: 3], *yfwd, K1, rep from * to last st, K1. 75 [82: 89: 96: 104] sts.
Row 2: P to end, turn and cast on 6 sts.
81 [88: 95: 102: 110] sts.
Beg with a K row, now work in st st throughout as folls:
Work 4 rows, ending with RS facing for next row.
Row 7 (RS): K3, yfwd, K2tog tbl (to make first buttonhole of this pair), K2, K2tog, yfwd (to make 2nd buttonhole of this pair), K to end.
Making a further 5 pairs of buttonholes in this way to correspond with positions marked for buttons on left front and noting that no further reference will be made to buttonholes, cont as folls:
Work 9 rows, ending with RS facing for next row.
Dec 1 st at end of next and 3 foll 16th rows.
77 [84: 91: 98: 106] sts.
Complete to match left front, reversing shapings and working first row of neck shaping as folls:
Shape front neck
Next row (RS): K6 and slip these 6 sts onto a holder, K16 and slip these 16 sts onto another

holder (for neckband), K to end.
36 [39: 43: 47: 52] sts.

SLEEVES

Using 3mm (US 2/3) needles cast on as folls: cast on 5 sts, *cast off 2 sts, slip st on right needle back onto left needle**, cast on 3 sts, rep from * until there are 32 [34: 35: 35: 36] sts on left needle (ending last rep at **), cast on 1 st.
33 [35: 36: 36: 37] sts.
Row 1 (RS): K2, *yfwd, K1, rep from * to last st, K1. 63 [67: 69: 69: 71] sts.
Beg with a P row, now work in st st throughout as folls:
Inc 1 st at each end of 8th [8th: 6th: 4th: 4th] and every foll 10th [10th: 8th: 6th: 6th] row to 83 [99: 85: 73: 91] sts, then on every foll 12th [-: 10th: 8th: 8th] row until there are 93 [-: 105: 111: 117] sts.
Cont straight until sleeve meas 45 [45: 46: 46: 46] cm, ending with RS facing for next row.
Shape top
Cast off 6 [7: 8: 9: 10] sts at beg of next 2 rows
81 [85: 89: 93: 97] sts.
Dec 1 st at each end of next 3 rows, then on foll 4 alt rows, then on 5 foll 4th rows.
57 [61: 65: 69: 73] sts.
Work 1 row.
Dec 1 st at each end of next and every foll alt row until 45 sts rem, then on foll 11 rows, ending with RS facing for next row.
Cast off rem 23 sts.

MAKING UP

Press as described on the information page.
Join both shoulder seams using back stitch, or mattress stitch if preferred.
Neckband
At left front neck edge, slip 6 sts nearest front opening edge onto another holder, leaving 16 sts on original holder. Fold 6 sts to inside along both front opening edges (to form front facings) and neatly sew row-end edge in place and, when picking up sts for neckband, pick up sts through both sets of sts so that facing is secured to inside. Along right front opening edge, neatly sew around buttonholes to secure buttonholes of both layers in same place.
With RS facing and using 3mm (US 2/3) needles, K across 16 sts on right front holder (working through facing 6 sts at same time for 6 sts nearest fold), pick up and knit 23 [23: 26: 26: 29] sts up right side of front neck, and 7 sts down right side of back neck, K across 41 [41: 43: 43: 45] sts on back holder, pick up and knit 7 sts up left side of back neck, and 23 [23: 26: 26: 29] sts down left side of front neck, then K across 16 sts on left front holder (working through facing 6 sts at same time for 6 sts nearest fold).
133 [133: 141: 141: 149] sts.
Work in g st for 2 rows, ending with **WS** facing for next row.
Cast off knitwise (on **WS**).
See information page for finishing instructions, setting in sleeves using the set-in method.

SHEELER

Emma Wright

Main image page **86, 87**

SIZE

To fit bust

81-86 91-97 102-107 112-117 122-127cm

32-34 36-38 40-42 44-46 48-50 in

Actual bust measurement of garment

93.5 100 113.5 120 133.5 cm

36¾ 39¼ 44¾ 47¼ 52½ in

YARN

Cotton Cashmere and Fine Lace

A CC Silver Lining 224

    3   3   3   4   4   x 50gm

B CC Stormy Sky 225

    2   2   2   3   3   x 50gm

C *FL Cameo 920

    6   6   7   7   7   x 50gm

*Use Fine Lace DOUBLE throughout

Alternatively you could use Rowan Handknit Cotton in the following shade(s):

A HK Feather 373

    5   5   5   7   7   x 50gm

B HK Slate 347

    4   4   4   5   5   x 50gm

C *FL Cameo 920

    6   6   7   7   7   x 50gm

*Use Fine Lace DOUBLE throughout

CROCHET HOOK

4.00mm (no 8) (US G6) crochet hook
4.50mm (no 7) (US 7) crochet hook

TENSION

2 patt reps to **13** cm and 8 rows to 10 cm measured over chevron patt using 4.50mm (US 7) crochet hook. 6 patt reps and 16 rows to 10 cm measured over main patt using 4.00mm (US G6) crochet hook and Fine Lace DOUBLE.

CROCHET ABBREVIATIONS

ch = chain; **dc** = double crochet; **htr** = half

treble; **sp(s)** = space(s); **ss** = slip stitch; **tr** = treble; **tr3tog** = (yoh and insert hook as indicated, yoh and draw loop through, yoh and draw through 2 loops) 3 times, yoh and draw through all 4 loops on hook; **yoh** = yarn over hook.

BACK

Using 4.50mm (US 7) crochet hook and yarn A make 114 [124: 134: 144: 154] ch.

Row 1 (RS): 1 tr into 4th ch from hook, *1 tr into each of next 3 ch, tr3tog over next 3 ch, 1 tr into each of next 3 ch**, 3 tr into next ch, rep from * to end, ending last rep at **, 2 tr into last ch, turn. 111 [121: 131: 141: 151] sts, 11 [12: 13: 14: 15] patt reps.

Now work in chevron patt as folls:

Row 2: 3 ch (counts as first tr), 1 tr into tr at base of 3 ch, *1 tr into each of next 3 tr, tr3tog over next 3 sts, 1 tr into each of next 3 tr**, 3 tr into next tr, rep from * to end, ending last rep at **, 2 tr into top of 3 ch at beg of previous row, turn.

Last row forms chevron patt.

Keeping chevron patt correct and joining in and breaking off colours as required, cont in chevron patt in stripes as folls:

Row 3: Using yarn B.

Row 4: Using yarn C DOUBLE.

Row 5: Using yarn A.

Rows 6 and 7: Using yarn B.

Row 8: Using yarn A.

Row 9: Using yarn C DOUBLE.

Row 10: Using yarn A.

Row 11: Using yarn C DOUBLE.

Rows 12 and 13: Using yarn A.

Row 14: Using yarn B.

Row 15: Using yarn C DOUBLE.

Row 16: Using yarn A.

Row 17: Using yarn B.

Row 18: Using yarn C DOUBLE.

Break off yarns A and B and cont using yarn C DOUBLE **only** as folls:

Change to 4.00mm (US G6) crochet hook.

Row 19: 1 ch (does NOT count as st), 1 dc into each st to end, working 2 dc into 3 [1: 7: 5: 11] sts evenly spaced across row and working last dc into top of 3 ch at beg of previous row, turn. 114 [122: 138: 146: 162] sts.

Row 20: 2 ch (counts as first st), miss st at base of 2 ch and next dc, *2 dc into next dc, 2 ch,

2 dc into next dc**, miss 2 dc, rep from * to end, ending last rep at **, miss 1 dc, 1 dc into last dc, turn. 28 [30: 34: 36: 40] patt reps.

Now work in main patt as folls:

Row 21: 3 ch (counts as first st), miss st at base of 3 ch and next 2 dc, *(2 dc, 2 ch and 2 dc) into next ch sp**, miss 4 dc, rep from * to end, ending last rep at **, miss 2 dc, 1 dc into turning ch at beg of previous row, turn.

Last row forms main patt.

Cont in main patt until back meas 54 [56: 58: 60: 62] cm.

Shape shoulders

Fasten off, placing markers either side of centre 10 [10: 12: 12: 12] patt reps (to denote back neck).

FRONT

Work as given for back until 12 [12: 13: 13: 14] rows less have been worked than on back to shoulder.

Shape front neck

Next row: 3 ch (counts as first st), miss dc at base of 3 ch and next 2 dc, *(2 dc, 2 ch and 2 dc) into next ch sp, miss 4 dc, rep from * 10 [11: 12: 13: 15] times more, 1 tr into next ch sp and turn, leaving rem sts unworked.

Work on this set of 11 [12: 13: 14: 16] patt reps only for first side of neck as folls:

Work 1 row.

Next row: 3 ch (counts as first st), miss dc at base of 3 ch and next 2 dc, *(2 dc, 2 ch and 2 dc) into next ch sp, miss 4 dc, rep from * 9 [10: 11: 12: 14] times more, 1 tr into next ch sp, turn. 10 [11: 12: 13: 15] patt reps.

Work 1 row.

Next row: 3 ch (counts as first st), miss dc at base of 3 ch and next 2 dc, *(2 dc, 2 ch and 2 dc) into next ch sp, miss 4 dc, rep from * 8 [9: 10: 11: 13] times more, 1 tr into next ch sp, turn. 9 [10: 11: 12: 14] patt reps.

Work 7 [7: 8: 8: 9] rows.

Shape shoulder

Fasten off.

Return to last complete row worked, miss 4 [4: 6: 6: 6] ch sps at centre of row, then rejoin yarn to next ch sp, 3 ch (counts as first st), miss 4 dc, (2 dc, 2 ch and 2 dc) into next ch sp, patt to end, turn. 11 [12: 13: 14: 16] patt reps.

Work 1 row.

Next row: Ss across and into first ch sp, 3 ch

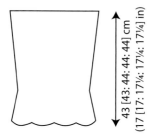

43 [43: 44: 44: 44] cm
(17 [17: 17¼: 17¼: 17¼] in)

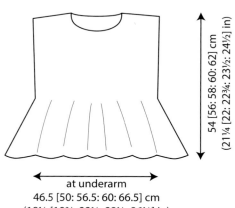

54 [56: 58: 60: 62] cm
(21¼ [22: 22¾: 23½: 24½] in)

at underarm
46.5 [50: 56.5: 60: 66.5] cm
(18¼ [19¾: 22¼: 23½: 26¼] in)

(counts as first st), miss 4 dc, (2 dc, 2 ch and 2 dc) into next ch sp, patt to end, turn. 10 [11: 12: 13: 15] patt reps.
Rep last 2 rows once more. 9 [10: 11: 12: 14] patt reps.
Work 7 [7: 8: 8: 9] rows.
Shape shoulder
Fasten off.

SLEEVES
Using 4.50mm (US 7) crochet hook and yarn A make 44 ch.
Work row 1 as given for back. 41 sts, 4 patt reps.
Now work rows 2 to 8 as given for back.
Break off yarns A and B and cont using yarn C DOUBLE **only** as folls:
Change to 4.00mm (US G6) crochet hook.
Row 9: 1 ch (does NOT count as st), 1 dc into each st to end, working 2 dc into 9 [13: 13: 17: 17] sts evenly spaced across row and working last dc into top of 3 ch at beg of previous row, turn. 50 [54: 54: 58: 58] sts.
Row 10: Work as given for row 20 of back. 12 [13: 13: 14: 14] patt reps.
Now working in main patt as given for back,

cont as folls:
Work 6 [4: 3: 3: 2] rows.
Inc row 1: 4 ch (counts as first st), miss st at base of 4 ch and next 2 dc, ★(2 dc, 2 ch and 2 dc) into next ch sp★★, miss 4 dc, rep from ★ to end, ending last rep at ★★, miss 2 dc, 1 ch, 1 htr into turning ch at beg of previous row, turn.
Inc row 2: 3 ch (counts as first st), miss st at base of 3 ch, 2 dc into first ch sp, miss 2 dc, ★(2 dc, 2 ch and 2 dc) into next ch sp★★, miss 4 dc, rep from ★ to end, ending last rep at ★★, miss 2 dc, (2 dc, 1 ch and 1 dc) into turning ch at beg of previous row, turn.
Inc row 3: 3 ch (counts as first st), miss st at base of 3 ch, ★(2 dc, 2 ch and 2 dc) into next ch sp, miss 4 dc, rep from ★ until only the turning ch remains, (2 dc, 2 ch and 3 dc) into turning ch at beg of previous row, turn. 14 [15: 15: 16: 16] patt reps.
Last 3 rows inc 1 patt rep at each end of row.
Work 7 [6: 4: 4: 3] rows, then rep inc rows 1 to 3 again. 16 [17: 17: 18: 18] patt reps.
Work 8 [6: 5: 5: 4] rows, then rep inc rows 1 to 3 again.
Rep last 11 [9: 8: 8: 7] rows 1 [2: 3: 3: 4] times

more. 20 [23: 25: 26: 28] patt reps.
Cont straight until sleeve meas 43 [43: 44: 44: 44] cm.
Fasten off.

MAKING UP
Press as described on the information page.
Join both shoulder seams.
Neck edging
With RS facing, using 4.00mm (US G6) crochet hook and yarn C DOUBLE, attach yarn at one shoulder seam and work one round of dc evenly around entire neck edge, ending with ss to first dc, do NOT turn.
Next round: 1 ch (does NOT count as st), 1 dc into each dc to end, ss to first dc, do NOT turn.
Rep last round once more.
Fasten off.
Mark points along side seam edges 18 [19.5: 21: 22.5: 24] cm either side of shoulder seams (to denote base of armhole openings). See information page for finishing instructions, setting in sleeves using the straight cast-off method.

YOKO
Sharon Miller
Main image page **102, 103**
● ● ●

YARN
Fine Lace

A White 944	4	x 50gm
B Pigeon 950	4	x 50gm

NEEDLES
1 pair 4½mm (no 7) (US 7) needles
4½mm (no 7) (US 7) circular needle at least 120 cm long

TENSION
22 sts and 30 rows to 10 cm measured over st st using 4½mm (US 7) needles and one strand each of yarns A and B held together.

FINISHED SIZE
Completed shawl is 61.5 cm (24¼ in) deep and meas 245.5 cm (96½ in) along upper edge, excluding triangles.

SHAWL
First band of triangles
Using 4½mm (US 7) needles and yarn A cast on 4 sts.
Row 1 (RS): K2, yfwd, K2. 5 sts.
Row 2 and every foll alt row: Knit.
Row 3: K3, yfwd, K2. 6 sts.
Row 5: K2, yfwd, K2tog tbl, yfwd, K2. 7 sts.
Row 7: K3, yfwd, K2tog tbl, yfwd, K2. 8 sts.
Row 9: K2, (yfwd, K2tog tbl) twice, yfwd, K2. 9 sts.
Row 11: K3, (yfwd, K2tog tbl) twice, yfwd, K2. 10 sts.
Row 13: K2, (yfwd, K2tog tbl) 3 times, yfwd, K2. 11 sts.
Row 15: K3, (yfwd, K2tog tbl) 3 times, yfwd, K2. 12 sts.
Row 17: K2, (yfwd, K2tog tbl) 4 times, yfwd, K2. 13 sts.
Row 19: K3, (yfwd, K2tog tbl) 4 times, yfwd,

K2. 14 sts.
Row 21: K2, (yfwd, K2tog tbl) 5 times, yfwd, K2. 15 sts.
Row 23: K3, (yfwd, K2tog tbl) 5 times, yfwd, K2. 16 sts.
Row 25: K2, (yfwd, K2tog tbl) 6 times, yfwd, K2. 17 sts.
Row 27: K3, (yfwd, K2tog tbl) 6 times, yfwd, K2. 18 sts.
Row 29: K2, (yfwd, K2tog tbl) 7 times, yfwd, K2. 19 sts.
Row 31: K2, (K2tog, yfwd) 7 times, K2tog, K1. 18 sts.
Row 33: K1, (K2tog, yfwd) 7 times, K2tog, K1. 17 sts.
Row 35: K2, (K2tog, yfwd) 6 times, K2tog, K1. 16 sts.
Row 37: K1, (K2tog, yfwd) 6 times, K2tog, K1. 15 sts.
Row 39: K2, (K2tog, yfwd) 5 times, K2tog, K1. 14 sts.
Row 41: K1, (K2tog, yfwd) 5 times, K2tog, K1. 13 sts.
Row 43: K2, (K2tog, yfwd) 4 times, K2tog, K1. 12 sts.
Row 45: K1, (K2tog, yfwd) 4 times, K2tog, K1. 11 sts.
Row 47: K2, (K2tog, yfwd) 3 times, K2tog, K1. 10 sts.
Row 49: K1, (K2tog, yfwd) 3 times, K2tog, K1. 9 sts.
Row 51: K2, (K2tog, yfwd) twice, K2tog, K1. 8 sts.
Row 53: K1, (K2tog, yfwd) twice, K2tog, K1. 7 sts.

Row 55: K2, K2tog, yfwd, K2tog, K1. 6 sts.
Row 57: K1, K2tog, yfwd, K2tog, K1. 5 sts.
Row 59: K2, K2tog, K1. 4 sts.
Row 60: Knit.
These 60 rows form one triangle.
Rep last 60 rows 26 times more, ending with RS facing for next row – 27 triangles in total.
Cast off rem 4 sts.

Second band of triangles
Work as given for first band of triangles **but using yarn B**.

Main section
Lay the 2 bands of triangles together with their **WS** tog (so that RS of each band is on outside) and straight row-end edges are level.
Using 4½mm (US 7) circular needle and one strand each of yarns A and B held together, beg at one end of doubled triangle band, picking up sts through row-end sts of **both** triangles together and picking up one st for every 2 rows of triangles, now pick up and knit sts along straight row-end edge of doubled triangle band as folls: with RS of end triangle in yarn B facing, pick up and knit 29 sts along row-end edge of first triangle, *twist doubled triangle band so that RS of next triangle in yarn A is facing and pick up and knit one st working over point where bands were twisted tog – this is row 60 of triangles, pick up and knit 29 sts along row-end edges of this next triangle, twist doubled triangle band so that RS of next triangle in yarn B is facing and pick up and knit one st working over point where bands were twisted tog – this is row 60 of triangles, pick up and knit 29 sts along row-end edges of this next triangle, rep from * 12 times more, then pick up and knit one st from last row-end edge of end triangle. 810 sts.
Next row (WS): *P1, P2tog, rep from * to end. 540 sts.
Now shape main section as folls:
Row 1 (RS): K360 and turn.
Row 2: P180 and turn.
Row 3: K182 and turn.
Row 4: P184 and turn.
Row 5: K186 and turn.
Row 6: P188 and turn.
Row 7: K190 and turn.
Row 8: P192 and turn.
Row 9: K194 and turn.
Row 10: P196 and turn.
Cont in this way, working 2 more sts on every row before turning, until the foll row has been worked:
Row 181 (RS): K538 (end of row) and turn.
Now cont as folls:
Row 182: P to end. 540 sts.
Working all sts **very loosely**, now complete main section as folls:
Row 183 (RS): *K2tog and slip st on right needle back onto left needle, K2tog tbl and slip st on right needle back onto left needle, rep from * until there are 2 sts on left needle, K2tog and fasten off.

MAKING UP
Press as described on the information page.
See information page for finishing instructions.

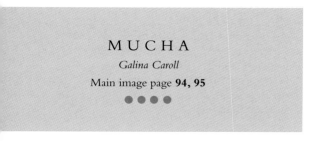

MUCHA

Galina Caroll

Main image page **94, 95**

●●●●

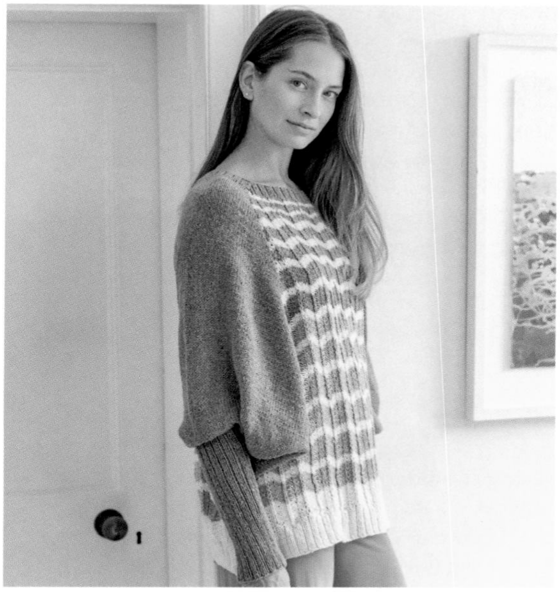

SIZE

To fit bust

81-86	91-97	102-107	112-117	122-127	cm
32-34	36-38	40-42	44-46	48-50	in

Actual bust measurement of garment

112	122.5	131.5	141.5	152	cm
44	48¼	51¾	55¾	59¾	in

YARN

Cotton Cashmere

A Paper 210					
3	4	4	4	5	x 50gm
B Silver Lining 224					
4	4	5	5	5	x 50gm
C Stormy Sky 225					
7	8	9	9	10	x 50gm

Alternatively, you could use Rowan Handknit Cotton in the following shade(s):

A Bleached 263					
5	7	7	7	8	x 50gm
B Feather 373					
7	7	8	8	8	x 50gm
C Slate 347					
11	13	14	14	16	x 50gm

NEEDLES

1 pair 3¼mm (no 10) (US 3) needles
1 pair 4mm (no 8) (US 6) needles
3¼mm (no 10) (US 3) circular needle no more than 40 cm long
4.00mm (no 8) (US G6) crochet hook

TENSION

23 sts and 28 rows to 10 cm measured over patt, 20 sts and 28 rows to 10 cm measured over st st, both using 4mm (US 6) needles.

SPECIAL ABBREVIATION

sL2togK = slip next 2 sts as though to K2tog.

STRIPE SEQUENCE

Rows 1 to 12: Using yarn A.
Rows 13 to 24: Using yarn B.
Rows 25 to 28: Using yarn A.
Rows 29 to 38: Using yarn B.
Rows 39 to 42: Using yarn A.
Rows 43 to 52: Using yarn B.
Rows 53 to 56: Using yarn A.
Rows 57 to 66: Using yarn B.
Rows 67 to 70: Using yarn A.
Rows 71 to 78: Using yarn B.
Rows 79 to 82: Using yarn A.
Rows 83 to 90: Using yarn B.
Rows 91 to 94: Using yarn A.
Rows 95 to 102: Using yarn C.
Rows 103 to 106: Using yarn A.
Rows 107 to 114: Using yarn C.
Rows 115 to 118: Using yarn A.
Rows 119 to 124: Using yarn C.
Rows 125 to 128: Using yarn A.
Rows 129 to 134: Using yarn C.
Rows 135 to 138: Using yarn A.
Rows 139 to 142: Using yarn C.
Rows 143 and 144: Using yarn A.
Rows 145 to 148: Using yarn C.
Rows 149 and 150: Using yarn A.
Rows 151 and 152: Using yarn C.
Now rep rows 149 to 152 as and if required.

BACK and FRONT (both alike)

Using 3¼mm (US 3) needles and yarn A cast on 128 [140: 152: 164: 176] sts.
Row 1 (RS): K2, *P1, K2, rep from * to end.
Row 2: P2, *K1, P2, rep from * to end.
These 2 rows form rib.
Work in rib for a further 14 rows, inc [inc: dec: dec: dec] 1 st at centre of last row and ending with RS facing for next row.
129 [141: 151: 163: 175] sts.
Change to 4mm (US 6) needles.
Next row (RS): K4 [4: 3: 3: 3], *yfwd, sl 1 and mark this st, K2, M1, K2, sL2togK, K1, p2sso, K2, M1, K2, rep from * to last 5 [5: 4: 4: 4] sts, yfwd, sl 1 and mark this st, K4 [4: 3: 3: 3].
Note: From this point onwards, the marked st will be slipped on WS rows and knitted on RS rows. On every row a "yfwd" or "yrn" will be worked directly after the st is either slipped or knitted **but this does NOT count as a st** and is **NOT** included in any st counts.
Next row: P4 [4: 3: 3: 3], *slip marked st, drop yfwd of previous row, yrn, P11, rep from * to last 5 [5: 4: 4: 4] sts, slip marked st, drop yfwd of previous row, yrn, P4 [4: 3: 3: 3].
Now work in patt as folls:
Row 1 (RS): K4 [4: 3: 3: 3], *K tog yrn and marked st, yfwd, K2, M1, K2, sL2togK, K1, p2sso, K2, M1, K2, rep from * to last 5 [5: 4: 4: 4] sts, K tog yrn and marked st, yfwd, K4 [4: 3: 3: 3].
Row 2: P4 [4: 3: 3: 3], *drop yfwd of previous row, slip marked st, yrn, P11, rep from * to last 5 [5: 4: 4: 4] sts, drop yfwd of previous row, slip marked st, yrn, P4 [4: 3: 3: 3].
Last 2 rows form patt, and last 4 rows form rows 1 to 4 of stripe sequence.
Beg with stripe sequence row 5 (so another 8 rows are to be worked using yarn A before yarn B is joined in), cont in patt until work meas 15 [15.5: 16: 16.5: 17] cm, ending with RS facing for next row.

Shape raglan armholes

Place markers at both ends of last row (to denote base of raglan armhole openings).
Note: While raglan shaping is being worked, and as the marked st becomes one of the sts to be decreased at end of row, marked st needs to be unravelled and crocheted back up to the required point. To do this, drop the marked st off left needle and unravel the st back to top of rib. Pick up st at top of rib using the crochet hook and, working from RS, draw the next 2 "bars" of yarn through st on hook. Cont in this way, picking up 2 "bars" of yarn and drawing this double st through loops on hook, until all "bars" have been worked. Place double st back onto left needle and treat this double st as one st when working the decrease.**
Keeping patt correct (and crocheting vertical lines along marked sts as detailed above), dec 1 st at each end of next and 15 [11: 9: 5: 2] foll 4th rows, then on foll 28 [38: 44: 54: 62] alt rows.
41 [41: 43: 43: 45] sts.
Work 1 row, ending with RS facing for next row.
Break yarn and leave sts on a holder (for neckband), unravelling all rem marked sts and crocheting these sts back up to last row.

SLEEVES

Using 3¼mm (US 3) needles and yarn C cast on 50 [50: 53: 53: 56] sts.
Work in rib as given for back for 46 [46: 48: 48: 48] rows, ending with RS facing for next row.
Inc 1 st at each end of next and foll 10th row, then on foll 8th row, then on foll 6th row, then on foll alt row, taking inc sts into rib and ending

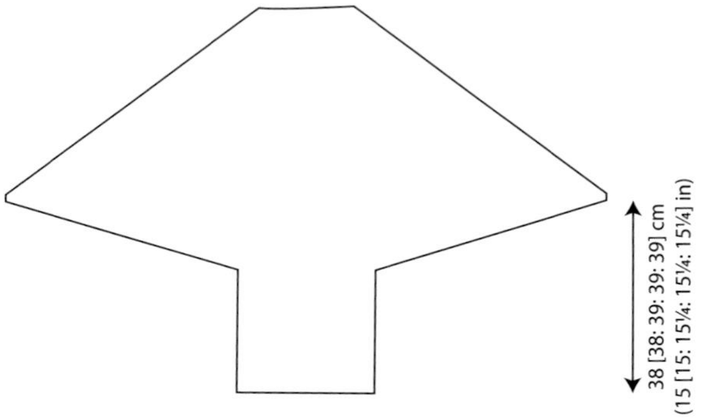
38 [38: 39: 39: 39] cm
(15 [15: 15¼: 15¼: 15¼] in)

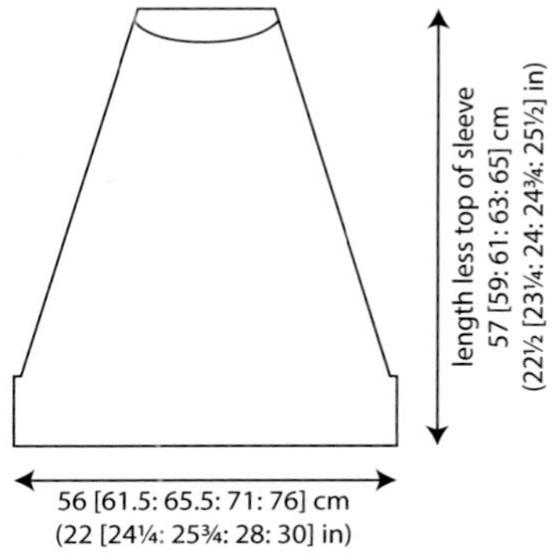
length less top of sleeve
57 [59: 61: 63: 65] cm
(22½ [23¼: 24: 24¾: 25½] in)
56 [61.5: 65.5: 71: 76] cm
(22 [24¼: 25¾: 28: 30] in)

with **WS** facing for next row.
60 [60: 63: 63: 66] sts.
Work 1 row, dec 2 [0: 1: 1: 2] sts evenly across
row and ending with RS facing for next row.
58 [60: 62: 62: 64] sts.
Change to 4mm (US 6) needles.
Beg with a K row, now work in st st throughout
as folls:
Cast on 3 sts at beg of next 6 [2: 6: 0: 0] rows,
then 4 sts at beg of foll 28 [32: 30: 36: 32] rows,
then 5 sts at beg of foll 0 [0: 0: 0: 4] rows.
188 [194: 200: 206: 212] sts.
Work 2 rows, ending with RS facing for next
row. (Sleeve should meas approx 38 [38: 39: 39:
39] cm.)
Shape raglan
Place markers at both ends of last row (to denote
base of raglan armhole).

Dec 1 st at each end of next 47 [49: 51: 53: 55]
rows, then on every foll alt row until 36 sts rem.
Work 1 row, ending with RS facing for next row.
Break yarn and leave sts on a holder (for
neckband).

MAKING UP
Press as described on the information page.
Join all raglan seams using back stitch, or mattress
stitch if preferred.
Neckband
With RS facing, using 3¼mm (US 3) circular
needle and yarn C, K across 36 sts on left sleeve
holder, place marker on needle, K across 41 [41:
43: 43: 45] sts on front holder inc 1 [1: 2: 2: 0] sts
evenly, place second marker on needle, K across
36 sts on right sleeve holder, place 3rd marker
on needle, K across 41 [41: 43: 43: 45] sts on

back holder inc 1 [1: 2: 2: 0] sts evenly, place 4th
marker on needle. 156 [156: 162: 162: 162] sts.
Round 1 (RS): ★K1, (P1, K2) to within 2 sts
of next marker, P1, K1, slip marker onto right
needle, rep from ★ to end.
This round forms rib.
Keeping rib correct, cont as folls:
Round 2: ★Sl 1, K1, psso, rib to within 2 sts
of next marker, K2tog, slip marker onto right
needle, rep from ★ to end.
Round 3: ★K1, rib to within 1 st of next
marker, K1, slip marker onto right needle, rep
from ★ to end.
Rep last 2 rounds twice more.
132 [132: 138: 138: 138] sts.
Cast off in rib, still decreasing either side of all 4
markers as before.
See information page for finishing instructions.

YATLEN
Grace Jones
Main image page **14, 15**
● ● ●

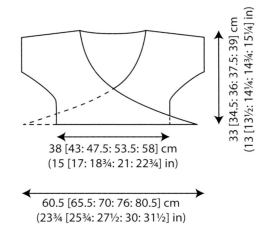

SIZE
To fit bust
81-86 91-97 102-107 112-117 122-127cm

32-34 36-38 40-42 44-46 48-50 in
Actual bust measurement of garment
88   97.5   107   119   128   cm
34½   38½   42¼   46¾   50½   in
YARN
Kidsilk Haze
2   2   3   3   3   x 25gm
(photographed in Drab 611)

NEEDLES
1 pair 5mm (no 6) (US 8) needles
5mm (no 6) (US 8) circular needle at least 90 cm
long

TENSION
17 sts and 25 rows to 10 cm measured over patt
using 5mm (US 8) needles.

Pattern note: Take care to ensure each dec of
patt is matched by an inc. If there are insufficient
sts to work both, work end sts of rows in st st.

BACK
Using 5mm (US 8) needles cast on 65 [73: 81:
91: 99] sts **very loosely**.
Beg and ending rows as indicated and repeating
the 8 row patt repeat throughout, cont in patt
from chart as folls:
Work 4 rows, ending with RS facing for next
row.
Inc 1 st at each end of next and 2 foll 4th rows,
then on foll 2 alt rows, then on foll 5 rows, taking
inc sts into patt and ending with RS facing for
next row. 85 [93: 101: 111: 119] sts.
Cast on 9 sts **very loosely** at beg of next 2 rows,
taking these sts into patt.
103 [111: 119: 129: 137] sts.
Work 48 [52: 56: 60: 64] rows, ending with
RS facing for next row. (Work should meas
approx 20 [21.5: 23: 24.5: 26] cm from last set
of cast-on sts.)

Shape shoulders and back neck
Next row (RS): Cast off 6 [7: 8: 9: 9] sts, patt
until there are 33 [36: 38: 42: 45] sts on right
needle and turn, leaving rem sts on a holder.
Work each side of neck separately.
Keeping patt correct, dec 1 st at neck edge of
next 6 rows **and at same time** cast off 6 [7: 8:
9: 9] sts at beg of 2nd row and foll 0 [1: 2: 2: 0] alt
rows, then 7 [8: –: –: 10] sts at beg of foll 2 [1: –:
–: 2] alt rows.
Work 1 row.
Cast off rem 7 [8: 8: 9: 10] sts.
With RS facing, slip centre 25 [25: 27: 27: 29] sts
onto a holder, rejoin yarn and patt to end.
Complete to match first side, reversing shapings.

LEFT FRONT
Using 5mm (US 8) needles cast on 68 [76: 84:
94: 102] sts **very loosely**.
Beg and ending rows as indicated, cont in patt
from chart as folls:
Work 4 rows, ending with RS facing for next
row.
Inc 1 st at beg of next row, taking inc st into patt.
69 [77: 85: 95: 103] sts.
Work 1 row, ending with RS facing for next row.

33 [34.5: 36: 37.5: 39] cm
(13 [13½: 14¼: 14¾: 15¼] in)

38 [43: 47.5: 53.5: 58] cm
(15 [17: 18¾: 21: 22¾] in)

60.5 [65.5: 70: 76: 80.5] cm
(23¾ [25¾: 27½: 30: 31½] in)

Shape front slope

Keeping patt correct, dec 1 st at end of next row and at same (front slope) edge on foll 15 rows **and at same time** inc 1 st at beg of 3rd and foll 4th row, then on foll 2 alt rows, then at same (side seam) edge on foll 5 rows, taking inc sts into patt and ending with RS facing for next row. 62 [70: 78: 88: 96] sts.

Cast on 9 sts **very loosely** at beg and dec 1 st at end of next row, taking cast-on sts into patt. 70 [78: 86: 96: 104] sts.

Keeping patt correct, dec 1 st at front slope edge on next 28 [32: 38: 44: 50] rows, then on foll 8 [8: 7: 6: 5] alt rows, then on foll 4th row. 33 [37: 40: 45: 48] sts.

Work 1 row, ending with RS facing for next row.

Shape shoulder

Cast off 6 [7: 8: 9: 9] sts at beg of next and foll 1 [2: 3: 3: 1] alt rows, then 7 [8: –: –: 10] sts at beg of foll 2 [1: –: –: 2] alt rows.

Work 1 row.

Cast off rem 7 [8: 8: 9: 10] sts.

RIGHT FRONT

Using 5mm (US 8) needles cast on 68 [76: 84: 94: 102] sts **very loosely**.

Beg and ending rows as indicated, cont in patt from chart as folls:

Work 4 rows, ending with RS facing for next row.

Inc 1 st at end of next row, taking inc st into patt. 69 [77: 85: 95: 103] sts.

Work 1 row, ending with RS facing for next row.

Shape front slope

Keeping patt correct, dec 1 st at beg of next row and at same (front slope) edge on foll 15 rows **and at same time** inc 1 st at end of 3rd and foll 4th row, then on foll 2 alt rows, then at same (side seam) edge on foll 5 rows, taking inc sts into patt and ending with RS facing for next row. 62 [70: 78: 88: 96] sts.

Complete to match left front, reversing shapings.

MAKING UP

Press as described on the information page.

Join both shoulder seams using back stitch, or mattress stitch if preferred.

Front band

With RS facing and using 5mm (US 8) circular needle, beg and ending at beg of front slope shaping, pick up and knit 74 [77: 80: 83: 86] sts up right front slope, and 7 sts down right side of back neck, K across 25 [25: 27: 27: 29] sts on back holder, then pick up and knit 7 sts up left side of back neck, and 74 [77: 80: 83: 86] sts down left front slope. 187 [193: 201: 207: 215] sts.

Cast off knitwise (on **WS**).

Ties (both alike)

With RS facing and using 5mm (US 8) needles, pick up and knit 5 sts along straight row-end edge of front, between cast-off edge of front band and cast-on edge of front.

Work in g st until tie meas 120 [130: 140: 150: 160] cm, ending with RS facing for next row.

Cast off.

See information page for finishing instructions.

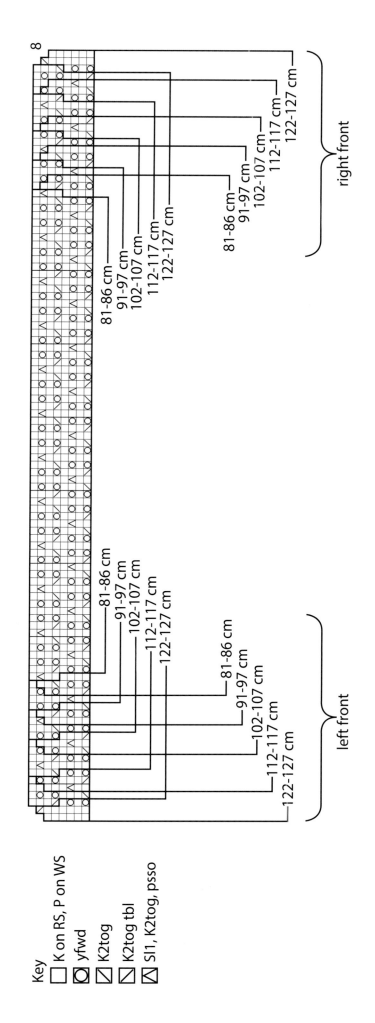

Key
- □ K on RS, P on WS
- ⊘ yfwd
- ◪ K2tog
- ◨ K2tog tbl
- ◩ Sl1, K2tog, psso

PURPOSE

Lisa Richardson

Main image page **52, 53**

●●

SIZE

To fit bust

81–86 91–97 102–107 112–117 122–127cm

32–34 36–38 40–42 44–46 48–50 in

Actual bust measurement of garment

89.5   100   110.5   121   129.5   cm

35¼   39¼   43½   47½   51   in

YARN

Creative Linen

3   4   4   5   5   x 100gm

(photographed in Apple 629)

NEEDLES

1 pair 4mm (no 8) (US 6) needles

1 pair 4½mm (no 7) (US 7) needles

BUTTONS – 2 x BN1800 from Bedecked.

Please see information page for contact details.

TENSION

19 sts and 33 rows to 10 cm measured over moss st using 4½mm (US 7) needles.

FRONT

Using 4½mm (US 7) needles cast on 85 [95: 105: 115: 123] sts.

Row 1 (RS): K1, *P1, K1, rep from * to end.

Row 2: As row 1.

These 2 rows form moss st.

Working in moss st throughout, cont as folls:

Work 8 [8: 10: 10: 12] rows, ending with RS facing for next row.

Dec 1 st at each end of next and 2 foll 6th rows. 79 [89: 99: 109: 117] sts.

Work 11 rows, ending with RS facing for next row.

Inc 1 st at each end of next and 2 foll 8th rows. 85 [95: 105: 115: 123] sts.

Work 9 [9: 9: 9: 11] rows, ending with RS facing for next row. (Front should meas approx 18 [18: 19: 19: 20] cm.)

Shape for cap sleeve extensions

Inc 1 st at each end of next and foll 6th row, then on 2 foll 4th rows, then on foll 3 alt rows. 99 [109: 119: 129: 137] sts.

Place markers at both ends of last row (to denote base of armhole openings).

Work 51 [57: 61: 67: 71] rows, ending with RS facing for next row. (Armhole should meas approx 16 [17.5: 19: 20.5: 22] cm.)

Shape shoulders and front neck

Cast off 2 [2: 3: 3: 3] sts at beg of next 4 rows. 91 [101: 107: 117: 125] sts.

Next row (RS): Cast off 2 [2: 3: 3: 3] sts, moss st until there are 34 [39: 40: 45: 48] sts on right needle and turn.

Work each side of neck separately.

Cast off 2 [2: 3: 3: 3] sts at beg of 2nd and foll 5 [0: 8: 4: 1] alt rows, then 3 [3: –: 4: 4] sts at beg of foll 3 [8: –: 4: 7] alt rows **and at same time** dec 1 st at neck edge of next 6 rows, then on foll 3 alt rows, then on foll 4th row.

Work 1 row.

Cast off rem 3 [3: 3: 4: 4] sts.

With RS facing, slip centre 19 [19: 21: 21: 23] sts onto a holder (for neckband), rejoin yarn and moss st to end.

Complete to match first side, reversing shapings.

RIGHT BACK

Using 4½mm (US 7) needles cast on 22 [27: 32: 37: 41] sts.

Row 1 (RS): *K1, P1, rep from * to last 0 [1: 0: 1: 1] st, K0 [1: 0: 1: 1].

Row 2: K0 [1: 0: 1: 1], *P1, K1, rep from * to end.

These 2 rows form moss st.

Working in moss st throughout, cont as folls:

Work 2 rows, ending with RS facing for next row.

Shape back opening edge

Next row (RS): Moss st to last 2 sts, inc **twice** in next st, moss st 1 st.

Working all back opening edge increases as set by last row, cont as folls:

Work 5 [5: 7: 7: 9] rows, inc 0 [0: 0: 0: 2] sts at end of – [–: –: –: 8th] of these rows and ending with RS facing for next row. 24 [29: 34: 39: 45] sts.

Dec 1 st at beg of next and 2 foll 6th rows **and at same time** inc 2 sts at back opening edge of next [next: next: next: 7th] and 2 [2: 1: 1: 0] foll 6th [6th: 8th: 8th: –] rows. 27 [32: 35: 40: 44] sts.

Work 11 rows, inc 2 sts at back opening edge of 6th [8th: 4th: 4th: 2nd] and 0 [0: 0: 0: 1] foll 8th row and ending with RS facing for next row. 29 [34: 37: 42: 48] sts.

Inc 1 st at beg of next and 2 foll 8th rows **and at same time** inc 2 sts at back opening edge of next [5th: next: next: 7th] and 1 [0: 0: 0: 0] foll 6th row, then on 1 [1: 2: 2: 1] foll 8th rows. 38 [41: 46: 51: 55] sts.

Work 9 [9: 9: 9: 11] rows, inc 2 sts at back opening edge of 6th [4th: 8th: 8th: 6th] of these rows and ending with RS facing for next row. 40 [43: 48: 53: 57] sts.

Shape for cap sleeve extension

Inc 1 st at beg of next and foll 6th row, then on 2 foll 4th rows, then on foll 3 alt rows **and at same time** inc 2 sts at back opening edge of 5th [3rd: 7th: 7th: 3rd] and 2 [2: 1: 1: 2] foll 8th rows. 53 [56: 59: 64: 70] sts.

Place marker at beg of last row (to denote base of armhole opening).

Inc 2 sts at back opening edge of 8th [6th: 2nd: 2nd: 6th] and 5 [6: 7: 5: 0] foll 8th rows, then on 0 [0: 0: 2: 6] foll 10th rows.

Back

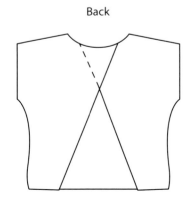

Front

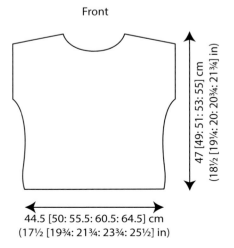

47 [49: 51: 53: 55] cm
(18½ [19¼: 20: 20¾: 21¾] in)

44.5 [50: 55.5: 60.5: 64.5] cm
(17½ [19¾: 21¾: 23¾: 25½] in)

65 [70: 75: 80: 84] sts.

Work 3 [3: 3: 5: 5] rows, ending with RS facing for next row.

Shape shoulder and back neck

Cast off 2 [2: 3: 3: 3] sts at beg of next and foll alt row. 61 [66: 69: 74: 78] sts.

Work 1 row.

Next row (RS): Cast off 2 [2: 3: 3: 3] sts, moss st until there are 34 [39: 40: 45: 48] sts on right needle and turn, leaving rem 25 [25: 26: 26: 27] sts on a holder (for neckband).

Cast off 2 [2: 3: 3: 3] sts at beg of 2nd and foll 5 [0: 8: 4: 1] alt rows, then 3 [3: –: 4: 4] sts at beg of foll 3 [8: –: 4: 7] alt rows **and at same time** dec 1 st at neck edge of next 6 rows, then on foll 3 alt rows, then on foll 4th row.

Work 1 row.

Cast off rem 3 [3: 3: 4: 4] sts.

LEFT BACK

Using 4½mm (US 7) needles cast on 22 [27: 32: 37: 41] sts.

Row 1 (RS): K0 [1: 0: 1: 1], *P1, K1, rep from * to end.

Row 2: *K1, P1, rep from * to last 0 [1: 0: 1: 1] st, K0 [1: 0: 1: 1].

These 2 rows form moss st.

Working in moss st throughout, cont as folls:
Work 2 rows, ending with RS facing for next row.

Shape back opening edge

Next row (RS): Moss st 1 st, inc **twice** in next st, moss st to end.

Working all back opening edge increases as set by last row, cont as folls:
Work 5 [5: 7: 7: 9] rows, inc 0 [0: 0: 0: 2] sts at beg of – [–: –: –: 8th] of these rows and ending with RS facing for next row.
24 [29: 34: 39: 45] sts.

Dec 1 st at end of next and 2 foll 6th rows **and at same time** inc 2 sts at back opening edge of next [next: next: next: 7th] and 2 [2: 1: 1: 0] foll 6th [6th: 8th: 8th: –] rows. 27 [32: 35: 40: 44] sts.
Reversing shapings, now work as given for right back to beg of shoulder shaping.

Shape shoulder and back neck

Work 1 row.

Cast off 2 [2: 3: 3: 3] sts at beg of next row.

Next row (RS): Moss st 2 sts, cast off 2 sts (to make first buttonhole – cast on 2 sts over these cast-off sts on next row), moss st until there are 23 sts on right needle after cast-off, cast off 2 sts (to make second buttonhole – cast on 2 sts over these cast-off sts on next row), moss st to end.

Cast off 2 [2: 3: 3: 3] sts at beg of next row.
61 [66: 69: 74: 78] sts.

Next row (RS): K25 [25: 26: 26: 27] and slip these sts onto a holder (for neckband), moss st to end.

Complete to match right back, reversing shapings.

MAKING UP

Press as described on the information page.
Join both shoulder seams using back stitch, or mattress stitch if preferred.

Neckband

With RS facing and using 4mm (US 6) needles, slip 25 [25: 26: 26: 27] sts on left back holder onto right needle, rejoin yarn and pick up and knit 16 sts up left side of back neck, and 16 sts down left side of front neck, K across 19 [19: 21: 21: 23] sts on front holder, pick up and knit 16 sts up right side of front neck, and 16 sts down right side of back neck, then K across 25 [25: 26: 26: 27] sts on right back holder.
133 [133: 137: 137: 141] sts.

Work in g st for 4 rows, ending with **WS** facing for next row.

Cast off knitwise (on **WS**).

See information page for finishing instructions.

MONDRIAN

Annika Andrea Wolke

Main image page **92, 93**

● ● ●

SIZE

To fit bust

81-86	91-97	102-107	112-117	122-127	cm
32-34	36-38	40-42	44-46	48-50	in

Actual bust measurement of garment

88	97.5	108	117.5	128	cm
34½	38½	42½	46¼	50½	in

YARN

Fine Lace

4	4	4	5	5	x 50gm

(photographed in Pigeon 950)

NEEDLES

1 pair 3¼mm (no 10) (US 3) needles

Cable needle

TENSION

42 sts and 36 rows to 10 cm measured over rib patt using 3¼mm (US 3) needles and yarn DOUBLE.

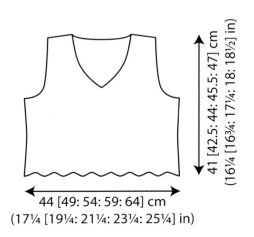

41 [42.5: 44: 45.5: 47] cm
(16¼ [16¾: 17¼: 18: 18½] in)

44 [49: 54: 59: 64] cm
(17¼ [19¼: 21¼: 23¼: 25¼] in)

BACK

Using 3¼mm (US 3) needles and yarn DOUBLE cast on 173 [193: 215: 235: 257] sts.
Work border patt as folls:

Row 1 (RS): Knit.

Row 2: K1 [1: 0: 0: 1], (P1 tbl, K1) 3 [0: 2: 3: 0] times, *P7, K1, rep from * to last 6 [0: 3: 5: 0] sts, (P1 tbl, K1) 3 [0: 1: 2: 0] times, (P1 tbl) 0 [0: 1: 1: 0] time.

Row 3: (K1 tbl) 0 [0: 1: 1: 0] time, (P1, K1 tbl) 3 [0: 1: 2: 0] times, *P1, sl 1, K1, psso, K5, yfrn, P1, yon, K5, K2tog, rep from * to last 7 [1: 4: 6: 1] sts, (P1, K1 tbl) 3 [0: 2: 3: 0] times, P1 [1: 0: 0: 1].

Row 4: K1 [1: 0: 0: 1], (P1 tbl, K1) 3 [0: 2: 3: 0] times, *P2tog, P4, yon, K3, yfrn, P4, P2tog tbl, K1, rep from * to last 6 [0: 3: 5: 0] sts, (P1 tbl, K1) 3 [0: 1: 2: 0] times, (P1 tbl) 0 [0: 1: 1: 0] time.

Row 5: (K1 tbl) 0 [0: 1: 1: 0] time, (P1, K1 tbl) 3 [0: 1: 2: 0] times, *P1, sl 1, K1, psso, K3, yfwd, K1, P3, K1, yfwd, K3, K2tog, rep from * to last 7 [1: 4: 6: 1] sts, (P1, K1 tbl) 3 [0: 2: 3: 0] times, P1 [1: 0: 0: 1].

Row 6: K1 [1: 0: 0: 1], (P1 tbl, K1) 3 [0: 2: 3: 0] times, *P2tog, P2, yrn, P2, K3, P2, yrn, P2, P2tog tbl, K1, rep from * to last 6 [0: 3: 5: 0] sts, (P1 tbl, K1) 3 [0: 1: 2: 0] times, (P1 tbl) 0 [0: 1: 1: 0] time.

Row 7: (K1 tbl) 0 [0: 1: 1: 0] time, (P1, K1 tbl) 3 [0: 1: 2: 0] times, *P1, sl 1, K1, psso, K1, yfrn, P1, K2, P3, K2, P1, yon, K1, K2tog, rep from * to last 7 [1: 4: 6: 1] sts, (P1, K1 tbl) 3 [0: 2: 3: 0] times, P1 [1: 0: 0: 1].

Row 8: K1 [1: 0: 0: 1], (P1 tbl, K1) 3 [0: 2: 3: 0] times, *P2tog, yon, K2, P2, K3, P2, K2, yfrn, P2tog tbl, K1, rep from * to last 6 [0: 3: 5: 0] sts, (P1 tbl, K1) 3 [0: 1: 2: 0] times, (P1 tbl) 0 [0: 1: 1: 0] time.

Row 9: (K1 tbl) 0 [0: 1: 1: 0] time, (P1, K1 tbl) 3 [0: 1: 2: 0] times, *P1, yon, sl 1, K1, psso, P2, yon, K1, sl 1, K1, psso, P1, K2tog, K1, yfrn, P2, K2tog, yfrn, rep from * to last 7 [1: 4: 6: 1] sts, (P1, K1 tbl) 3 [0: 2: 3: 0] times, P1 [1: 0: 0: 1].

Row 10: K1 [1: 0: 0: 1], (P1 tbl, K1) 3 [0: 2: 3: 0] times, *P2, K2, K1 tbl, P2, K1, P2, K1 tbl, K2, P2, K1, rep from * to last 6 [0: 3: 5: 0] sts, (P1 tbl, K1) 3 [0: 1: 2: 0] times, (P1 tbl) 0 [0: 1: 1: 0] time.

Row 11: (K1 tbl) 0 [0: 1: 1: 0] time, (P1, K1 tbl) 3 [0: 1: 2: 0] times, *P1, K1 tbl, yfwd, sl 1, K1, psso, P2, slip next 5 sts onto cable needle, wind yarn 3 times anti-clockwise around these 5 sts and then slip these 5 sts onto right needle, P2, K2tog, yfwd, K1 tbl, rep from * to last 7 [1: 4: 6: 1] sts, (P1, K1 tbl) 3 [0: 2: 3: 0] times, P1 [1: 0: 0: 1].

Row 12: K1 [1: 0: 0: 1], (P1 tbl, K1) 3 [0: 2: 3: 0] times, *P1 tbl, K1, P1, K2, P2, K1, P2, K2, P1, K1, P1 tbl, K1, rep from * to last 6 [0: 3: 5: 0] sts, (P1 tbl, K1) 3 [0: 1: 2: 0] times, (P1 tbl) 0 [0: 1: 1: 0] time.

Row 13: (K1 tbl) 0 [0: 1: 1: 0] time, (P1, K1 tbl) 3 [0: 1: 2: 0] times, *P1, K1 tbl, P1, yon, sl 1, K1, psso, K2tog, K1, yfrn, P1, yon, K1, sl 1, K1, psso, K2tog, yfrn, P1, K1 tbl, rep from * to last 7 [1: 4:

6: 1] sts, (P1, K1 tbl) 3 [0: 2: 3: 0] times, P1 [1: 0: 0: 1].

Row 14: K1 [1: 0: 0: 1], (P1 tbl, K1) 3 [0: 2: 3: 0] times, *P1 tbl, K1, P4, K1 tbl, K1, K1 tbl, P4, K1, P1 tbl, K1, rep from * to last 6 [0: 3: 5: 0] sts, (P1 tbl, K1) 3 [0: 1: 2: 0] times, (P1 tbl) 0 [0: 1: 1: 0] time.

Row 15: (K1 tbl) 0 [0: 1: 1: 0] time, (P1, K1 tbl) 3 [0: 1: 2: 0] times, *(P1, K1 tbl) twice, yfwd, sl 1, K1, psso, K1, P3, K1, K2tog, yfwd, K1 tbl, P1, K1 tbl, rep from * to last 7 [1: 4: 6: 1] sts, (P1, K1 tbl) 3 [0: 2: 3: 0] times, P1 [1: 0: 0: 1].

Row 16: K1 [1: 0: 0: 1], (P1 tbl, K1) 3 [0: 2: 3: 0] times, *(P1 tbl, K1) twice, P2, K3, P2, (K1, P1 tbl) twice, K1, rep from * to last 6 [0: 3: 5: 0] sts, (P1 tbl, K1) 3 [0: 1: 2: 0] times, (P1 tbl) 0 [0: 1: 1: 0] time.

Row 17: (K1 tbl) 0 [0: 1: 1: 0] time, (P1, K1 tbl) 3 [0: 1: 2: 0] times, *(P1, K1 tbl) twice, P1, yon, sl 1, K1, psso, P3, K2tog, yfrn, (P1, K1 tbl) twice, rep from * to last 7 [1: 4: 6: 1] sts, (P1, K1 tbl) 3 [0: 2: 3: 0] times, P1 [1: 0: 0: 1].

Row 18: K1 [1: 0: 0: 1], (P1 tbl, K1) 3 [0: 2: 3: 0] times, *(P1 tbl, K1) twice, P2, K3, P2, (K1, P1 tbl) twice, K1, rep from * to last 6 [0: 3: 5: 0] sts, (P1 tbl, K1) 3 [0: 1: 2: 0] times, (P1 tbl) 0 [0: 1: 1: 0] time.

Row 19: (K1 tbl) 0 [0: 1: 1: 0] time, (P1, K1 tbl) 3 [0: 1: 2: 0] times, *(P1, K1 tbl) 3 times, yfwd, sl 1, K1, psso, P1, K2tog, yfwd, K1 tbl, (P1, K1 tbl) twice, rep from * to last 7 [1: 4: 6: 1] sts, (P1, K1 tbl) 3 [0: 2: 3: 0] times, P1 [1: 0: 0: 1].

Row 20: K1 [1: 0: 0: 1], (P1 tbl, K1) 3 [0: 2: 3: 0] times, *(P1 tbl, K1) 3 times, (P1, K1) twice, (P1 tbl, K1) 3 times, rep from * to last 6 [0: 3: 5: 0] sts, (P1 tbl, K1) 3 [0: 1: 2: 0] times, (P1 tbl) 0 [0: 1: 1: 0] time.

These 20 rows complete border patt.
Now work in rib patt as folls:

Row 1 (RS): (K1 tbl) 0 [0: 1: 1: 0] time, *P1, K1 tbl, rep from * to last 1 [1: 0: 0: 1] st, P1 [1: 0: 0: 1].

Row 2: (P1 tbl) 0 [0: 1: 1: 0] time, *K1, P1 tbl, rep from * to last 1 [1: 0: 0: 1] st, K1 [1: 0: 0: 1].
These 2 rows form rib patt.
Cont in rib patt, shaping side seams by inc 1 st at each end of next and 5 foll 8th rows, taking inc sts into rib patt. 185 [205: 227: 247: 269] sts.
Cont straight until back meas 20 cm, ending with RS facing for next row.

Shape armholes
Keeping patt correct, cast off 10 [12: 13: 15: 16] sts at beg of next 2 rows.
165 [181: 201: 217: 237] sts.

Next row (RS): K1, K1 tbl, P2tog, patt to last 4 sts, P2tog tbl, K1 tbl, K1.

Next row: K1, P1 tbl, sl 1, K1, psso, patt to last 4 sts, K2tog, P1 tbl, K1.
161 [177: 197: 213: 233] sts.
Working all decreases as set by last 2 rows and now working first and last st of every row as a K st, cont as folls:★★
Dec 1 st at each end of next 7 [9: 11: 11: 13]

rows, then on foll 9 [11: 13: 13: 15] alt rows.
129 [137: 149: 165: 177] sts.
Cont straight until armhole meas 19 [20.5: 22: 23.5: 25] cm, ending with RS facing for next row.

Shape back neck and shoulders
Next row (RS): Cast off 5 [6: 7: 9: 9] sts, patt until there are 30 [33: 36: 42: 46] sts on right needle and turn, leaving rem sts on a holder.
Work each side of neck separately.
Keeping patt correct and working all neck decreases in same way as armhole decreases, dec 1 st at neck edge of next 6 rows **and at same time** cast off 6 [6: 7: 9: 10] sts at beg of 2nd and foll 2 [0: 1: 2: 2] alt rows, then - [7: 8: -: -] sts at beg of foll - [2: 1: -: -] alt rows.
Work 1 row.
Cast off rem 6 [7: 8: 9: 10] sts.
With RS facing, rejoin yarn and cast off centre 59 [59: 63: 63: 67] sts, patt to end.
Complete to match first side, reversing shapings.

FRONT

Work as given for back to ★★.
Dec 1 st at each end of next 5 rows, ending with **WS** facing for next row.
151 [167: 187: 203: 223] sts.

Next row (WS): K1, P1 tbl, sl 1, K1, psso, patt 71 [79: 89: 97: 107] sts, inc in next st, patt 71 [79: 89: 97: 107] sts, K2tog, P1 tbl, K1.
150 [166: 186: 202: 222] sts.

Divide for front neck
Next row (RS): K1, K1 tbl, P2tog, patt 70 [78: 88: 96: 106] sts, K1 and turn, leaving rem sts on a holder. 74 [82: 92: 100: 110] sts.
Work each side of neck separately.
Working all decreases as set by armhole decreases and now working first and last st of every row as a K st, cont as folls:
Dec 1 st at neck edge of next 28 [22: 20: 16: 14] rows, then on foll 6 [12: 16: 20: 24] alt rows, then on 2 foll 4th rows **and at same time** dec 1 st at armhole edge of 2nd [next: next: next: next] and foll 0 [1: 3: 3: 5] rows, then on foll 8 [11: 13: 13: 15] alt rows. 29 [33: 37: 45: 49] sts.
Cont straight until front matches back to beg of shoulder shaping, ending with RS facing for next row.

Shape shoulder
Cast off 5 [6: 7: 9: 9] sts at beg of next and foll 0 [1: 2: 3: 0] alt rows, then 6 [7: 8: -: 10] sts at beg of foll 3 [2: 1: -: 3] alt rows.
Work 1 row.
Cast off rem 6 [7: 8: 9: 10] sts.
With RS facing, rejoin yarn and K1, patt to end.
Complete to match first side, reversing shapings.

MAKING UP

Press as described on the information page.
Join both shoulder seams using back stitch, or mattress stitch if preferred.
See information page for finishing instructions.

SIMPLE

Martin Storey

Main image page **58, 59**

● ● ●

SIZE

To fit bust

81-86 91-97 102-107 112-117 122-127cm

32-34 36-38 40-42 44-46 48-50 in

Actual bust measurement of garment

87.5 97.5 107.5 117.5 127.5 cm

34½ 38½ 42¼ 46¼ 50¼ in

YARN

Kidsilk Haze and Fine Lace

A KSH Pearl 590

| 5 | 5 | 6 | 6 | 7 | x 25gm |

B FL Cameo 920

| 3 | 3 | 3 | 4 | 4 | x 50gm |

NEEDLES

1 pair 2¾mm (no 12) (US 2) needles

1 pair 3¼mm (no 10) (US 3) needles

TENSION

24 sts and 33 rows to 10 cm measured over st st,
24 sts and 40 rows to 10 cm measured over patt,
both using 3¼mm (US 3) needles and one strand
each of yarns A and B held together.

BACK

Using 2¾mm (US 2) needles and one strand
each of yarns A and B held together cast on
109 [121: 133: 145: 157] sts.

Row 1 (RS): K1, *P1, K1, rep from * to end.

Row 2: P1, *K1, P1, rep from * to end.

These 2 rows form rib.

Work in rib for a further 8 rows, ending with RS
facing for next row.

Change to 3¼mm (US 3) needles.

Beg with a K row, now work in st st throughout
as folls:

Work 12 [12: 14: 14: 16] rows, ending with RS
facing for next row.

Dec 1 st at each end of next and 5 foll 8th rows.
97 [109: 121: 133: 145] sts.

Work 19 rows, ending with RS facing for next
row.

Inc 1 st at each end of next and 3 foll 10th rows.
105 [117: 129: 141: 153] sts.

Cont straight until back meas 38 [38.5: 39: 39.5:
40] cm, ending with RS facing for next row.

Shape raglan armholes

Cast off 3 sts at beg of next 2 rows.

99 [111: 123: 135: 147] sts.

Now work in patt and shape raglans as folls:

Row 1 (RS): K2, sl 1, K1, psso, K to last 4 sts,
K2tog, K2.

Row 2: P3 [3: 3: 2: 2], (P2tog) 0 [0: 0: 1: 1] times,
K to last 3 [3: 3: 4: 4] sts, (P2tog tbl) 0 [0: 0: 1: 1]
times, P3 [3: 3: 2: 2]. 97 [109: 121: 131: 143] sts.

Row 3: K3 [3: 3: 2: 2], (sl 1, K1, psso) 0 [0: 0:
1: 1] times, P2 [2: 2: 0: 0], P2tog, yrn, *P4, P2tog,
yrn, rep from * to last 6 [6: 6: 5: 5] sts, P3 [3: 3:
1: 1], (K2tog) 0 [0: 0: 1: 1] times, K3 [3: 3: 2: 2].

Row 4: (P2, P2tog) 0 [0: 0: 0: 1] times, P to last
0 [0: 0: 0: 4] sts, (P2tog tbl, P2) 0 [0: 0: 0: 1] times.
97 [109: 121: 129: 139] sts.

Row 5: As row 1.

Row 6: As row 4. 95 [107: 119: 127: 135] sts.

Row 7: (K2, sl 1, K1, psso) 0 [0: 0: 1: 1] times, K
to last 0 [0: 0: 4: 4] sts, (K2tog, K2) 0 [0: 0: 1: 1]
times.

Row 8: Purl. 95 [107: 119: 125: 133] sts.

Last 8 rows form patt and beg raglan shaping.

Working all raglan decreases as set by last 8 rows
and keeping patt correct, dec 1 st at each end of
next and 5 [2: 0: 0: 0] foll 4th rows, then on foll
22 [31: 38: 41: 44] alt rows. 39 [39: 41: 41: 43] sts.

Work 1 row, ending with RS facing for next row.

Break yarn and leave sts on a holder (for
neckband).

FRONT

Work as given for back until 63 [63: 69: 69: 75] sts
rem in raglan armhole shaping.

Work 1 row, ending with RS facing for next row.

Shape front neck

Next row (RS): K2, sl 1, K1, psso, patt 12 [12:
15: 15: 18] sts and turn, leaving rem sts on a
holder. 15 [15: 18: 18: 21] sts.

Work each side of neck separately.

Keeping patt correct and working all raglan
armhole decreases as set, dec 1 st at raglan
armhole edge of 2nd and foll 3 [3: 5: 5: 7] alt

rows **and at same time** dec 1 st at neck edge
of next 6 rows, then on foll 1 [1: 2: 2: 2] alt rows,
then on 0 [0: 0: 0: 1] foll 4th row. 4 sts.

Work 1 row.

Next row (RS): K1, sl 1, K2tog, psso.

Next row: P2.

Next row: K2tog and fasten off.

With RS facing, slip centre 31 sts onto a holder
(for neckband), rejoin yarn and patt to last 4 sts,
K2tog, K2. 15 [15: 18: 18: 21] sts.

Complete to match first side, reversing shapings.

SLEEVES

Using 2¾mm (US 2) needles and one strand
each of yarns A and B held together cast on
57 [63: 69: 75: 81] sts.

Work in rib as given for back for 10 rows, ending
with RS facing for next row.

Change to 3¼mm (US 3) needles.

Now work in patt as folls:

Row 1 (RS): Knit.

Row 2: Purl.

Row 3: Inc in first st, K to last st, inc in last st.
59 [65: 71: 77: 83] sts.

Row 4: Knit.

Row 5: *P4, P2tog, yrn, rep from * to last 5 sts,
P5.

Row 6: Purl.

Row 7: As row 3. 61 [67: 73: 79: 85] sts.

Row 8: Purl.

These 8 rows form patt and beg sleeve shaping.

Cont in patt, shaping sides by inc 1 st at each
end of 3rd and 5 foll 4th rows, then on 2 foll 6th
rows, taking inc sts into patt.

77 [83: 89: 95: 101] sts.

Work 5 rows, ending after patt row 8 and with
RS facing for next row. (Sleeve should meas
approx 15 cm.)

Shape raglan

Keeping patt correct, cast off 3 sts at beg of next
2 rows. 71 [77: 83: 89: 95] sts.

Working all raglan decreases in same way as
raglan armhole decreases, dec 1 st at each end of
next and every foll alt row until 65 sts rem, then
on 14 foll 4th rows. 37 sts.

Work 1 row, ending with RS facing for next row.

Left sleeve only

Work 1 row, ending with **WS** facing for next
row.

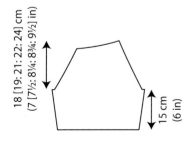

18 [19: 21: 22: 24] cm
(7 [7½: 8¼: 8¾: 9½] in)

15 cm
(6 in)

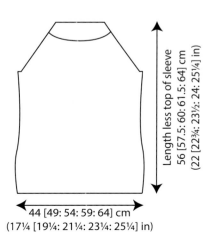

Length less top of sleeve
56 [57.5: 60: 61.5: 64] cm
(22 [22¾: 23½: 24: 25¼] in)

44 [49: 54: 59: 64] cm
(17¼ [19¼: 21¼: 23¼: 25¼] in)

Cast off 4 sts at beg of next row, then 5 sts at beg of foll 5 alt rows **and at same time** dec 1 st at beg of 2nd and 2 foll 4th rows. 5 sts.

Right sleeve only

Cast off 4 sts at beg of next row, then 5 sts at beg of foll 5 alt rows **and at same time** dec 1 st at end of 3rd and 2 foll 4th rows. 5 sts.

Work 1 row, ending with RS facing for next row.

Both sleeves

Cast off rem 5 sts.

MAKING UP

Press as described on the information page.

Join both front and right back raglan seams using back stitch, or mattress stitch if preferred.

Neckband

With RS facing, using 2¾mm (US 2) needles and one strand each of yarns A and B held together, pick up and knit 31 sts from top of left sleeve, and 10 [10: 12: 12: 14] sts down left side of front neck, K across 31 sts on front holder, pick up and knit 10 [10: 12: 12: 14] sts up right side of front neck, and 31 sts from top of right sleeve, then K across 39 [39: 41: 41: 43] sts on back holder dec 1 st at centre.

151 [151: 157: 157: 163] sts.

Beg with row 2, work in rib as given for back for 9 rows, ending with RS facing for next row.

Cast off in rib.

See information page for finishing instructions.

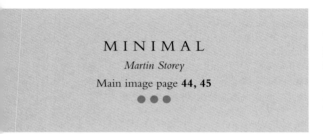

MINIMAL

Martin Storey

Main image page **44, 45**

● ● ●

SIZE

To fit bust

81–86 91–97 102–107 112–117 122–127cm

32–34 36–38 40–42 44–46 48–50 in

Actual bust measurement of garment

| 90 | 101 | 110 | 121 | 130 | cm |
| 35½ | 39¾ | 43¼ | 47¾ | 51¼ | in |

YARN

Cotton Glacé

| 9 | 10 | 11 | 12 | 13 | x 50gm |

(photographed in Oyster 730)

NEEDLES

1 pair 2¾mm (no 12) (US 2) needles
1 pair 3¼mm (no 10) (US 3) needles

BUTTONS – 7 x G427224190 (metal shank) from Groves. Please see information page for contact details.

TENSION

22 sts and 31 rows to 10 cm measured over patt using 3¼mm (US 3) needles.

BACK

Using 2¾mm (US 2) needles cast on 99 [111: 121: 133: 143] sts.

Row 1 (RS): K1, ★P1, K1, rep from ★ to end.

Row 2: P1, ★K1, P1, rep from ★ to end.

These 2 rows form rib.

Work in rib for a further 18 rows, ending with RS facing for next row.

Change to 3¼mm (US 3) needles.

Now work in patt as folls:

Row 1 (RS): Knit.

Row 2 and every foll alt row: Purl.

Row 3: K1 [7: 4: 2: 7], yfwd, sl 1, K1, psso, ★K6, yfwd, sl 1, K1, psso, rep from ★ to last 0 [6: 3: 1: 6] sts, K0 [6: 3: 1: 6].

Row 5: Knit.

Row 7: K5 [3: 8: 6: 3], yfwd, sl 1, K1, psso, ★K6, yfwd, sl 1, K1, psso, rep from ★ to last 4 [2: 7: 5: 2] sts, K4 [2: 7: 5: 2].

Row 8: As row 2.

These 8 rows form patt.

Cont in patt until back meas 31 [31.5: 32: 32.5: 33] cm, ending with RS facing for next row.

Shape armholes

Keeping patt correct, cast off 4 [5: 6: 7: 8] sts at beg of next 2 rows. 91 [101: 109: 119: 127] sts.

Next row (RS): K1, sl 1, K1, psso, patt to last 3 sts, K2tog, K1.

Next row: P1, P2tog, patt to last 3 sts, P2tog tbl, P1.

Working all armhole decreases as set by last 2 rows, dec 1 st at each end of next 3 [5: 5: 7: 7] rows, then on foll 4 [5: 6: 5: 6] alt rows. 73 [77: 83: 91: 97] sts.

Cont straight until armhole meas 19 [20.5: 22: 23.5: 25] cm, ending with RS facing for next row.

Shape shoulders and back neck

Keeping patt correct, cast off 4 [5: 5: 6: 7] sts at beg of next 2 rows. 65 [67: 73: 79: 83] sts.

Next row (RS): Cast off 5 [5: 6: 7: 7] sts, patt until there are 13 [14: 15: 17: 18] sts on right needle and turn, leaving rem sts on a holder.

Work each side of neck separately.

Keeping patt correct, dec 1 st at neck edge of next 3 rows **and at same time** cast off 5 [5: 6: 7: 7] sts at beg of 2nd row.

Cast off rem 5 [6: 6: 7: 8] sts.

With RS facing, slip centre 29 [29: 31: 31: 33] sts onto a holder (for neckband), rejoin yarn and

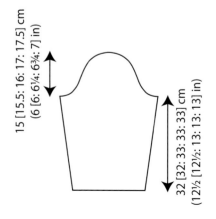

15 [15.5: 16: 17: 17.5] cm
(6 [6: 6¼: 6¾: 7] in)

32 [32: 33: 33: 33] cm
(12½ [12½: 13: 13: 13] in)

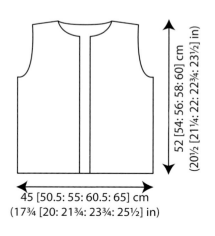

52 [54: 56: 58: 60] cm
(20½ [21¼: 22: 22¾: 23½] in)

45 [50.5: 55: 60.5: 65] cm
(17¾ [20: 21¾: 23¾: 25½] in)

patt to end.
Complete to match first side, reversing shapings.

LEFT FRONT

Using 2¾mm (US 2) needles cast on 58 [64: 68: 74: 80] sts.
Row 1 (RS): ★K1, P1, rep from ★ to last 2 sts, K2.
Row 2: ★K1, P1, rep from ★ to end.
These 2 rows form rib.
Work in rib for a further 17 rows, ending with **WS** facing for next row.
Row 20 (WS): Rib 9 and slip these 9 sts onto a holder (for button band), M1, rib to last 2 [2: 0: 0: 2] sts, (K2tog) 1 [1: 0: 0: 1] times.
49 [55: 60: 66: 71] sts.
Change to 3¼mm (US 3) needles.
Now work in patt as folls:
Row 1 (RS): Knit.
Row 2 and every foll alt row: Purl.
Row 3: K1 [7: 4: 2: 7], ★yfwd, sl 1, K1, psso, K6, rep from ★ to end.
Row 5: Knit.
Row 7: K5 [3: 8: 6: 3], yfwd, sl 1, K1, psso, ★K6, yfwd, sl 1, K1, psso, rep from ★ to last 2 sts, K2.
Row 8: As row 2.
These 8 rows form patt.
Cont in patt until left front matches back to beg of armhole shaping, ending with RS facing for next row.
Shape armhole
Keeping patt correct, cast off 4 [5: 6: 7: 8] sts at beg of next row. 45 [50: 54: 59: 63] sts.
Work 1 row.
Working all armhole decreases in same way as given for back, dec 1 st at armhole edge of next 5 [7: 7: 9: 9] rows, then on foll 4 [5: 6: 5: 6] alt rows. 36 [38: 41: 45: 48] sts.
Cont straight until 26 [26: 28: 28: 30] rows less have been worked than on back to beg of shoulder shaping, ending with RS facing for next row.
Shape front neck
Next row (RS): Patt 31 [33: 36: 40: 43] sts and turn, leaving rem 5 sts on a holder (for neckband).
Keeping patt correct and working all neck decreases in same way as armhole decreases, dec 1 st at neck edge of next 6 rows, then on foll 4 [4: 5: 5: 6] alt rows, then on 2 foll 4th rows. 19 [21: 23: 27: 29] sts.
Work 3 rows, ending with RS facing for next row.
Shape shoulder
Keeping patt correct, cast off 4 [5: 5: 6: 7] sts at beg of next row, then 5 [5: 6: 7: 7] sts at beg of foll 2 alt rows.
Work 1 row.
Cast off rem 5 [6: 6: 7: 8] sts.

RIGHT FRONT

Using 2¾mm (US 2) needles cast on 58 [64: 68: 74: 80] sts.
Row 1 (RS): K2, ★P1, K1, rep from ★ to end.
Row 2: ★P1, K1, rep from ★ to end.

These 2 rows form rib.
Work in rib for a further 4 rows, ending with **RS** facing for next row.
Row 7 (RS): K2, P1, sl 1, K1, psso, yfwd (to make first buttonhole), rib to end.
Work in rib for a further 12 rows, ending with **WS** facing for next row.
Row 20 (WS): (K2tog) 1 [1: 0: 0: 1] times, rib to last 9 sts, M1 and turn, leaving rem 9 sts on a holder (for buttonhole band).
49 [55: 60: 66: 71] sts.
Change to 3¼mm (US 3) needles.
Now work in patt as folls:
Row 1 (RS): Knit.
Row 2 and every foll alt row: Purl.
Row 3: K7, yfwd, sl 1, K1, psso, ★K6, yfwd, sl 1, K1, psso, rep from ★ to last 0 [6: 3: 1: 6] sts, K0 [6: 3: 1: 6].
Row 5: Knit.
Row 7: K3, yfwd, sl 1, K1, psso, ★K6, yfwd, sl 1, K1, psso, rep from ★ to last 4 [2: 7: 5: 2] sts, K4 [2: 7: 5: 2].
Row 8: As row 2.
These 8 rows form patt.
Complete to match left front, reversing shapings and working first row of neck shaping as folls:
Shape front neck
Next row (RS): Break yarn and slip first 5 sts onto a holder (for neckband). Rejoin yarn and patt to end. 31 [33: 36: 40: 43] sts.

SLEEVES

Using 2¾mm (US 2) needles cast on 49 [51: 53: 53: 55] sts.
Work in rib as given for back for 20 rows, ending with RS facing for next row.
Change to 3¼mm (US 3) needles.
Now work in patt as folls:
Row 1 (RS): Knit.
Row 2 and every foll alt row: Purl.
Row 3: (Inc in first st) 0 [1: 1: 1: 1] times, K4 [4: 5: 5: 6], yfwd, sl 1, K1, psso, ★K6, yfwd, sl 1, K1, psso, rep from ★ to last 3 [4: 5: 5: 6] sts, K3 [3: 4: 4: 5], (inc in last st) 0 [1: 1: 1: 1] times.
49 [53: 55: 55: 57] sts.
Row 5: (Inc in first st) 1 [0: 0: 0: 0] times, K to last 1 [0: 0: 0: 0] st, (inc in last st) 1 [0: 0: 0: 0] times. 51 [53: 55: 55: 57] sts.
Row 7: (Inc in first st) 0 [1: 1: 1: 1] times, K1 [1: 2: 2: 3], yfwd, sl 1, K1, psso, ★K6, yfwd, sl 1, K1, psso, rep from ★ to last 0 [1: 2: 2: 3] sts, K0 [0: 1: 1: 2], (inc in last st) 0 [1: 1: 1: 1] times.
51 [55: 57: 57: 59] sts.
Row 8: As row 2.
These 8 rows form patt and beg sleeve shaping.
Cont in patt, shaping sides by inc 1 st at each end of 3rd and 0 [0: 2: 8: 11] foll 4th rows, then on every foll 6th row until there are 71 [75: 79: 83: 87] sts, taking inc sts into patt.
Cont straight until sleeve meas 32 [32: 33: 33: 33] cm, ending with RS facing for next row.
Shape top
Keeping patt correct, cast off 4 [5: 6: 7: 8] sts at beg of next 2 rows. 63 [65: 67: 69: 71] sts.
Working all decreases in same way as armhole

decreases, dec 1 st at each end of next 3 rows, then on foll 2 alt rows, then on 5 foll 4th rows. 43 [45: 47: 49: 51] sts.
Work 1 row.
Dec 1 st at each end of next and every foll alt row until 33 sts rem, then on foll 7 rows, ending with RS facing for next row.
Cast off rem 19 sts.

MAKING UP

Press as described on the information page.
Join both shoulder seams using back stitch, or mattress stitch if preferred.
Button band
Slip 9 sts on left front holder onto 2¾mm (US 2) needles and rejoin yarn with RS facing.
Row 1 (RS): K2, ★P1, K1, rep from ★ to last st, K1.
Row 2: K1, ★P1, K1, rep from ★ to end.
These 2 rows form rib.
Cont in rib until button band, when slightly stretched, fits up left front opening edge to neck shaping, sewing in place as you go along and ending with RS facing for next row.
Break yarn and leave sts on a holder.
Mark positions for 7 buttons on this band – first to come level with buttonhole already worked in right front, last to come just above neck shaping and rem 5 buttons evenly spaced between.
Buttonhole band
Slip 9 sts on right front holder onto 2¾mm (US 2) needles and rejoin yarn with **WS** facing.
Beg with row 2, complete to match button band with the addition of a further 5 buttonholes worked to correspond with positions marked for buttons as folls:
Buttonhole row (RS): K2, P1, sl 1, K1, psso, yfwd (to make a buttonhole), K1, P1, K2.
When buttonhole band is complete, ending with RS facing for next row, do NOT break yarn.
Neckband
With RS facing, using 2¾mm (US 2) needles and yarn still attached to buttonhole band, rib across 9 sts of buttonhole band as folls: K1, (K1, P1) 4 times, K across 5 sts on right front holder, pick up and knit 26 [26: 28: 28: 30] sts up right side of front neck, and 3 sts down right side of back neck, K across 29 [29: 31: 31: 33] sts on back holder, pick up and knit 3 sts up left side of back neck, and 26 [26: 28: 28: 30] sts down left side of front neck, K across 5 sts on left front holder, then work across 9 sts on button band holder as folls: (P1, K1) 4 times, K1.
115 [115: 121: 121: 127] sts.
Beg with row 2, work in rib as given for button band for 1 row, ending with RS facing for next row.
Row 2 (RS): K2, P1, sl 1, K1, psso, yfwd (to make 7th buttonhole), rib to end.
Work in rib for a further 4 rows, ending with **WS** facing for next row.
Cast off in rib (on **WS**).
See information page for finishing instructions, setting in sleeves using the set-in method.

PICASSO

Lisa Richardson

Main image page **96**

● ● ●

SIZE

To fit bust

81–86 91–97 102–107 112–117 122–127cm

32–34 36–38 40–42 44–46 48–50 in

Actual bust measurement of garment

| 91 | 100 | 111 | 120 | 131 | cm |
| 35¾ | 39¼ | 43¾ | 47¼ | 51½ | in |

YARN

Cotton Cashmere

| 7 | 7 | 8 | 9 | 9 | x 50gm |

(photographed in Charcoal 232)

Alternatively, you could use Rowan Handknit Cotton in the following shade(s):

Black 252

| 11 | 11 | 13 | 14 | 14 | x 50gm |

NEEDLES

1 pair 4mm (no 8) (US 6) needles

BUTTONS – 5 x BN1709/15 from Bedecked. Please see information page for contact details.

TENSION

22 sts and 25 rows to 10 cm measured over patt using 4mm (US 6) needles.

Pattern note: Take care to ensure each dec of patt is matched by an inc. If there are insufficient sts to work both, work end sts of rows in st st.

BACK

Using 4mm (US 6) needles cast on 102 [112: 124: 134: 146] sts.

Work in patt as folls:

Row 1 (RS): K1 [2: 0: 1: 3], *K2tog, (yfwd) twice, sl 1, K1, psso, rep from * to last 1 [2: 0: 1: 3] sts, K1 [2: 0: 1: 3].

Row 2: P1 [2: 0: 1: 3], *P1, P into front and back of double yfwd of previous row, P1, rep

from * to last 1 [2: 0: 1: 3] sts, P1 [2: 0: 1: 3].

These 2 rows form patt.

Cont in patt, shaping side seams by dec 1 st at each end of 11th and 4 foll 6th rows.

92 [102: 114: 124: 136] sts.

Work 13 rows, ending with RS facing for next row.

Inc 1 st at each end of next and 3 foll 10th rows, taking inc sts into patt.

100 [110: 122: 132: 144] sts.

Cont straight until back meas 37.5 [38: 38.5: 39: 39.5] cm, ending with RS facing for next row.

Shape armholes

Keeping patt correct, cast off 4 [5: 6: 7: 8] sts at beg of next 2 rows. 92 [100: 110: 118: 128] sts.

Dec 1 st at each end of next 5 [5: 7: 7: 9] rows, then on foll 4 [5: 5: 6: 5] alt rows.

74 [80: 86: 92: 100] sts.

Cont straight until armhole meas 19 [20.5: 22: 23.5: 25] cm, ending with RS facing for next row.

Shape shoulders and back neck

Next row (RS): Cast off 7 [8: 8: 9: 10] sts, patt until there are 16 [18: 20: 22: 24] sts on right needle and turn, leaving rem sts on a holder.

Work each side of neck separately.

Keeping patt correct, dec 1 st at neck edge of next 3 rows, ending with RS facing for next row, **and at same time** cast off 7 [8: 8: 9: 10] sts at beg of 2nd row.

Cast off rem 6 [7: 9: 10: 11] sts.

With RS facing, rejoin yarn, cast off centre 28 [28: 30: 30: 32] sts and patt to end.

Complete to match first side, reversing shapings.

LEFT FRONT

Using 4mm (US 6) needles cast on 54 [59: 65: 70: 76] sts.

Work in patt as folls:

Row 1 (RS): K1 [2: 0: 1: 3], *K2tog, (yfwd) twice, sl 1, K1, psso, rep from * to last st, K1.

Row 2: K1, *P1, P into front and back of double yfwd of previous row, P1, rep from * to last 1 [2: 0: 1: 3] sts, P1 [2: 0: 1: 3].

These 2 rows form patt.

Cont in patt, shaping side seam by dec 1 st at beg of 11th and 4 foll 6th rows. 49 [54: 60: 65: 71] sts.

Work 13 rows, ending with RS facing for next row.

Inc 1 st at beg of next and 3 foll 10th rows, taking inc sts into patt. 53 [58: 64: 69: 75] sts.

Cont straight until 4 rows less have been worked than on back to beg of armhole shaping, ending with RS facing for next row.

Shape front slope

Next row (RS): Patt to last 7 sts, K2tog (for front slope dec), patt 5 sts.

Working all front slope decreases as set by last row, cont as folls:

Work 3 rows, dec 1 st at front slope edge of 2nd of these rows and ending with RS facing for next row. 51 [56: 62: 67: 73] sts.

Shape armhole

Keeping patt correct, cast off 4 [5: 6: 7: 8] sts at beg and dec 1 st at front slope edge of next row. 46 [50: 55: 59: 64] sts.

Work 1 row.

Dec 1 st at armhole edge of next 5 [5: 7: 7: 9] rows, then on foll 4 [5: 5: 6: 5] alt rows **and at same time** dec 1 st at front slope edge of next and foll 3 [1: 1: 0: 0] alt rows, then on 1 [3: 3: 4: 4] foll 4th rows. 32 [35: 38: 41: 45] sts.

Dec 1 st at front slope edge **only** on 2nd [4th: 2nd: 2nd: 2nd] and 6 [6: 7: 7: 8] foll 4th rows. 25 [28: 30: 33: 36] sts.

Cont straight until left front matches back to beg of shoulder shaping, ending with RS facing for next row.

Shape shoulder

Cast off 7 [8: 8: 9: 10] sts at beg of next and foll alt row, then 6 [7: 9: 10: 11] sts at beg of foll alt row. 5 sts.

Inc 1 st at end of next row. 6 sts.

Now working first and last st of every row as a K sts and rem 4 sts in patt as set, cont on these 6 sts only (for back neck border extension) until this strip meas 7.5 [7.5: 8: 8: 8.5] cm, ending with RS facing for next row.

Cast off.

RIGHT FRONT

Using 4mm (US 6) needles cast on 54 [59: 65: 70: 76] sts.

Work in patt as folls:

Row 1 (RS): K1, *K2tog, (yfwd) twice, sl 1, K1, psso, rep from * to last 1 [2: 0: 1: 3] sts, K1 [2: 0: 1: 3].

Row 2: P1 [2: 0: 1: 3], *P1, P into front and back of double yfwd of previous row, P1, rep from * to last st, K1.

These 2 rows form patt.

Cont in patt, shaping side seam by dec 1 st at end

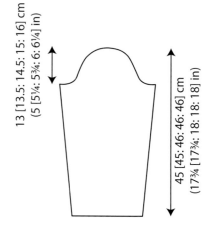

13 [13.5: 14.5: 15: 16] cm
(5 [5¼: 5¾: 6: 6¼] in)

45 [45: 46: 46: 46] cm
(17¾ [17¾: 18: 18: 18] in)

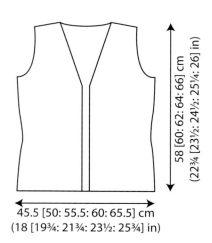

58 [60: 62: 64: 66] cm
(22¾ [23½: 24½: 25¼: 26] in)

45.5 [50: 55.5: 60: 65.5] cm
(18 [19¾: 21¾: 23½: 25¾] in)

of 11th and 4 foll 6th rows. 49 [54: 60: 65: 71] sts.
Work 13 rows, ending with RS facing for next row.
Inc 1 st at end of next and 3 foll 10th rows, taking inc sts into patt. 53 [58: 64: 69: 75] sts.
Cont straight until 4 rows less have been worked than on back to beg of armhole shaping, ending with RS facing for next row.

Shape front slope

Next row (RS): Patt 5 sts, sl 1, K1, psso (for front slope dec), patt to end.
Working all front slope decreases as set by last row, complete to match left front, reversing shapings.

SLEEVES

Using 4mm (US 6) needles cast on 48 [50: 52: 52: 56] sts.

Work in patt as folls:

Row 1 (RS): K0 [1: 0: 0: 0], ★K2tog, (yfwd) twice, sl 1, K1, psso, rep from ★ to last 0 [1: 0: 0: 0] st, K0 [1: 0: 0: 0].

Row 2: P0 [1: 0: 0: 0], ★P1, P into front and back of double yfwd of previous row, P1, rep from ★ to last 0 [1: 0: 0: 0] st, P0 [1: 0: 0: 0].
These 2 rows form patt.
Cont in patt, shaping sides by inc 1 st at each end of 5th [5th: 3rd: 3rd: 3rd] and every foll 8th [8th: 8th: 6th: 6th] row to 58 [70: 78: 70: 74] sts, then on every foll 10th [10th: –: 8th: 8th] row until there are 70 [74: –: 82: 86] sts, taking inc sts into patt.
Cont straight until sleeve meas 45 [45: 46: 46: 46] cm, ending with RS facing for next row.

Shape top

Keeping patt correct, cast off 4 [5: 6: 7: 8] sts at beg of next 2 rows. 62 [64: 66: 68: 70] sts.
Dec 1 st at each end of next 5 rows, then on every foll alt row until 34 sts rem, then on foll 7 rows, ending with RS facing for next row.
Cast off rem 20 sts.

MAKING UP

Press as described on the information page.
Join both shoulder seams using back stitch, or mattress stitch if preferred. Join cast-off ends of back neck border extensions, then sew one edge to back neck.
See information page for finishing instructions, setting in sleeves using the set-in method. Using photograph as a guide, attach buttons along left front opening edge, using "holes" of lace patt of right front as buttonholes.

KIRKIN

Sasha Kagan

Main image page **8, 9**

● ● ●

YARN

Summerlite 4ply and Kidsilk Haze

A	4ply Green Bay 445	2	x 50gm
B	4ply Sand Dune 438	2	x 50gm
C	KSH Jelly 587	1	x 25gm
D	4ply Touch of Gold 439	2	x 50gm
E	4ply Buttermilk 421	1	x 50gm
F	KSH Cream 634	1	x 25gm

NEEDLES

1 pair 3¾mm (no 9) (US 5) needles

TENSION

30 sts and 32 rows to 10 cm measured over patt using 3¾mm (US 5) needles.

FINISHED SIZE

Completed wrap is 40.5 cm (16 in) wide and 186 cm (73¼ in) long.

WRAP

First section

Using 3¾mm (US 5) needles and yarn A cast on 121 sts.
Work in patt as folls:

Row 1 (RS): Using yarn A, K1, ★yfwd, K3, K3tog, K3, yfwd, K1, rep from ★ to end.

Row 2: Using yarn A, knit.
These 2 rows form patt.
Keeping patt correct, now work in stripe sequence as folls:

Rows 2 to 8: Using yarn A.
Rows 9 and 10: Using yarn B.
Rows 11 to 14: Using yarn C.
Rows 15 to 18: Using yarn D.
Rows 19 and 20: Using yarn E.
Rows 21 and 22: Using yarn F.

Rows 23 and 24: Using yarn E.
Rows 25 and 26: Using yarn B.
Rows 27 and 28: Using yarn E.
Rows 29 and 30: Using yarn F.
Rows 31 and 32: Using yarn E.
Rows 33 to 40: Using yarn A.
Rows 41 to 44: Using yarn E.
Rows 45 and 46: Using yarn D.
Rows 47 and 48: Using yarn C.
Rows 49 to 56: As rows 45 to 48, twice.
Rows 57 and 58: Using yarn D.
Rows 59 to 66: Using yarn B.
Rows 67 and 68: Using yarn F.
Rows 69 to 76: Using yarn D.
Rows 77 and 78: Using yarn F.
Rows 79 and 80: Using yarn A.
Rows 81 to 84: As rows 77 to 80.
Rows 85 to 88: Using yarn B.
These 88 rows form stripe sequence.
Cont in patt in stripe sequence as now set until work meas 93 cm, ending with RS facing for next row.★★
Break yarn and leave sts on a holder.

Second section

Work as given for first section to ★★.

Join sections

Slip sts of first section onto a spare 3¾mm (US 5) needle and, holding first and second sections with their RS together, cast off both sets of sts at same time, taking one st from first section with corresponding st from second section.

MAKING UP

Press as described on the information page.
See information page for finishing instructions.

KINETIC

Lisa Richardson

Main image page **79, 80**

● ●

SIZE

To fit bust

81-86	91-97	102-107	112-117	122-127	cm
32-34	36-38	40-42	44-46	48-50	in

Actual bust measurement of garment

96	106	116	126	136	cm
37¾	41¾	45¾	49½	53½	in

YARN

Cotton Cashmere and Kidsilk Haze

A CC Stormy Sky 225

5	5	6	6	7	x 50gm

B CC Silver Lining 224

5	5	5	6	6	x 50gm

C *KSH White 612

2	2	3	3	3	x 25gm

*Kidsilk Haze is used DOUBLE throughout

Alternatively, you could use Rowan Handknit
Cotton in the following shades:

A HK Slate 347

8	8	10	10	11	x 50gm

B HK Feather 373

8	8	8	10	10	x 50gm

C *KSH White 612

2	2	3	3	3	x 25gm

*Kidsilk Haze is used DOUBLE throughout

NEEDLES

1 pair 3¼mm (no 10) (US 3) needles
1 pair 4mm (no 8) (US 6) needles
3¼mm (no 10) (US 3) circular needle at least
160 cm long

BUTTONS – 8 x RW5030 from Bedecked.
Please see information page for contact details.

TENSION

20 sts and 29 rows to 10 cm measured over
striped st st using 4mm (US 6) needles.

STRIPE SEQUENCE

Rows 1 to 16: Using yarn A.
Rows 17 to 20: Using yarn C DOUBLE.
Rows 21 to 36: Using yarn B.
Rows 37 to 40: Using yarn C DOUBLE.
These 40 rows form stripe sequence and are
repeated throughout.

BACK

Using 3¼mm (US 3) needles and yarn A cast on
102 [110: 122: 130: 142] sts.
Row 1 (RS): K2, *P2, K2, rep from * to end.
Row 2: P2, *K2, P2, rep from * to end.
These 2 rows form rib and rows 1 and 2 of stripe
sequence (see above).
Keeping stripe sequence correct throughout as
now set and beg with row 3, cont as folls:
Work in rib for a further 6 rows, dec 1 [0: 1: 0:
1] st at each end of last row and ending with RS
facing for next row. 100 [110: 120: 130: 140] sts.
Change to 4mm (US 6) needles.
Beg with a K row and keeping stripe sequence
correct, now work in st st throughout as folls:
Work 60 rows, ending with RS facing for next
row.
Dec 1 st at each end of next and foll 40th row.
96 [106: 116: 126: 136] sts.
Cont straight until back meas approx 58 [58.5:
59: 59.5: 60] cm, ending after stripe sequence
row 8 [10: 12: 12: 14] and with RS facing for
next row.

Shape armholes

Keeping stripes correct, cast off 3 [4: 5: 6: 7] sts at
beg of next 2 rows. 90 [98: 106: 114: 122] sts.
Dec 1 st at each end of next 5 [5: 7: 7: 9] rows,
then on foll 4 [6: 5: 6: 4] alt rows.
72 [76: 82: 88: 96] sts.
Cont straight until armhole meas 22 [23.5: 25:
26.5: 28] cm, ending with RS facing for next
row.

Shape shoulders and back neck

Next row (RS): Cast off 4 [5: 5: 6: 7] sts, K
until there are 19 [20: 22: 24: 26] sts on right
needle and turn, leaving rem sts on a holder.
Work each side of neck separately.
Keeping stripes correct, dec 1 st at neck edge of
next 4 rows **and at same time** cast off 5 [5: 6:
6: 7] sts at beg of 2nd row and 5 [5: 6: 7: 7] sts at
beg of foll alt row.
Work 1 row.
Cast off rem 5 [6: 6: 7: 8] sts.
With RS facing, slip centre 26 [26: 28: 28: 30] sts
onto a holder (for front band), rejoin appropriate
yarn and K to end.
Complete to match first side, reversing shapings.

LEFT FRONT

Using 3¼mm (US 3) needles and yarn A cast on
51 [55: 63: 67: 71] sts.
Row 1 (RS): K2, *P2, K2, rep from * to last st,
K1.
Row 2: K1, P2, *K2, P2, rep from * to end.
These 2 rows form rib and rows 1 and 2 of stripe
sequence (see above).
Keeping stripe sequence correct throughout as
now set and beg with row 3, cont as folls:
Work in rib for a further 6 rows, dec 1 [0: 3: 2:
1] sts evenly across last row and ending with RS
facing for next row. 50 [55: 60: 65: 70] sts.
Change to 4mm (US 6) needles.

Beg with a K row and keeping stripe sequence
correct, now work in st st throughout as folls:
Work 60 rows, ending with RS facing for next
row.
Dec 1 st at beg of next and foll 40th row.
48 [53: 58: 63: 68] sts.
Cont straight until 18 rows less have been
worked than on back to beg of armhole shaping,
ending with RS facing for next row.

Shape front slope

Keeping stripes correct, dec 1 st at end of next
and 4 foll 4th rows. 43 [48: 53: 58: 63] sts.
Work 1 row, ending with RS facing for next row.

Shape armhole

Keeping stripes correct, cast off 3 [4: 5: 6: 7] sts at
beg of next row. 40 [44: 48: 52: 56] sts.
Work 1 row.
Dec 1 st at armhole edge of next 5 [5: 7: 7: 9]
rows, then on foll 4 [6: 5: 6: 4] alt rows **and at
same time** dec 1 st at front slope edge of next
and 3 [4: 4: 3: 3] foll 4th rows, then on 0 [0: 0: 1:
0] foll 6th row. 27 [28: 31: 34: 39] sts.
Dec 1 st at front slope edge **only** on 4th [6th:
4th: 6th: 2nd] and 2 [0: 0: 0: 0] foll 4th rows, then
on 5 [6: 7: 7: 9] foll 6th rows.
19 [21: 23: 26: 29] sts.
Cont straight until left front matches back to beg
of shoulder shaping, ending with RS facing for
next row.

Shape shoulder

Cast off 4 [5: 5: 6: 7] sts at beg of next and foll 0
[2: 0: 1: 2] alt rows, then 5 [-: 6: 7: -] sts at beg of

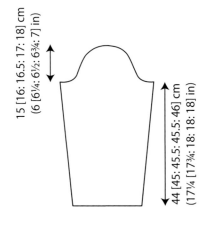

15 [16: 16.5: 17: 18] cm
(6 [6¼: 6½: 6¾: 7] in)

44 [45: 45.5: 45.5: 46] cm
(17¼ [17¾: 18: 18: 18] in)

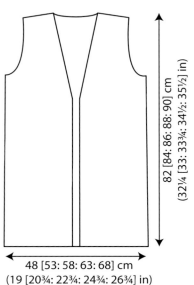

82 [84: 86: 88: 90] cm
(32¼ [33: 33¾: 34½: 35½] in)

48 [53: 58: 63: 68] cm
(19 [20¾: 22¾: 24¾: 26¾] in)

foll 2 [-: 2: 1: -] alt rows.
Work 1 row.
Cast off rem 5 [6: 6: 7: 8] sts.

RIGHT FRONT

Using 3¼mm (US 3) needles and yarn A cast on 51 [55: 63: 67: 71] sts.
Row 1 (RS): K3, *P2, K2, rep from * to end.
Row 2: P2, *K2, P2, rep from * to last st, K1.
These 2 rows form rib and rows 1 and 2 of stripe sequence (see above).
Keeping stripe sequence correct throughout as now set and beg with row 3, cont as folls:
Work in rib for a further 6 rows, dec 1 [0: 3: 2: 1] sts evenly across last row and ending with RS facing for next row. 50 [55: 60: 65: 70] sts.
Change to 4mm (US 6) needles.
Beg with a K row and keeping stripe sequence correct, now work in st st throughout as folls:
Work 60 rows, ending with RS facing for next row.
Dec 1 st at end of next and foll 40th row.
48 [53: 58: 63: 68] sts.
Complete to match left front, reversing shapings.

SLEEVES

Using 3¼mm (US 3) needles and yarn A cast on 46 [46: 50: 50: 50] sts.
Work in rib as given for back for 7 cm, dec 1 [0: 1: 1: 0] st at each end of last row and ending with RS facing for next row. 44 [46: 48: 48: 50] sts.
Change to 4mm (US 6) needles.
Beg with a K row and stripe sequence row 21, now work in st st in stripe sequence (see above)

as folls:
Inc 1 st at each end of 5th [5th: 5th: 5th: 3rd] and every foll 6th [6th: 6th: 6th: 4th] row to 48 [54: 62: 78: 54] sts, then on every foll 8th [8th: 8th: 8th: 6th] row until there are 68 [72: 76: 80: 84] sts.
Cont straight until sleeve meas approx 44 [45: 45.5: 45.5: 46] cm, ending after stripe sequence row 8 [10: 12: 12: 14] and with RS facing for next row.

Shape top
Keeping stripes correct, cast off 3 [4: 5: 6: 7] sts at beg of next 2 rows. 62 [64: 66: 68: 70] sts.
Dec 1 st at each end of next 3 rows, then on foll 2 alt rows, then on 4 foll 4th rows.
44 [46: 48: 50: 52] sts.
Work 1 row.
Dec 1 st at each end of next and every foll alt row until 32 sts rem, then on foll 7 rows, ending with RS facing for next row.
Cast off rem 18 sts.

MAKING UP

Press as described on the information page.
Join both shoulder seams using back stitch, or mattress stitch if preferred.

Front band
With RS facing, using 3¼mm (US 3) circular needle and yarn A, beg and ending at front cast-on edges, pick up and knit 111 [111: 111: 118: 118] sts up right front opening edge to beg of front slope shaping, 69 [71: 74: 77: 80] sts up right front slope, and 5 sts down right side of back neck, K across 26 [26: 28: 28: 30] sts on back holder, pick up and knit 5 sts up left side of

back neck, 69 [71: 74: 77: 80] sts down left front slope to beg of front slope shaping, and 111 [111: 111: 118: 118] sts down left front opening edge. 396 [400: 408: 428: 436] sts.
Row 1 (WS): K1, P2, *K2, P2, rep from * to last st, K1.
Row 2: K3, *P2, K2, rep from * to last st, K1.
These 2 rows form rib.
Keeping rib correct, cont as folls:
Row 3 (WS): Rib to last 111 [111: 111: 118: 118] sts, *work 2 tog, yrn (to make a buttonhole), rib 13 [13: 13: 14: 14], rep from * 6 times more, work 2 tog, yrn (to make 8th buttonhole), rib 4.
Work in rib for 2 rows more, ending with RS facing for next row.
Cast off in rib.

Pockets (make 2)
Using 4mm (US 6) needles and yarn B cast on 28 sts.
Row 1 (RS): Knit.
Row 2: K1, P to last st, K1.
Rep last 2 rows 23 times more, ending with RS facing for next row.
Row 49 (RS): (K3, inc in next st, K3) 4 times. 32 sts.
Change to 3¼mm (US 3) needles.
Beg with row 1, work in rib as given for front band for 5 rows, ending with RS facing for next row.
Cast off in rib.
See information page for finishing instructions, setting in sleeves using the set-in method. Using photograph as a guide, sew pockets onto fronts.

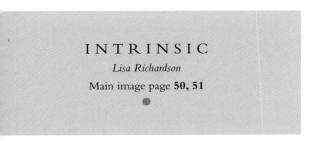

INTRINSIC
Lisa Richardson
Main image page **50, 51**
●

YARN
Creative Linen
   5   x 100gm
(photographed in Natural 621)

NEEDLES
1 pair 4½mm (no 7) (US 7) needles

TENSION
19 sts and 33 rows to 10 cm measured over patt using 4½mm (US 7) needles.

FINISHED SIZE
Completed shawl is 54 cm (21¼ in) wide and 175 cm (69 in) long.

SHAWL
Using 4½mm (US 7) needles cast on 103 sts.
Work in patt as folls:
Row 1 (RS): *K6, P3, rep from * to last 4 sts, K4.

Row 2: K2, *P3, K6, rep from * to last 2 sts, P2.
Row 3: P1, *K6, P3, rep from * to last 3 sts, K3.
Row 4: K3, *P3, K6, rep from * to last st, K1.
Row 5: P2, *K6, P3, rep from * to last 2 sts, K2.
Row 6: K4, *P3, K6, rep from * to end.
Row 7: *P3, K6, rep from * to last 4 sts, P3, K1.
Row 8: K5, *P3, K6, rep from * to last 8 sts, P3, K5.
Row 9: K1, *P3, K6, rep from * to last 3 sts, P3.
Rows 10 to 17: As rows 1 to 8.
Row 18: P4, *K6, P3, rep from * to end.
These 18 rows form patt.
Cont in patt until shawl meas 175 cm, ending with RS facing for next row.
Cast off.

MAKING UP
Press as described on the information page.
See information page for finishing instructions.

MARISOL

Lisa Richardson

Main image page **98, 99**

● ●

SIZE
To fit bust
81-86 91-97 102-107 112-117 122-127cm
32-34 36-38 40-42 44-46 48-50 in
Actual bust measurement of garment

90	100	110	120	130	cm
35½	39¼	43¼	47¼	51¼	in

YARN
Cotton Cashmere

5	5	6	7	8	x 50gm

(photographed in Paper 210)

Alternatively, you could use Rowan Handknit
Cotton in the following shade(s):
Bleached 263

8	8	10	11	13	x 50gm

NEEDLES
3¼mm (no 10) (US 3) circular needle no more
than 70 [80: 90: 100: 110] cm long
4mm (no 8) (US 6) circular needles – shortest no
more than 40 cm long, longest no more than
70 [80: 90: 100: 110] cm long, and lengths
between as required
Set of 4 double-pointed 3¼mm (no 10) (US 3)
needles
Set of 4 double-pointed 4mm (no 8) (US 6)
needles

TENSION
20 sts and 28 rounds to 10 cm measured over st
st using 4mm (US 6) needles.

BODY
Using 3¼mm (US 3) circular needle cast on
180 [200: 220: 240: 260] sts.
Taking care not to twist cast-on edge, now work
in st st (K every round) as folls:
Round 1 (RS): Place marker on needle (to
denote left side "seam" and beg of rounds), K90

[100: 110: 120: 130], place 2nd marker on needle
(to denote right side "seam"), K90 [100: 110:
120: 130].
Work in st st for a further 3 rounds.
Change to 4mm (US 6) circular needle. (**Note**:
Start using longest circular needle and change
to different lengths of needle as and when
required.)
Now work in patt as folls:
Round 1 (RS): ★K1, sl 1, K1, psso, (yfwd) twice,
K2tog, K to within 5 sts of next marker,
sl 1, K1, psso, (yfwd) twice, K2tog, K1, slip
marker onto right needle, rep from ★ once more.
Round 2: K to end, working into front and
back of double yfwd of previous round.
These 2 rounds form patt.
Keeping patt correct throughout, cont as folls:
Work 8 rounds.
Next round: ★K1, sl 1, K1, psso, (yfwd) twice,
K3tog (to form eyelet **and** side "seam" dec), K to
within 6 sts of next marker, sl 1, K2tog, psso (to
form eyelet **and** side "seam" dec), (yfwd) twice,
K2tog, K1, slip marker onto right needle, rep
from ★ once more.
This round sets side "seam" decreases – 1 st
is decreased at each side of both side "seam"
markers, decreasing a total of 4 sts on every dec
round.
Working all side seam decreases as now set and
keeping patt correct, dec 1 st at each side of both
side "seam" markers on 4th and 3 foll 4th rounds.
160 [180: 200: 220: 240] sts.
Work 11 rounds.
Next round: ★Patt 5 sts, M1 (for side "seam"
inc), K to within 5 sts of next marker, M1 (for
side "seam" inc), patt 5 sts, slip marker onto right
needle, rep from ★ once more.
This round sets side "seam" increases – 1 st
is increased at each side of both side "seam"
markers, increasing a total of 4 sts on every inc
round.
Working all side seam increases as now set and
keeping patt correct, inc 1 st at each side of both
side "seam" markers on 8th and 3 foll 8th rounds.
180 [200: 220: 240: 260] sts.
Work 15 rounds, ending after patt round 2.
Divide for armholes
Next round (RS): K3 and slip these sts onto
a holder (for left underarm), K until there are
84 [94: 104: 114: 124] sts on right needle and
slip these sts onto another holder (for front), K6

and slip these sts onto another holder (for right
underarm), K until there are 84 [94: 104: 114:
124] sts on right needle and slip these sts onto
another holder (for back), K rem 3 sts and slip
these 3 sts onto same underarm holder as first
3 sts (so there are 6 sts on left underarm holder).
Break yarn.

SLEEVES
Using set of 4 double-pointed 3¼mm (US 3)
needles cast on 64 [68: 72: 78: 82] sts.
Taking care not to twist cast-on edge, work in
rounds as folls:
Round 1 (RS): Knit.
Place marker on first st of round just knitted to
denote beg and end of rounds – this marker "sits"
along sleeve "seam".
Work in st st for a further 3 rounds.
Change to double-pointed 4mm (US 6) needles.
Next round: K3 and slip these sts onto a holder
(for underarm), K to last 3 sts, K rem 3 sts and
slip these 3 sts onto same holder as first 3 sts (so
there are 6 sts on underarm holder).
Break yarn and leave rem 58 [62: 66: 72: 76] sts
on another holder.

YOKE
With RS facing and using 4mm (US 6) circular
needle, work across all sts from holders as folls:
K 58 [62: 66: 72: 76] sts on left sleeve holder,
place marker on needle, K 84 [94: 104:
114: 124] sts on front holder, place 2nd marker
on needle, K 58 [62: 66: 72: 76] sts on right
sleeve holder, place 3rd marker on needle, then
K 84 [94: 104: 114: 124] sts on back holder,
and place 4th marker on needle.
284 [312: 340: 372: 400] sts.
There are now 4 markers, with each marker
denoting a raglan "seam" position.
Now cont as folls:
Round 1 (RS): ★K1, sl 1, K1, psso, (yfwd) twice,
K3tog (to form eyelet **and** dec), K to within 6 sts
of next marker, sl 1, K2tog, psso (to form eyelet
and dec), (yfwd) twice, K2tog, K1, slip marker
onto right needle, rep from ★ 3 times more.
276 [304: 332: 364: 392] sts.
This round sets decreases next to raglan markers
and sets position of patt as given for body.
Now working eyelets on every alt round as now
set (and remembering to work twice into each
double yfwd of previous round on round after

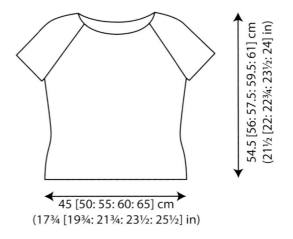

54.5 [56: 57.5: 59.5: 61] cm
(21½ [22: 22¾: 23½: 24] in)

45 [50: 55: 60: 65] cm
(17¾ [19¾: 21¾: 23½: 25½] in)

eyelets are made), cont as folls:

Round 2: ★Work across sleeve sts as folls: K2, K into front and back of double yfwd, K to within 4 sts of next marker, K into front and back of double yfwd, K2, slip marker onto right needle, working raglan decreases, work across next set of sts as folls: K2, K into front and back of double yfwd, K2tog (for raglan dec), K to within 6 sts of next marker, sl 1, K1, psso (for raglan dec), K into front and back of double yfwd, K2, slip marker onto right needle, rep from ★ once more.
272 [300: 328: 360: 388] sts.
This round sets decreases on rounds that do

NOT have eyelets.
Now keeping patt correct as set and working all decreases as now set, cont as folls:
Dec 1 st near each raglan "seam" marker of both front and back sections on next 1 [7: 11: 15: 19] rounds, then on foll 22 [21: 21: 22: 22] alt rounds **and at same time** dec 1 st near each raglan "seam" marker of both sleeve sections on 3rd and 3 foll 4th rounds, then on foll 15 [17: 19: 22: 24] alt rounds. 104 [104: 108: 108: 112] sts.
(**Note**: As number of sts decreases, change to shorter circular needle or to set of 4 double-pointed needles).

Work 1 round.
Remove all raglan markers.
Work neckband
Change to 4 double-pointed 3¼mm (US 3) needles.
Work in st st for 5 rounds.
Cast off.

MAKING UP
Press as described on the information page.
Graft together the 2 sets of 6 sts left on holders at underarms.
See information page for finishing instructions.

GENNER
ARNE & CARLOS
Main image page **30, 31**
● ● ●

YARN
Cotton Cashmere

A Paper 210	3	x 50gm
B Morning Sky 221	1	x 50gm
C Harbour Blue 223	1	x 50gm
D Cinnabar 215	1	x 50gm

NEEDLES
3¼mm (no 10) (US 3) circular needle at least 120 cm long
4mm (no 8) (US 6) circular needle at least 120 cm long

TENSION
22 sts and 24 rows to 10 cm measured over patterned st st using 4mm (US 6) needles.

FINISHED SIZE
Completed infinity scarf is 25 cm (9¾ in) deep and measures 163.5 cm (64¼ in) all round.

SCARF
Using 3¼mm (US 3) circular needle and yarn A cast on 360 sts.
Taking care not to twist cast-on edge, work in rounds as folls:
Round 1 (RS): ★K2, P2, rep from ★ to end.
This round forms rib.
Work in rib for a further 10 rounds.
Change to 4mm (US 6) circular needle.

Beg and ending rows as indicated, using the **fairisle** technique as described on the information page and repeating the 12 st patt repeat 30 times around each round, cont in patt from chart, which is worked entirely in st st (K every round), as folls:
Work chart rounds 1 to 41.
Change to 3¼mm (US) circular needles.
Break off contrasts and cont using yarn A **only**.
Next round: Knit.
Now work in rib as given for cast-on edge for 10 rounds.
Cast off in rib.

MAKING UP
Press as described on the information page.
See information page for finishing instructions.

Key
□ A
◉ B
⊠ C
⊘ D

12 st patt rep

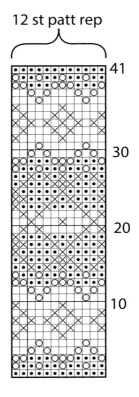

MAREEL

Sarah Hatton

Main image page **26, 27**

● ● ●

SIZE
To fit bust

81-86 91-97 102-107 112-117 122-127cm

32-34 36-38 40-42 44-46 48-50 in

Actual bust measurement of garment

| 106 | 116 | 126 | 136 | 146 | cm |
| 41¾ | 45¾ | 49½ | 53½ | 57½ | in |

YARN
Cotton Cashmere

| 8 | 9 | 10 | 10 | 11 | x 50gm |

(photographed in Sea Spray 219)

NEEDLES
1 pair 3¼mm (no 10) (US 3) needles
1 pair 4mm (no 8) (US 6) needles

TENSION
20 sts and 28 rows to 10 cm measured over st st using 4mm (US 6) needles. Body panel (45 sts) measures 19 cm.

BACK
Using 3¼mm (US 3) needles cast on 113 [123: 133: 143: 153] sts.
Row 1 (RS): K1, *P1, K1, rep from * to end.
Row 2: P1, *K1, P1, rep from * to end.
These 2 rows form rib.
Work in rib for a further 6 rows, ending with RS facing for next row.
Change to 4mm (US 6) needles.
Now work in patt, placing body panel chart as folls:
Row 1 (RS): P1, (K1, P1) 8 [10: 12: 14: 16] times, K1, yfwd, sl 1, K1, psso, K14 [15: 16: 17: 18], work next 45 sts as row 1 of chart for body panel, K14 [15: 16: 17: 18], K2tog, yfwd, K1, (P1, K1) 8 [10: 12: 14: 16] times, P1.
Row 2: K1, (P1, K1) 8 [10: 12: 14: 16] times, P17 [18: 19: 20: 21], work next 45 sts as row 2 of chart for body panel, P17 [18: 19: 20: 21], (K1,

P1) 8 [10: 12: 14: 16] times, K1.
Row 3: K1, (P1, K1) 8 [10: 12: 14: 16] times, K1, yfwd, sl 1, K1, psso, K14 [15: 16: 17: 18], work next 45 sts as row 3 of chart for body panel, K14 [15: 16: 17: 18], K2tog, yfwd, K1, (K1, P1) 8 [10: 12: 14: 16] times, K1.
Row 4: P1, (K1, P1) 8 [10: 12: 14: 16] times, P17 [18: 19: 20: 21], work next 45 sts as row 4 of chart for body panel, P17 [18: 19: 20: 21], (P1, K1) 8 [10: 12: 14: 16] times, P1.
These 4 rows set the sts – centre 45 sts in patt from chart with st st, eyelet line and irish moss st at sides.
Working chart rows 1 to 8 **once only** and then repeating chart rows 9 to 68 as required and keeping all sts correct throughout as now set, cont as folls:
Cont straight until back meas 33 [33.5: 34: 34.5: 35] cm, ending with RS facing for next row.
Shape raglan armholes
Keeping patt correct, cast off 3 sts at beg of next 2 rows. 107 [117: 127: 137: 147] sts.
Next row (RS): K2, P1, K1, P1, sl 1, K1, psso, patt to last 7 sts, K2tog, P1, K1, P1, K2.
Next row: P2, K1, P1, K1, P2tog, patt to last 7 sts, P2tog tbl, K1, P1, K1, P2.
Rep last 2 rows 13 [16: 18: 21: 23] times more. 51 [49: 51: 49: 51] sts.
Next row (RS): K2, P1, K1, P1, sl 1, K1, psso, patt to last 7 sts, K2tog, P1, K1, P1, K2.
Next row: P2, (K1, P1) twice, patt to last 6 sts, (P1, K1) twice, P2.
Rep last 2 rows 9 [8: 8: 7: 7] times more, ending with RS facing for next row.
31 [31: 33: 33: 35] sts.
Break yarn and leave sts on a holder (for neckband).

FRONT
Work as given for back until 43 [43: 47: 47: 51] sts rem in raglan armhole shaping.
Work 1 [1: 1: 1: 0] row, ending with RS facing for next row.
Shape front neck
Next row (RS): K2, P1, K1, P1, sl 1, K1, psso, patt 2 [2: 4: 4: 6] sts and turn, leaving rem sts on a holder. 8 [8: 10: 10: 12] sts.
Work each side of neck separately.

81-86 and 91-97 cm sizes only
Next row (WS): Work 2 tog, (P1, K1) twice, P2. 7 sts.
Next row: K2, P1, K1, sl 1, K2tog, psso. 5 sts.
Next row: P2tog tbl, K1, P2. 4 sts.
102-107 and 112-117 cm sizes only
Next row (WS): Work 2 tog, patt 2 sts, (P1, K1) twice, P2. 9 sts.
Next row: K2, P1, K1, P1, sl 1, K1, psso, work 2 tog. 7 sts.
Next row: P2tog tbl, K1, P1, K1, P2. 6 sts.
122-127 cm size only
Next row (WS): Work 2 tog, patt 4 sts, (P1, K1) twice, P2. 11 sts.
Next row: K2, P1, K1, P1, sl 1, K1, psso, patt 2 sts, work 2 tog. 9 sts.
Next row: Work 2 tog, patt 1 st, (P1, K1) twice, P2. 8 sts.
Next row: K2, P1, K1, P1, sl 1, K2tog, psso. 6 sts.
Next row: (P1, K1) twice, P2.
102-107, 112-117 and 122-127 cm sizes only
Next row (RS): K2, P1, sl 1, K2tog, psso. 4 sts.
Next row: P1, K1, P2.
All sizes
Next row (RS): K1, sl 1, K2tog, psso. 2 sts.
Next row: P2.
Next row: K2tog and fasten off.
With RS facing, slip centre 25 sts onto a holder (for neckband), rejoin yarn and patt to last 7 sts, K2tog, P1, K1, P1, K2. 8 [8: 10: 10: 12] sts.
Complete to match first side, reversing shapings.

SLEEVES
Using 3¼mm (US 3) needles cast on 39 [41: 43: 43: 45] sts.
Row 1 (RS): P1 [0: 1: 1: 0], *K1, P1, rep from * to last 0 [1: 0: 0: 1] st, K0 [1: 0: 0: 1].
Row 2: K1 [0: 1: 1: 0], *P1, K1, rep from * to last 0 [1: 0: 0: 1] st, P0 [1: 0: 0: 1].
These 2 rows form rib.
Work in rib for a further 6 rows, ending with RS facing for next row.
Change to 4mm (US 6) needles.
Now work in patt as folls:
Row 1 (RS): K12 [13: 14: 14: 15], K2tog, yfwd, (K1, P1) 5 times, K1, yfwd, sl 1, K1, psso, K12 [13: 14: 14: 15].
Row 2: P15 [16: 17: 17: 18], (K1, P1) 4 times,

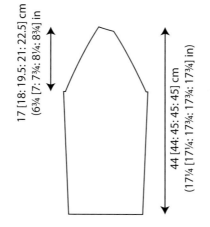

17 [18: 19.5: 21: 22.5] cm (6¾ [7: 7¾: 8¼: 8¾] in)

44 [44: 45: 45: 45] cm (17¼ [17¼: 17¾: 17¾: 17¾] in)

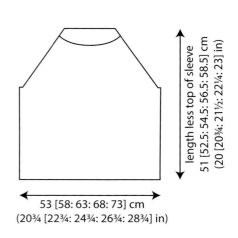

length less top of sleeve
51 [52.5: 54.5: 56.5: 58.5] cm (20 [20¾: 21½: 22¼: 23] in)

53 [58: 63: 68: 73] cm (20¾ [22¾: 24¾: 26¾: 28¾] in)

K1, P15 [16: 17: 17: 18].

Row 3: (Inc in first st) 0 [0: 0: 1: 1] times, K12 [13: 14: 13: 14], K2tog, yfwd, K2, (P1, K1) 3 times, P1, K2, yfwd, sl 1, K1, psso, K12 [13: 14: 13: 14], (inc in last st) 0 [0: 0: 1: 1] times. 39 [41: 43: 45: 47] sts.

Row 4: P16 [17: 18: 19: 20], (K1, P1) 3 times, K1, P16 [17: 18: 19: 20].

These 4 rows form patt and beg sleeve shaping for largest 2 sizes.

Cont in patt as now set, inc 1 st at each end of next [next: next: 3rd: 3rd] and every foll 6th [6th: 6th: 4th: 4th] row to 57 [67: 73: 51: 59] sts, then on every foll 8th [8th: 8th: 6th: 6th] row until there are 69 [73: 77: 81: 85] sts, taking inc sts into st st.

Cont straight until sleeve meas 44 [44: 45: 45: 45] cm, ending with RS facing for next row.

Shape raglan

Keeping patt correct, cast off 3 sts at beg of next 2 rows. 63 [67: 71: 75: 79] sts.

Next row (RS): K2, P1, K1, P1, sl 1, K1, psso, patt to last 7 sts, K2tog, P1, K1, P1, K2.

Next row: P2, (K1, P1) twice, patt to last 6 sts, (P1, K1) twice, P2.

Rep last 2 rows 20 [22: 24: 26: 28] times more, ending with RS facing for next row. 21 sts.

Keeping all raglan decreases correct as set, complete top of sleeve as folls:

Left sleeve only

Dec 1 st at each end of next row, then cast off 4 sts at beg of foll row. 15 sts.

Dec 1 st at beg of next row, then cast off 5 sts at beg of foll row. 9 sts.

Dec 1 st at beg of next row, then cast off 4 sts at beg of foll row. 4 sts.

Right sleeve only

Cast off 5 sts at beg and dec 1 st at end of next row. 15 sts.

Work 1 row.

Rep last 2 rows once more. 9 sts.

Cast off 5 sts at beg of next row. 4 sts.

Work 1 row.

Both sleeves

Cast off rem 4 sts.

MAKING UP

Press as described on the information page.

Join both front and right back raglan seams using back stitch, or mattress stitch if preferred.

Neckband

With RS facing and using 3¼mm (US 3) needles, pick up and knit 15 sts from top of left sleeve, and 5 [5: 7: 7: 9] sts down left side of front neck, K across 25 sts on front holder, pick up and knit 5 [5: 7: 7: 9] sts up right side of front neck, and 15 sts from top of right sleeve, then K across 31 [31: 33: 33: 35] sts on back holder. 96 [96: 102: 102: 108] sts.

Work in g st until neckband meas 4 cm from pick-up row, ending with RS facing for next row. Cast off.

See information page for finishing instructions.

Key

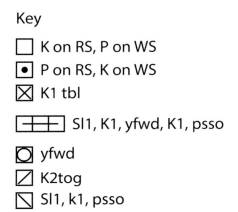

- ☐ K on RS, P on WS
- ☒ P on RS, K on WS
- ☒ K1 tbl
- ┼┼┼ Sl1, K1, yfwd, K1, psso
- ○ yfwd
- ╱ K2tog
- ╲ Sl1, k1, psso

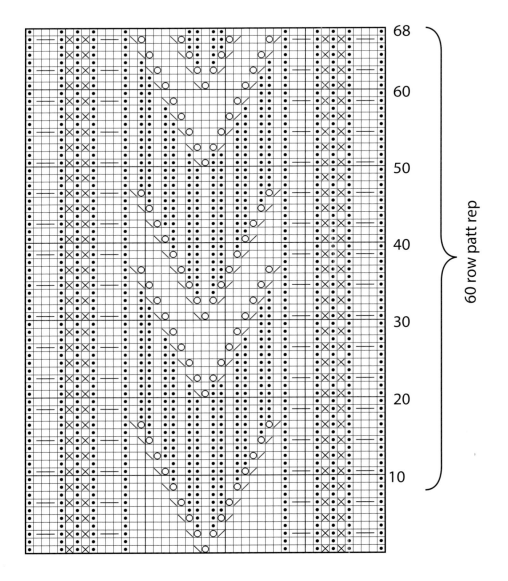

68
60
50
40
30
20
10

60 row patt rep

PIA

Martin Storey

Main image page **68, 69, 70**

● ● ●

SIZE

To fit bust

81-86	91-97	102-107	112-117	122-127cm
32-34	36-38	40-42	44-46	48-50 in

Actual bust measurement of garment

115.5	126	136.5	145	155.5 cm
45½	49½	53¾	57	61¼ in

YARN

Cotton Cashmere

A Stormy Sky 225

6	6	7	8	8	x 50gm

B Charcoal 232

7	7	8	9	9	x 50gm

C Silver Lining 224

3	3	3	3	4	x 50gm

Alternatively, you could use Rowan Handknit
Cotton in the following shade(s):

A Slate 347

10	10	11	13	13	x 50gm

B Black 252

11	11	13	14	14	x 50gm

C Feather 373

5	5	5	5	7	x 50gm

NEEDLES

1 pair 3¼mm (no 10) (US 3) needles
1 pair 4mm (no 8) (US 6) needles
3¼mm (no 10) (US 3) circular needle at least
160 cm long

TENSION

20 sts and 31 rows to 10 cm measured over stripe
patt, 23 sts and 24 rows to 10 cm measured over
patterned st st, both using 4mm (US 6) needles.

BACK

Using 3¼mm (US 3) needles and yarn A cast on
117 [127: 137: 145: 155] sts.
Work in g st for 12 rows, ending with RS facing
for next row.
Change to 4mm (US 6) needles.
Now work in stripe patt as folls:
Join in yarn B.
Row 1 (RS): Using yarn B, knit.
Row 2: Using yarn B, purl.
Rows 3 and 4: Using yarn A, knit.
These 4 rows form stripe patt.
Work in stripe patt for a further 89 rows, ending
after stripe patt row 1 and with **WS** facing for
next row.
Next row (WS): Using yarn B, P6 [4: 2: 9: 8],
M1P, (P7 [7: 7: 6: 6], M1P) 15 [17: 19: 21: 23]
times, P6 [4: 2: 10: 9]. 133 [145: 157: 167: 179] sts.
Beg and ending rows as indicated, using
the **fairisle** technique as described on the
information page and repeating the 60 row patt
repeat throughout, cont in patt from chart, which
is worked entirely in st st beg with a K row, as
folls:
Cont straight until back meas approx 62 [62.5:
63: 63.5: 64] cm, ending after chart row 10 [10:
12: 14: 14] and with RS facing for next row.
Shape armholes
Keeping patt correct, cast off 9 [10: 11: 12: 13] sts
at beg of next 2 rows.
115 [125: 135: 143: 153] sts.
Dec 1 st at each end of next 9 [11: 11: 13: 13]
rows, then on foll 9 [10: 12: 10: 11] alt rows.
79 [83: 89: 97: 105] sts.
Cont straight until armhole meas 20 [21.5: 23:
24.5: 26] cm, ending with RS facing for next
row.
Shape shoulders and back neck
Keeping patt correct, cast off 4 [4: 5: 6: 6] sts at
beg of next 2 rows, then 4 [5: 5: 6: 6] sts at beg of
foll 2 rows. 63 [65: 69: 73: 81] sts.
Next row (RS): Cast off 4 [5: 5: 6: 7] sts, patt
until there are 13 [13: 14: 15: 17] sts on right
needle and turn, leaving rem sts on a holder.
Work each side of neck separately.
Dec 1 st at neck edge of next 3 rows, ending
with RS facing for next row, **and at same time**
cast off 5 [5: 5: 6: 7] sts at beg of 2nd row.
Cast off rem 5 [5: 6: 6: 7] sts.
With RS facing, slip centre 29 [29: 31: 31: 33] sts

onto a holder (for front band), rejoin yarns and
patt to end.
Complete to match first side, reversing shapings.

LEFT FRONT

Using 3¼mm (US 3) needles and yarn A cast on
43 [48: 52: 57: 61] sts.
Work in g st for 12 rows, ending with RS facing
for next row.
Change to 4mm (US 6) needles.
Join in yarn B.
Beg with row 1, now work in stripe patt as given
for back for 93 rows, ending after stripe patt row
1 and with **WS** facing for next row.
Next row (WS): Using yarn B, P4 [3: 5: 4: 2],
M1P, (P7 [7: 6: 7: 7], M1P) 5 [6: 7: 7: 8] times,
P4 [3: 5: 4: 3]. 49 [55: 60: 65: 70] sts.
Beg and ending rows as indicated, cont in patt
from chart as folls:
Cont straight until left front matches back to beg
of armhole shaping, ending after chart row
10 [10: 12: 14: 14] and with RS facing for
next row.
Shape armhole
Keeping patt correct, cast off 9 [10: 11: 12: 13] sts
at beg of next row. 40 [45: 49: 53: 57] sts.
Work 1 row.
Dec 1 st at armhole edge of next 9 [11: 11: 13:
13] rows, then on foll 9 [10: 12: 10: 11] alt rows.
22 [24: 26: 30: 33] sts.
Cont straight until left front matches back to beg
of shoulder shaping, ending with RS facing for
next row.
Shape shoulder
Keeping patt correct, cast off 4 [4: 5: 6: 6] sts at
beg of next and foll 2 [0: 3: 3: 1] alt rows, then
5 [5: -: -: 7] sts at beg of foll 1 [3: -: -: 2] alt rows.
Work 1 row.
Cast off rem 5 [5: 6: 6: 7] sts.

RIGHT FRONT

Work to match left front, reversing shapings.

SLEEVES

Using 3¼mm (US 3) needles and yarn A cast on
50 [52: 54: 54: 56] sts.

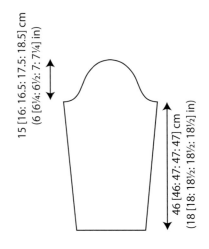

15 [16: 16.5: 17.5: 18.5] cm
(6 [6¼: 6½: 7: 7¼] in)

46 [46: 47: 47: 47] cm
(18 [18: 18½: 18½: 18½] in)

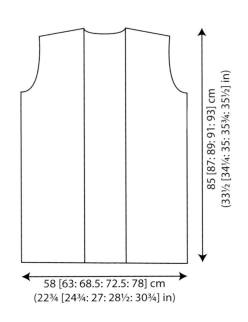

85 [87: 89: 91: 93] cm
(33½ [34¼: 35: 35¾: 35½] in)

58 [63: 68.5: 72.5: 78] cm
(22¾ [24¾: 27: 28½: 30¾] in)

Work in g st for 12 rows, ending with RS facing for next row.

Change to 4mm (US 6) needles.

Join in yarn B.

Beg with row 1, now work in stripe patt as given for back as folls:

Inc 1 st at each end of 11th [9th: 9th: 7th: 7th] and 4 [1: 1: 4: 4] foll 12th [10th: 8th: 8th: 8th] rows, then on – [3: 4: 2: 2] foll – [12th: 10th: 10th: 10th] rows, taking inc sts into patt. 60 [62: 66: 68: 70] sts.

Work 2 [6: 4: 2: 2] rows, ending after stripe patt row 1 and with **WS** facing for next row.

Next row (WS): Using yarn B, P2 [3: 5: 4: 5], M1P, (P7 [7: 7: 6: 6], M1P) 8 [8: 8: 10: 10] times, P2 [3: 5: 4: 5]. 69 [71: 75: 79: 81] sts.

Beg and ending rows as indicated and beg with chart row 15 [15: 15: 17: 17], cont in patt from chart as folls:

Inc 1 st at each end of 7th [3rd: 5th: 5th: 5th] and every foll 8th [8th: 8th: 8th: 6th] row to 75 [83: 87: 91: 91] sts, then on every foll 10th [-: -: -: 8th] row until there are 79 [-: -: -: 95] sts, taking inc sts into patt.

Cont straight until sleeve meas approx 46 [46: 47: 47: 47] cm, ending after chart row 10 [10: 12: 14: 14] and with RS facing for next row.

Shape top

Keeping patt correct, cast off 9 [10: 11: 12: 13] sts at beg of next 2 rows. 61 [63: 65: 67: 69] sts.

Dec 1 st at each end of next 3 rows, then on foll alt row, then on 3 foll 4th rows.

47 [49: 51: 53: 55] sts.

Work 1 row.

Dec 1 st at each end of next and every foll alt row until 37 sts rem, then on foll 7 rows, ending with RS facing for next row.

Cast off rem 23 sts.

MAKING UP

Press as described on the information page.
Join both shoulder seams using back stitch, or mattress stitch if preferred.

Front band

With RS facing, using 3¼mm (US 3) circular needle and yarn A, beg and ending at front cast-on edges, pick up and knit 183 [187: 192: 196: 200] sts up entire right front opening edge, and 3 sts down right side of back neck, K across 29 [29: 31: 31: 33] sts on back holder dec [dec: dec: dec: inc] 1 st at centre, then pick up and knit 3 sts up left side of back neck, and 183 [187: 192: 196: 200] sts down entire left front opening edge. 400 [408: 420: 428: 440] sts.

Row 1 (WS): K1, P2, ★K2, P2, rep from ★ to last st, K1.

Row 2: K3, ★P2, K2, rep from ★ to last st, K1.

These 2 rows form rib.

Cont in rib until front band meas 5 cm, ending with RS facing for next row.

Cast off in rib.

See information page for finishing instructions, setting in sleeves using the set-in method.

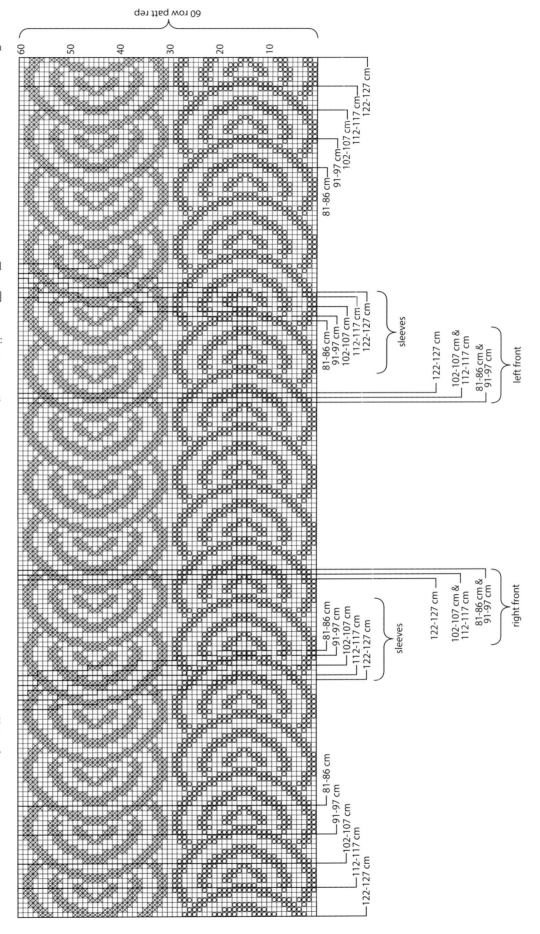

133

RAKKI

Martin Storey

Main image page **16, 17**

● ● ●

SIZE

One size

Actual bust measurement of garment

190 cm

74¾ in

YARN

Kidsilk Haze and Fine Lace

A	KSH Steel 664	17	x 25gm
B	FL Pigeon 950	3	x 50gm

NEEDLES

1 pair 2¾mm (no 12) (US 2) needles
1 pair 3¼mm (no 10) (US 3) needles
2¾mm (no 12) (US 2) circular needle no more than 40 cm long
Cable needle

TENSION

22 sts and 34 rows to 10 cm measured over lace patt using 3¼mm (US 3) needles and Kidsilk Haze DOUBLE. Central panel (93 sts) measures 29 cm.

SPECIAL ABBREVIATIONS

C2B = slip next st onto cable needle and leave at back of work, K1, then K1 from cable needle; **C2F** = slip next st onto cable needle and leave at front of work, K1, then K1 from cable needle; **C7B** = slip next 4 sts onto cable needle and leave at back of work, K3, slip centre st of this group of 7 sts back onto left needle and P this st, then K3 from cable needle; **C7F** = slip next 4 sts onto cable needle and leave at front of work, K3, slip centre st of this group of 7 sts back onto left needle and P this st, then K3 from cable needle; **Cr2L** = slip next st onto cable needle and leave at front of work, P1, then K1 from cable needle; **Cr2R** = slip next st onto cable needle and leave at back of work, K1, then P1 from cable needle; **Cr4L** = slip next 3 sts onto cable needle and

leave at front of work, P1, then K3 from cable needle; **Cr4R** = slip next st onto cable needle and leave at back of work, K3, then P1 from cable needle; **MB** = make bobble as folls: (K1, P1, K1, P1, K1) all into next st, turn, P5, turn, K5, turn, P2tog, P1, P2tog, turn, sl 1, K2tog, psso; **MK** = make knot as folls: (K1, P1, K1, P1, K1) all into next st, turn, P5, turn, lift 2nd, 3rd, 4th and 5th sts on left needle over first st then K tbl this rem 1 st.

CENTRE BACK PANEL

Using 2¾mm (US 2) needles and one strand each of yarns A and B held together cast on 95 sts.
Row 1 (RS): K1, P3, *K3, P3, rep from * to last st, K1.
Row 2: K4, *P3, K3, rep from * to last st, K1.
Rep last 2 rows 5 times more, ending with RS facing for next row.
Change to 3¼mm (US 3) needles.
Beg and ending rows as indicated and repeating the 16 row patt repeat throughout, cont in patt from chart for centre panel as folls:
Cont straight until centre back panel meas 78 cm, ending with RS facing for next row.
Shape shoulders
Next row (RS): Cast off first 10 sts, patt until there are 75 sts on right needle, cast off rem 10 sts.
Break yarns and leave rem 75 sts on a holder (for collar).

CENTRE FRONT PANEL

Work as given for centre back panel until 20 rows less have been worked than on back to shoulder cast-off, ending with RS facing for next row.
Shape front neck
Next row (RS): Patt 23 sts and turn, leaving rem sts on a holder.
Work each side of neck separately.
Keeping patt correct, dec 1 st at neck edge of next 10 rows, then on foll 3 alt rows. 10 sts.
Work 3 rows, ending with RS facing for next row.

Shape shoulder
Cast off.
With RS facing, slip centre 49 sts onto a holder (for collar), rejoin yarns and patt to end.
Complete to match first side, reversing shapings.

LEFT FRONT PANEL

Using 2¾mm (US 2) needles and yarn A DOUBLE cast on 77 sts.
Row 1 (RS): K4, *P3, K3, rep from * to last st, K1.
Row 2: K1, P3, *K3, P3, rep from * to last st, K1.
Rep last 2 rows 5 times more, dec 3 sts evenly across last row and ending with RS facing for next row. 74 sts.
Change to 3¼mm (US 3) needles.
Beg and ending rows as indicated and repeating the 16 row patt repeat throughout, cont in patt from chart for left front panel as folls:
Cont straight until left front panel meas 78 cm, ending with RS facing for next row.
Shape shoulder
Cast off.

RIGHT FRONT PANEL

Work as given for left front panel but foll chart for right front panel.

RIGHT BACK PANEL

Work as given for left front panel.

LEFT BACK PANEL

Work as given for right front panel.

MAKING UP

Press as described on the information page.
Join side panels to centre panels to form 3 joined panels for front and for back. Join both shoulder seams using back stitch, or mattress stitch if preferred.
Collar
With RS facing, using 2¾mm (US 2) circular needle and yarn A DOUBLE, pick up and knit

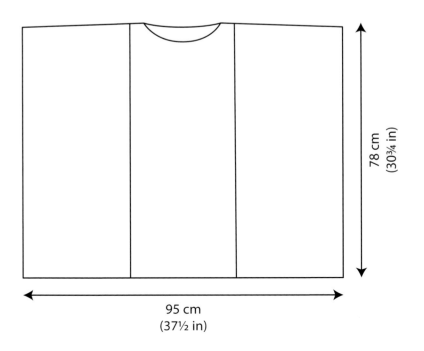

78 cm
(30¾ in)

95 cm
(37½ in)

Centre panel

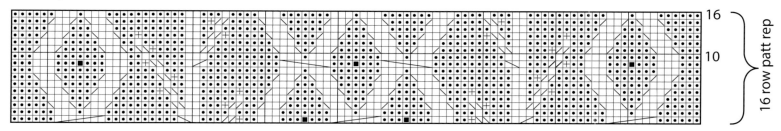

16

10

16 row patt rep

Right front panel

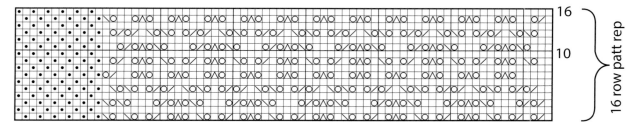

16

10

16 row patt rep

Left front panel

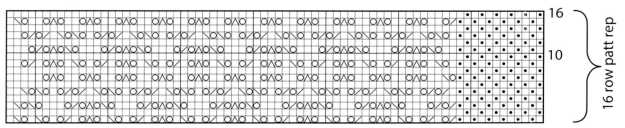

16

10

16 row patt rep

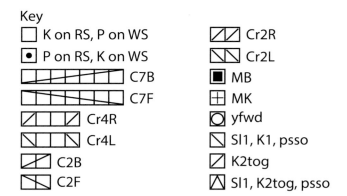

Key

☐ K on RS, P on WS	◪ Cr2R
▣ P on RS, K on WS	◺ Cr2L
▭ C7B	■ MB
▭ C7F	⊞ MK
◪ Cr4R	◯ yfwd
◺ Cr4L	◹ Sl1, K1, psso
◪ C2B	◩ K2tog
◺ C2F	△ Sl1, K2tog, psso

18 sts down left side of front neck, K across 49 sts on front holder dec 1 st at centre, pick up and knit 18 sts up right side of front neck, then K across 75 sts on back holder dec 3 sts evenly. 156 sts.

Round 1 (RS): ★K3, P3, rep from ★ to end.
Rep last round until collar meas 30 cm from pick-up round.
Cast off loosely in rib.
Mark points along side seam edges 35 cm and

45 cm below shoulder seams. Sew side seams between marked points. See information page for finishing instructions.

SIZE

To fit bust

81–86 91–97 102–107 112–117 122–127cm

32–34 36–38 40–42 44–46 48–50 in

Actual bust measurement of garment

| 88 | 98.5 | 108.5 | 117.5 | 128 | cm |
| 34½ | 38¾ | 42¾ | 46¼ | 50½ | in |

YARN

Cotton Glacé and Kidsilk Haze

A Glacé Heather 828

| 6 | 6 | 7 | 7 | 7 | x 50gm |

B KSH Dewberry 600

| 1 | 1 | 1 | 1 | 2 | x 25gm |

NEEDLES

1 pair 2¾mm (no 12) (US 2) needles

1 pair 3¼mm (no 10) (US 3) needles

TENSION

Using Cotton Glace, 23 sts and 32 rows to 10 cm measured over st st using 3¼mm (US 3) needles.

BACK

Using 2¾mm (US 2) needles cast on as folls: using yarn A cast on 61 [67: 73: 78: 84] sts, using yarn B cast on 41 sts **very loosely**, using yarn A cast on 61 [67: 73: 78: 84] sts.

163 [175: 187: 197: 209] sts.

Using the **intarsia** technique as described on the information page, cont as folls:

Row 1 (RS): Using yarn A P0 [0: 0: 1: 1], (K1, P1) 28 [31: 34: 36: 39] times, K next st and mark this st with a red thread – this st will form pleat fold line, (P1, K1) twice, using yarn B P1, (K1, P1) 3 times, P next st and mark this st with a blue thread – this st will form pleat fold line, P1, (K1, P1) 12 times, P next st and mark this st with a second blue thread – this st will form pleat fold line, P1, (K1, P1) 3 times, using yarn A (K1, P1) twice, K next st and mark this st with a second red thread – this st will form pleat fold line, (P1, K1) 28 [31: 34: 36: 39] times, P0 [0: 0: 1: 1].

Row 2: Using yarn A P0 [0: 0: 1: 1], (K1, P1) 28 [31: 34: 36: 39] times, slip red marked st, (P1, K1) twice, using yarn B P1, (K1, P1) 3 times, slip blue marked st, P1, (K1, P1) 12 times, slip blue marked st, P1, (K1, P1) 3 times, using yarn A (K1, P1) twice, slip red marked st, (P1, K1) 28 [31: 34: 36: 39] times, P0 [0: 0: 1: 1].

Row 3: Using yarn A P0 [0: 0: 1: 1], (K1, P1) 28 [31: 34: 36: 39] times, K red marked st, (P1, K1) twice, using yarn B P1, (K1, P1) 3 times, P blue marked st, P1, (K1, P1) 12 times, P blue marked st, P1, (K1, P1) 3 times, using yarn A (K1, P1) twice, K red marked st, (P1, K1) 28 [31: 34: 36: 39] times, P0 [0: 0: 1: 1].

Row 4: As row 2.

Change to 3¼mm (US 3) needles.

Now work in patt as folls:

Row 1 (RS): Using yarn A K to red marked st, K red marked st, K4, using yarn B K7, P blue marked st, K25, P blue marked st, K7, using yarn A K4, K red marked st, K to end.

Row 2: Using yarn A P to red marked st, slip red marked st, P4, using yarn B P7, slip blue marked st, P25, slip blue marked st, P7, using yarn A P4, slip red marked st, P to end.

Rows 3 to 16: As rows 1 and 2, 7 times.

Row 17: Using yarn A K2, sl 1, K1, psso, K to red marked st, K red marked st, K4, using yarn B K7, P blue marked st, K25, P blue marked st, K7, using yarn A K4, K red marked st, K to last 4 sts, K2tog, K2.

161 [173: 185: 195: 207] sts.

Row 18: As row 2.

Row 19: Using yarn A K to red marked st, K red marked st, K4, using yarn B K7, P blue marked st, K25, P blue marked st, K7, turn, sl 1, P6, slip blue marked st, P25, slip blue marked st, P7, turn, sl 1, K6, P blue marked st, K25, P blue marked st, K7, using yarn A K4, K red marked st, K to end. (**Note**: As row tension of Kidsilk Haze is different to that of Cotton Glace, you are working 2 extra rows in Kidsilk Haze at centre of this row, so that there are 34 rows in Kidsilk Haze for every 32 rows worked each side in Cotton Glace.)

Row 20: As row 2.

Rows 21 to 28: As rows 1 and 2, 4 times.

Row 29: As row 17. 159 [171: 183: 193: 205] sts.

Row 30: As row 2.

Rows 31 and 32: As rows 1 and 2.

These 32 rows form patt and beg side seam shaping.

Working all side seam shaping as set by row 17 and keeping patt correct, dec 1 st at each end of 9th and 3 foll 12th rows.

151 [163: 175: 185: 197] sts.

Cont straight until back meas 30 [30.5: 31: 31.5: 32] cm, ending with RS facing for next row.

Shape armholes

Keeping patt correct, cast off 7 [8: 9: 9: 10] sts at beg of next 2 rows. 137 [147: 157: 167: 177] sts.

Next row (RS): K2, sl 1, K1, psso, patt to last 4 sts, K2tog, K2.

Next row: P2, P2tog, patt to last 4 sts, P2tog tbl, P2.

Working all armhole decreases as set by last 2 rows, dec 1 st at each end of next 5 [7: 7: 9: 9] rows, then on foll 7 [7: 9: 8: 9] alt rows.

109 [115: 121: 129: 137] sts.

Work 33 [35: 37: 41: 45] rows, ending with RS facing for next row. (Armhole should meas approx 17.5 [19: 20.5: 22: 23.5] cm.)

Shape back neck

Next row (RS): K16 [19: 21: 25: 28] and turn,

Back

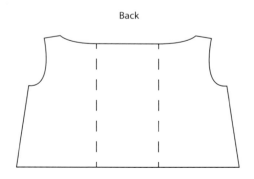

Front

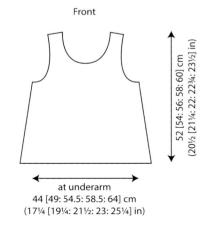

52 [54: 56: 58: 60] cm
(20½ [21¼: 22: 22¾: 23½] in)

at underarm
44 [49: 54.5: 58.5: 64] cm
(17¼ [19¼: 21½: 23: 25¼] in)

leaving rem sts on a holder.

Work each side of neck separately.

Dec 1 st at neck edge of next 6 rows.

10 [13: 15: 19: 22] sts.

Work 1 row, ending with RS facing for next row.

Shape shoulder

Cast off 3 [4: 4: 6: 7] sts at beg and dec 1 st at end of next row.

Work 1 row.

Rep last 2 rows once more.

Cast off rem 2 [3: 5: 5: 6] sts.

With RS facing, rejoin yarns and cast off centre 77 [77: 79: 79: 81] sts, then K to end.

Complete to match first side, reversing shapings.

FRONT

Using 2¾mm (US 2) needles and yarn A cast on 113 [125: 137: 147: 159] sts.

Row 1 (RS): P0 [0: 0: 1: 1], *K1, P1, rep from * to last 1 [1: 1: 0: 0] st, K1 [1: 1: 0: 0].

Row 2: As row 1.

These 2 rows form moss st.

Work in moss st for a further 2 rows, ending with RS facing for next row.

Change to 3¼mm (US 3) needles.

Beg with a K row, now work in st st throughout as folls:

Work 16 rows, ending with RS facing for next row.

Working all side seam shaping in same way as back side seam shaping, dec 1 st at each end of next and 5 foll 12th rows.

101 [113: 125: 135: 147] sts.

Cont straight until front matches back to beg of armhole shaping, ending with RS facing for next row.

Shape armholes

Cast off 7 [8: 9: 9: 10] sts at beg of next 2 rows.

87 [97: 107: 117: 127] sts.

Working all armhole decreases as set by back, dec 1 st at each end of next 7 [9: 9: 11: 11] rows, then on foll 7 [7: 9: 8: 9] alt rows.

59 [65: 71: 79: 87] sts.

Work 1 [3: 3: 7: 9] rows, ending with RS facing for next row.

Shape front neck

Next row (RS): K21 [24: 27: 31: 35] and turn, leaving rem sts on a holder.

Work each side of neck separately.

Dec 1 st at neck edge of next 8 rows, then on foll 2 [2: 3: 3: 4] alt rows, then on foll 4th row, then on foll 6th row, then on foll 8th row.

8 [11: 13: 17: 20] sts.

Work 9 rows, ending with RS facing for next row.

Shape shoulder

Cast off 3 [4: 4: 6: 7] sts at beg of next and foll alt row.

Work 1 row.

Cast off rem 2 [3: 5: 5: 6] sts.

With RS facing, slip centre 17 sts onto a holder (for neckband), rejoin yarn and K to end.

Complete to match first side, reversing shapings.

MAKING UP

Press as described on the information page.

Form back pleat as folls: Fold back along fold line sts to form a box pleat as shown in photograph, and then join folded edges indicated by red markers for 12 cm from back neck edge. Carefully sew cast-off edges together across back neck to hold pleat in place. When picking up sts for neckband, work through all 3 layers across top of pleat.

Join right shoulder seam using back stitch, or mattress stitch if preferred.

Neckband

With RS facing, using 2¾mm (US 2) needles and yarn A, pick up and knit 33 [33: 35: 35: 37] sts down left side of front neck, K across 17 sts on front holder, pick up and knit 33 [33: 35: 35: 37] sts up right side of front neck, and 11 sts down right side of back neck, 28 [28: 30: 30: 32] sts across back neck (remembering to work through all 3 layers across top of pleat), and 11 sts up left side of back neck.

133 [133: 139: 139: 145] sts.

Work in moss st as given for front for 4 rows, ending with **WS** facing for next row.

Cast off in moss st (on **WS**).

Join left shoulder and neckband seam.

Armhole borders (both alike)

With RS facing, using 2¾mm (US 2) needles and yarn A, pick up and knit 105 [113: 123: 129: 139] sts evenly all round armhole edge.

Work in moss st as given for front for 4 rows, ending with **WS** facing for next row.

Cast off in moss st (on **WS**).

See information page for finishing instructions.

RIVERA

Quail Studio

Main image page **70, 71**

● ●

SIZE
One size
Actual bust measurement of garment
237 cm
93¼ in

YARN
Cotton Cashmere

A	Silver Lining 224	10	x 50gm
B	Charcoal 232	6	x 50gm

Alternatively you could use Rowan Handknit
Cotton in the following shade(s):

A	Feather 373	16	x 50gm
B	Black 52	10	x 50gm

NEEDLES
1 pair 3¼mm (no 10) (US 3) needles
1 pair 4mm (no 8) (US 6) needles
3¼mm (no 10) (US 3) circular needle at least
100 cm long

TENSION
23 sts and 38 rows to 10 cm measured over patt
using 4mm (US 6) needles.

BACK
Using 3¼mm (US 3) needles and yarn A cast on
220 sts. (**Note**: Due to number of sts, you may
prefer to work on a circular needle.)
Work in g st for 13 rows, ending with **WS** facing
for next row.
Row 14 (WS): K2, (M1, K7, M1, K6) 16 times,
M1, K7, M1, K3. 254 sts.
Change to 4mm (US 6) needles.
Joining in yarn B when required, now work in
patt as folls:
Row 1 (RS): Using yarn A, knit.
Row 2: Using yarn A, purl.
Row 3: Using yarn B, K2, *keeping yarn at back
of work sl 1, K2, rep from * to end.
Row 4: Using yarn B, K2, *sl next st with yarn
at front (**WS**) of work, K2, rep from * to end.
These 4 rows form patt.
Cont in patt until back meas 59 cm, ending with
RS facing for next row.
Shape shoulders
Cast off all sts, placing markers either side of
centre 16 sts (to denote back neck) – there
should be 119 sts beyond markers at each side.

LEFT FRONT
Using 3¼mm (US 3) needles and yarn A cast on
103 sts.
Work in g st for 13 rows, ending with **WS** facing
for next row.
Row 14 (WS): K2, (M1, K7, M1, K6) 7 times,
M1, K7, M1, K3. 119 sts.

Change to 4mm (US 6) needles.
Joining in yarn B when required and beg with
row 1, now work in patt as given for back as folls:
Cont in patt until left front matches back to
shoulder cast-off, ending with RS facing for next
row.
Shape shoulder
Cast off.

RIGHT FRONT
Work as given for left front.

MAKING UP
Press as described on the information page.
Join both shoulder seams using back stitch, or
mattress stitch if preferred.
Front band
With RS facing, using 3¼mm (US 3) circular
needle and yarn A, beg and ending at front cast-
on edges, pick up and knit 118 sts up right front
opening edge, 14 sts from back neck, and 118 sts
down left front opening edge. 250 sts.
Work in g st for 12 rows, ending with **WS** facing
for next row.
Cast off knitwise (on **WS**).
Side borders (both alike)
With RS facing, using 3¼mm (US 3) circular
needle and yarn A, beg and ending at cast-on
edges, pick up and knit 118 sts up one row-end
edge to shoulder, and 118 sts down next row-
end edge. 236 sts.
Work in g st for 12 rows, ending with **WS** facing
for next row.
Cast off knitwise (on **WS**).
See information page for finishing instructions.

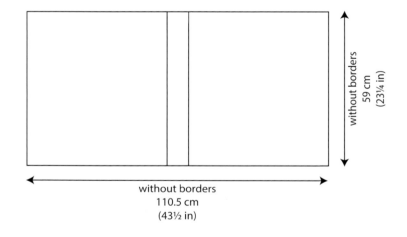

without borders
59 cm
(23¼ in)

without borders
110.5 cm
(43½ in)

OWRE

Vibe Ulrik

Main image page **12, 13**

● ● ● ●

SIZE
To fit bust

81-97	102-107	112-127	cm
32-38	40-42	44-50	in

Actual hem measurement of garment

320	352	384	cm
126	138½	151¼	in

YARN
Summerlite DK

12	12	13	50gm

(photographed in Plaster 452)

NEEDLES
Set of 4 double-pointed 3¼mm (no 10) (US 3) needles

4mm (no 8) (US 6) circular needle – one no more than 30 cm long, one at least 180 cm long, and lengths between as required

TENSION
20 sts and 29 rounds to 10 cm measured over patt using 4mm (US 6) needles.

BODY (worked in one piece, beg at neck edge)
Using double-pointed 3¼mm (US 3) needles cast on 80 [88: 96] sts.
Distribute sts evenly over 3 of the 4 needles and, using 4th needle and taking care not to twist cast-on edge, work in rounds as folls:
Round 1 (RS): ★K1, P1, rep from ★ to end.
This round forms rib.
Place marker after last st of last round (to denote beg and end of rounds – marker sits at centre back).
Work in rib for a further 5 rounds.
Change to shortest 4mm (US 6) circular needle.
Changing to a longer circular needle when

required, cont in patt as folls:
Rounds 1 and 2 (RS): Knit.
Round 3: ★K2, M1, rep from ★ to end.
120 [132: 144] sts.
Round 4: Knit.
Round 5: ★K3, P1, K2, rep from ★ to end.
Round 6: ★K2, P3, K1, rep from ★ to end.
Round 7: ★K1, P5, rep from ★ to end.
Round 8: ★P1, K5, rep from ★ to end.
Round 9: ★P2, K3, P1, rep from ★ to end.
Round 10: ★P3, K1, P2, rep from ★ to end.
Rounds 11 to 22: As rounds 5 to 10 twice.
Round 23: Knit.
Round 24: ★K3, M1, rep from ★ to end.
160 [176: 192] sts.
Round 25: Knit.
Round 26: ★M1, K4, rep from ★ to end.
200 [220: 240] sts.
Rounds 27 to 29: ★K1, P1, rep from ★ to end.
Round 30: ★K2tog, yfwd, rep from ★ to end.
Round 31: Knit.
Round 32: ★K2, (M1, K3) twice, M1, K2, rep from ★ to end. 260 [286: 312] sts.
Round 33: Knit.
Round 34: ★K3, M1, K4, (M1, K3) twice, rep from ★ to end. 320 [352: 384] sts.
Rounds 35 and 36: ★K4, P1, K3, rep from ★ to end.
Rounds 37 and 38: ★K3, P3, K2, rep from ★ to end.
Rounds 39 and 40: ★K2, P5, K1, rep from ★ to end.
Rounds 41 and 42: ★K1, P7, rep from ★ to end.
Rounds 43 to 46: Knit.
Rounds 47 to 49: ★K1, P1, rep from ★ to end.
Round 50: ★K8, M1, K8, rep from ★ to end.
340 [374: 408] sts.
Rounds 51 and 52: Knit.
Round 53: ★K17, M1, rep from ★ to end.
360 [396: 432] sts.
Rounds 54 to 71: As rounds 5 to 10, 3 times.
Rounds 72 to 74: Knit.
Round 75: ★K9, M1, rep from ★ to end.
400 [440: 480] sts.
Rounds 76 to 79: As rounds 27 to 30.
Round 80: ★M1, K10, rep from ★ to end.
440 [484: 528] sts.
Rounds 81 and 82: Knit.
Round 83: ★K11, M1, rep from ★ to end.

480 [528: 576] sts.
Rounds 84 to 91: As rounds 35 to 42.
Round 92: Knit.
Round 93: ★K12, M1, rep from ★ to end.
520 [572: 624] sts.
Rounds 94 and 95: Knit.
Rounds 96 to 98: ★K1, P1, rep from ★ to end.
Round 99: ★K13, M1, rep from ★ to end.
560 [616: 672] sts.
Rounds 100 and 101: Knit.
Round 102: ★M1, K14, rep from ★ to end.
600 [660: 720] sts.
Rounds 103 to 120: As rounds 5 to 10, 3 times.
Round 121: Knit.
Round 122: ★K30, M1, rep from ★ to end.
620 [682: 744] sts.
Rounds 123 and 124: Knit.
Rounds 125 to 128: As rounds 27 to 30.
Rounds 129 and 130: Knit.
Round 131: ★M1, K31, rep from ★ to end.
640 [704: 768] sts.
Round 132: Knit.
Rounds 133 to 140: As rounds 35 to 42.
Rounds 140 to 144: Knit.
Rounds 145 to 150: ★K1, P1, rep from ★ to end.
Keeping rib correct as set by last 6 rounds, now divide for cuffs as folls:
Next round (RS): Cast off first 140 [152: 164] sts in rib, rib until there are 40 [48: 56] sts on right needle and slip these sts onto a holder (for right cuff), cast off next 280 [304: 328] sts in rib, rib until there are 40 [48: 56] sts on right needle and slip these sts onto a holder (for left cuff), cast off rem 140 [152: 164] sts in rib.
Break yarn.

CUFFS (both alike)
Slip 40 [48: 56] sts from cuff holder onto double-pointed 3¼mm (US 3) needles.
Distribute sts evenly over 3 of the 4 needles and, using 4th needle and keeping rib correct as set, work in rounds of rib until cuff meas 14 [15: 16] cm from body cast-off edge.
Cast off in rib.

MAKING UP
Press as described on the information page.
See information page for finishing instructions.

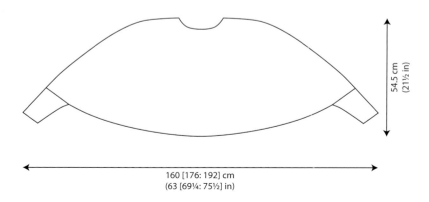

54.5 cm
(21½ in)

160 [176: 192] cm
(63 [69¼: 75½] in)

SIZE

To fit bust

81-86 91-97 102-107 112-117 122-127cm

32-34 36-38 40-42 44-46 48-50 in

Actual bust measurement of garment

89	99	109	119	129	cm
35	39	43	46¾	50¾	in

YARN

Cotton Cashmere

A Pearly Pink 216

4	4	5	6	6	x 50gm

B Sea Spray 219

1	1	1	1	1	x 50gm

C Morning Sky 221

1	1	1	1	1	x 50gm

D Harbour Blue 223

1	1	1	1	1	x 50gm

NEEDLES

1 pair 3¼mm (no 10) (US 3) needles
1 pair 4mm (no 8) (US 6) needles

TENSION

20 sts and 28 rows to 10 cm measured over patterned and plain st st using 4mm (US 6) needles.

BACK

Using 3¼mm (US 3) needles and yarn A cast on 90 [98: 110: 118: 130] sts.
Row 1 (RS): K2, *P2, K2, rep from * to end.
Row 2: P2, *K2, P2, rep from * to end.
These 2 rows form rib.
Work in rib for a further 6 rows, dec [inc: dec: inc: dec] 1 st at end of last row and ending with

RS facing for next row. 89 [99: 109: 119: 129] sts. Change to 4mm (US 6) needles.★★
Beg with a K row, now work in st st throughout as folls:
Work 78 [80: 82: 82: 84] rows, ending with RS facing for next row. (Back meas approx 31 [31.5: 32: 32.5: 33] cm.)

Shape armholes

Cast off 4 [5: 6: 6: 6] sts at beg of next 2 rows.
81 [89: 97: 107: 117] sts.
Dec 1 st at each end of next 3 [5: 5: 7: 7] rows, then on foll 4 [4: 5: 5: 6] alt rows.
67 [71: 77: 83: 91] sts.
Work 43 [45: 47: 49: 51] rows, ending with RS facing for next row. (Armhole should meas approx 20 [21.5: 23: 24.5: 26] cm.)

Shape shoulders and back neck

Next row (RS): Cast off 3 [4: 4: 5: 6] sts, K until there are 15 [16: 18: 20: 22] sts on right needle and turn, leaving rem sts on a holder.
Work each side of neck separately.
Dec 1 st at neck edge of next 4 rows **and at same time** cast off 3 [4: 4: 5: 6] sts at beg of 2nd row, then 4 [4: 5: 5: 6] sts at beg of foll alt row.
Work 1 row.
Cast off rem 4 [4: 5: 6: 6] sts.
With RS facing, slip centre 31 [31: 33: 33: 35] sts onto a holder (for neckband), rejoin yarn and K to end.
Complete to match first side, reversing shapings.

FRONT

Work as given for back to ★★.
Beg and ending rows as indicated and using the **intarsia** technique as described on the information page, cont in patt from chart, which is worked entirely in st st beg with a K row, as folls:
Cont straight until chart row 78 [80: 82: 82: 84] has been completed, ending with RS facing for next row.

Shape armholes

Keeping patt correct, cast off 4 [5: 6: 6: 6] sts at beg of next 2 rows. 81 [89: 97: 107: 117] sts.
Dec 1 st at each end of next 3 [5: 5: 7: 7] rows, then on foll 4 [4: 5: 5: 6] alt rows.
67 [71: 77: 83: 91] sts.
Work 3 [5: 5: 7: 7] rows, ending after chart row

94 [100: 104: 108: 112] and with RS facing for next row.

Shape front neck

Next row (RS): Patt 26 [28: 31: 34: 38] sts and turn, leaving rem sts on a holder.
Work each side of neck separately.
Keeping patt correct, dec 1 st at neck edge of next 4 rows, then on foll 4 [4: 5: 5: 6] alt rows, then on 2 foll 4th rows, then on 2 foll 6th rows.
14 [16: 18: 21: 24] sts.
Work 7 rows, ending after chart row 134 [140: 146: 150: 156] and with RS facing for next row.

Shape shoulder

Cast off 3 [4: 4: 5: 6] sts at beg of next and foll 1 [2: 1: 2: 2] alt rows, then 4 [-: 5: -: -] sts at beg of foll 1 [-: 1: -: -] alt rows.
Work 1 row.
Cast off rem 4 [4: 5: 6: 6] sts.
With RS facing, slip centre 15 sts onto a holder (for neckband), rejoin yarn and patt to end.
Complete to match first side, reversing shapings.

MAKING UP

Press as described on the information page.
Join right shoulder seam using back stitch, or mattress stitch if preferred.

Neckband

With RS facing, using 3¼mm (US 3) needles and yarn A, pick up and knit 35 [35: 38: 38: 39] sts down left side of front neck, K across 15 sts on front holder, pick up and knit 35 [35: 38: 38: 39] sts up right side of front neck, and 5 sts down right side of back neck, K across 31 [31: 33: 33: 35] sts on back holder, then pick up and knit 5 sts up left side of back neck.
126 [126: 134: 134: 138] sts.
Beg with row 2, work in rib as given for back for 5 rows, ending with RS facing for next row.
Cast off in rib.
Join left shoulder and neckband seam.

Armhole borders (both alike)

With RS facing, using 3¼mm (US 3) needles and yarn A, pick up and knit 90 [98: 106: 110: 118] sts evenly all round armhole edge.
Beg with row 2, work in rib as given for back for 5 rows, ending with RS facing for next row.
Cast off in rib.
See information page for finishing instructions.

44.5 [49.5: 54.5: 59.5: 64.5] cm
(17½ [19½: 21½: 23½: 25½] in)

53 [55: 57: 59: 61] cm
(20¾ [21½: 22½: 23¼: 24] in)

Key
□ A
⊠ B
◎ C
■ D

162
160
150
140
130
120
110
100
90
80
70
60
50
40
30
20
10

81-86 cm
91-97 cm
102-107 cm
112-117 cm
122-127 cm

81-86 cm
91-97 cm
102-107 cm
112-117 cm
122-127 cm

141

DADA
Lisa Richardson
Main image page **78, 79**

• •

SIZE
To fit bust
81-86 91-97 102-107 112-117 122-127cm
32-34 36-38 40-42 44-46 48-50 in
Actual bust measurement of garment

90	100	110	120	130	cm
35½	39¼	43¼	47¼	51¼	in

YARN
Cotton Cashmere and Kidsilk Haze
A CC Stormy Sky 225

3	3	3	3	4	x 50gm

B CC Silver Lining 224

2	2	2	2	3	x 50gm

C ★KSH White 612

1	2	2	2	2	x 25gm

★Kidsilk Haze is used DOUBLE throughout

Alternatively, you could use Rowan Handknit
Cotton in the following shade(s):
A HK Slate 347

5	5	5	5	7	x 50gm

B HK Feather 347

4	4	4	4	5	x 50 m

C ★KSH White 612

1	2	2	2	2	x 25gm

★Kidsilk Haze is used DOUBLE throughout

NEEDLES
1 pair 3¼mm (no 10) (US 3) needles
1 pair 4mm (no 8) (US 6) needles

TENSION
20 sts and 29 rows to 10 cm measured over
striped st st using 4mm (US 6) needles.

BACK
Using 3¼mm (US 3) needles and yarn A cast on
90 [102: 110: 122: 130] sts.
Row 1 (RS): K2, *P2, K2, rep from * to end.
Row 2: P2, *K2, P2, rep from * to end.

These 2 rows form rib.
Work in rib for a further 6 rows, dec 0 [1: 0: 1:
0] st at each end of last row and ending with RS
facing for next row. 90 [100: 110: 120: 130] sts.
Change to 4mm (US 6) needles.
Beg with a K row, now work in st st throughout
as folls:
Work 8 rows.
Joining in colours as required, now work in
striped st st as folls:
Using yarn C DOUBLE, work 4 rows, dec 1 st
at each end of 3rd of these rows.
88 [98: 108: 118: 128] sts.
Using yarn B, work 16 rows, dec 1 st at each end
of 7th and foll 8th row. 84 [94: 104: 114: 124] sts.
Using yarn C DOUBLE, work 4 rows.
Using yarn A, work 16 rows, inc 1 st at each end
of 11th of these row.
86 [96: 106: 116: 126] sts.
Last 40 rows form striped st st.
Keeping striped st st correct throughout, cont
as folls:
Inc 1 st at each end of 9th and foll 14th row.
90 [100: 110: 120: 130] sts.
Cont straight until back meas 34 [34.5: 35: 35.5:
36] cm, ending with RS facing for next row.
Shape armholes
Keeping striped st st correct, cast off 4 sts at beg
of next 2 rows. 82 [92: 102: 112: 122] sts.★★
Dec 1 st at each end of next 7 [9: 11: 9: 9] rows,
then on foll 7 [8: 7: 11: 11] alt rows, then on 3 [3:
4: 4: 5] foll 4th rows, then on foll 6th row, then
on foll 8th row. 44 [48: 54: 60: 68] sts.
Work 3 rows, ending with RS facing for next
row. (Armhole should meas approx 18 [19.5: 21:
22.5: 24] cm.)
Shape back neck
Next row (RS): K10 [12: 14: 17: 20] and turn,
leaving rem sts on a holder.
Work each side of neck separately.
Keeping stripes correct, dec 1 st at neck edge of
next 4 rows. 6 [8: 10: 13: 16] sts.
Work 1 row, ending with RS facing for next row.
Shape shoulder
Cast off.
With RS facing, slip centre 24 [24: 26: 26: 28] sts
onto a holder (for neckband), rejoin appropriate
yarn and K to end.
Complete to match first side, reversing shapings.

FRONT
Work as given for back to ★★.

Dec 1 st at each end of next 7 [9: 11: 9: 9] rows,
then on foll 7 [8: 7: 11: 11] alt rows, then on 3 [3:
4: 4: 4] foll 4th rows. 48 [52: 58: 64: 74] sts.
Work 3 [3: 1: 1: 3] rows, ending with RS facing
for next row.
Shape front neck
Next row (RS): (K2tog) 0 [0: 0: 0: 1] times,
K17 [19: 22: 25: 28] and turn, leaving rem sts on
a holder. 17 [19: 22: 25: 29] sts.
Work each side of neck separately.
Keeping stripes correct, dec 1 st at neck edge of
next 6 rows, then on foll 2 [2: 3: 3: 4] alt rows,
then on foll 4th row **and at same time** dec
1 st at armhole edge of 2nd [2nd: 4th: 4th: 6th]
and foll 8th row. 6 [8: 10: 13: 16] sts.
Work 5 rows, ending with RS facing for next
row.
Shape shoulder
Cast off.
With RS facing, slip centre 14 sts onto a holder
(for neckband), rejoin appropriate yarn and K to
last 0 [0: 0: 0: 2] sts, (K2tog) 0 [0: 0: 0: 1] times.
17 [19: 22: 25: 29] sts.
Complete to match first side, reversing shapings.

MAKING UP
Press as described on the information page.
Join right shoulder seam using back stitch, or
mattress stitch if preferred.
Neckband
With RS facing, using 3¼mm (US 3) needles
and yarn A, pick up and knit 17 [17: 18: 18: 21] sts
down left side of front neck, K across 14 sts
on front holder, pick up and knit 17 [17: 18:
18: 21] sts up right side of front neck, and 5 sts
down right side of back neck, K across 24 [24:
26: 26: 28] sts on back holder, then pick up and
knit 5 sts up left side of back neck.
82 [82: 86: 86: 94] sts.
Beg with row 2, work in rib as given for back for
5 rows, ending with RS facing for next row.
Cast off in rib.
Join left shoulder and neckband seam.
Armhole borders (both alike)
With RS facing, using 3¼mm (US 3) needles
and yarn A, pick up and knit 94 [102: 110:
114: 122] sts evenly all round armhole edge.
Beg with row 2, work in rib as given for back for
5 rows, ending with RS facing for next row.
Cast off in rib.
See information page for finishing instructions.

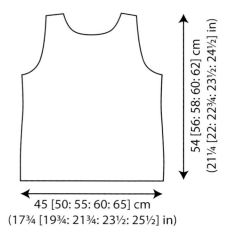

54 [56: 58: 60: 62] cm
(21¼ [22: 22¾: 23½: 24½] in)

45 [50: 55: 60: 65] cm
(17¾ [19¾: 21¾: 23½: 25½] in)

FRITZIA

Martin Storey

Main image page **72, 73**

● ●

SIZE
To fit bust
81-86 91-97 102-107 112-117 122-127cm
32-34 36-38 40-42 44-46 48-50 in
Actual bust measurement of garment
99.5   109.5   120   130.5   140.5   cm
39¼   43   47¼   51½   55¼   in

YARN
Cotton Cashmere
A Stormy Sky 225

4	5	5	6	6	x 50gm

B Silver Lining 224

4	4	4	5	5	x 50gm

C Paper 210

3	4	4	4	4	x 50gm

Alternatively, you could use Rowan Handknit
Cotton in the following shade(s):
A Slate 347

7	8	8	10	10	x 50gm

B Feather 373

7	7	7	8	8	x 50gm

C Bleached 263

5	7	7	7	7	x 50gm

NEEDLES
1 pair 3¼mm (no 10) (US 3) needles
1 pair 4mm (no 8) (US 6) needles
3¼mm (no 10) (US 3) circular needle no more
than 40 cm long

TENSION
19½ sts and 28 rows to 10 cm measured over
lower patt, 19½ sts and 29 rows to 10 cm
measured over moss st, 19½ sts and 34 rows to
10 cm measured over g st, all using 4mm (US 6)
needles.

BACK
Using 3¼mm (US 3) needles and yarn A cast on
98 [106: 118: 126: 138] sts.
Row 1 (RS): K2, *P2, K2, rep from * to end.
Row 2: P2, *K2, P2, rep from * to end.
These 2 rows form rib.
Cont in rib until back meas 7 cm, dec [inc: dec:
inc: dec] 1 st at centre of last row and ending
with RS facing for next row.
97 [107: 117: 127: 137] sts.
Change to 4mm (US 6) needles.
Now work in lower patt as folls:
Row 1 (RS): Knit.
Row 2: Purl.
Row 3: P0 [2: 1: 0: 2], K1, *P2, K1, rep from *
to last 0 [2: 1: 0: 2] sts, P0 [2: 1: 0: 2].
Row 4: K0 [2: 1: 0: 2], P1, *K2, P1, rep from *
to last 0 [2: 1: 0: 2] sts, K0 [2: 1: 0: 2].
These 4 rows form lower patt.
Work in lower patt for a further 49 rows, ending
after patt row 1 and with **WS** facing for next row.
Break off yarn A and join in yarn B.
Next row (WS): Purl.
Now work in moss st as folls:
Row 1 (RS): K1, *P1, K1, rep from * to end.
Row 2: As row 1.
These 2 rows form moss st.
Cont in moss st until back meas 46 [46.5: 47:
47.5: 48] cm, ending with RS facing for next row.
Break off yarn B and join in yarn C.
Shape armholes
Now working in g st throughout, cont as folls:
Cast off 5 [6: 7: 8: 9] sts at beg of next 2 rows.
87 [95: 103: 111: 119] sts.
Dec 1 st at each end of next 5 [7: 7: 9: 9] rows,
then on foll 5 [5: 6: 6: 6] alt rows.
67 [71: 77: 81: 89] sts.
Cont straight until armhole meas 20 [21.5: 23:
24.5: 26] cm, ending with RS facing for next
row.
Shape shoulders and back neck
Next row (RS): Cast off 4 [4: 5: 5: 6] sts, K
until there are 16 [18: 19: 21: 23] sts on right
needle and turn, leaving rem sts on a holder.
Work each side of neck separately.
Dec 1 st at neck edge of next 4 rows **and at
same time** cast off 4 [4: 5: 5: 6] sts at beg of 2nd
row and 4 [5: 5: 6: 6] sts at beg of foll alt row.
Work 1 row.
Cast off rem 4 [5: 5: 6: 7] sts.
With RS facing, slip centre 27 [27: 29: 29: 31] sts
onto a holder (for collar), rejoin yarn and K to
end.
Complete to match first side, reversing shapings.

FRONT
Work as given for back until 22 [22: 26: 26: 30]
rows less have been worked than on back to beg
of shoulder shaping, ending with RS facing for
next row.
Shape front neck
Next row (RS): K27 [29: 32: 34: 38] and turn,
leaving rem sts on a holder.
Work each side of neck separately.
Dec 1 st at neck edge of next 6 rows, then on
foll 3 alt rows, then on 2 [2: 3: 3: 4] foll 4th rows.
16 [18: 20: 22: 25] sts.
Work 1 row, ending with RS facing for next row.
Shape shoulder
Cast off 4 [4: 5: 5: 6] sts at beg of next and foll alt
row, then 4 [5: 5: 6: 6] sts at beg of foll alt row.
Work 1 row.
Cast off rem 4 [5: 5: 6: 7] sts.
With RS facing, slip centre 13 sts onto a holder
(for collar), rejoin yarn and K to end.
Complete to match first side, reversing shapings.

SLEEVES
Using 3¼mm (US 3) needles and yarn A cast on
46 [46: 50: 50: 50] sts.
Work in rib as given for back for 7 cm, dec [inc:
dec: dec: inc] 1 st at centre of last row and ending
with RS facing for next row.
45 [47: 49: 49: 51] sts.
Change to 4mm (US 6) needles.
Now work in lower patt as folls:
Row 1 (RS): Knit.
Row 2: Purl.
Row 3: P1 [2: 0: 0: 1], K1, *P2, K1, rep from *
to last 1 [2: 0: 0: 1] sts, P1 [2: 0: 0: 1].
Row 4: K1 [2: 0: 0: 1], P1, *K2, P1, rep from *
to last 1 [2: 0: 0: 1] sts, K1 [2: 0: 0: 1].
These 4 rows form lower patt.
Cont in lower patt, shaping sides by inc 1 st at
each end of 3rd [next: next: next: next] and 0 [0:
3: 8: 8] foll 6th rows, then on 5 [6: 3: 0: 0] foll 8th
rows, taking inc sts into patt.
57 [61: 63: 67: 69] sts.
Work 6 [0: 6: 0: 0] rows, ending after patt row 1
and with **WS** facing for next row.
Break off yarn A and join in yarn B.
Next row (WS): Purl.
Now work in moss st as given for back and cont
as folls:
Inc 1 st at each end of next [7th: next: 5th: 5th]
and every foll 8th [8th: 8th: 6th: 6th] row to
61 [71: 75: 73: 83] sts, then on every foll

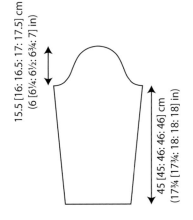

15.5 [16: 16.5: 17: 17.5] cm
(6 [6¼: 6½: 6¾: 7] in)

45 [45: 46: 46: 46] cm
(17¾ [17¾: 18: 18: 18] in)

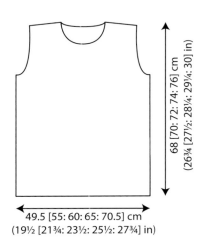

68 [70: 72: 74: 76] cm
(26¾ [27½: 28¼: 29¼: 30] in)

49.5 [55: 60: 65: 70.5] cm
(19½ [21¾: 23½: 25½: 27¾] in)

10th [-: -: 8th: -] row until there are 67 [-: -: 79: -] sts, taking inc sts into moss st.
Cont straight until sleeve meas 45 [45: 46: 46: 46] cm, ending with RS facing for next row.
Break off yarn B and join in yarn C.
Shape top
Now working in g st throughout, cont as folls:
Cast off 5 [6: 7: 8: 9] sts at beg of next 2 rows.
57 [59: 61: 63: 65] sts.
Dec 1 st at each end of next 3 rows, then on foll 2 alt rows, then on 7 foll 4th rows.
33 [35: 37: 39: 41] sts.
Work 1 row.

Dec 1 st at each end of next and every foll alt row until 23 sts rem, then on foll 5 rows, ending with RS facing for next row.
Cast off rem 13 sts.

MAKING UP
Press as described on the information page.
Join both shoulder seams using back stitch, or mattress stitch if preferred.
Collar
With RS facing, using 3¼mm (US 3) circular needle and yarn C, pick up and knit 21 [21: 22: 22: 25] sts down left side of front neck, K across

13 sts on front holder, pick up and knit 21 [21: 22: 22: 25] sts up right side of front neck, and 5 sts down right side of back neck, K across 27 [27: 29: 29: 31] sts on back holder, then pick up and knit 5 sts up left side of back neck.
92 [92: 96: 96: 104] sts.
Round 1: *K2, P2, rep from * to end.
Rep last round until collar meas 18 cm from pick-up round.
Cast off **loosely** in rib.
See information page for finishing instructions, setting in sleeves using the set-in method.

BERENICE
ARNE & CARLOS
Main image page **81**
● ● ●

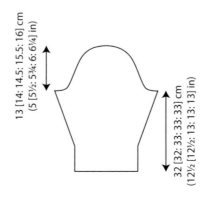

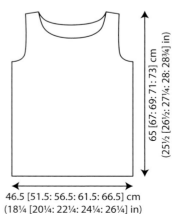

SIZE
To fit bust
81-86 91-97 102-107 112-117 122-127cm

32-34 36-38 40-42 44-46 48-50 in
Actual bust measurement of garment
92.5 102.5 112.5 122.5 132.5 cm
36½ 40¼ 44¼ 48¼ 52¼ in
YARN
Cotton Cashmere
A Stormy Sky 225
   5   6   6   7   8   x 50gm
B Paper 210
   4   5   5   6   6   x 50gm

Alternatively, you could use Rowan Handknit Cotton in the following shade(s):
A Slate 347
   8   10   10   11   13   x 50gm
B Bleached 263
   7   8   8   10   10   x 50gm

NEEDLES
1 pair 3¼mm (no 10) (US 3) needles
1 pair 4mm (no 8) (US 6) needles

TENSION
24 sts and 26 rows to 10 cm measured over patterned st st using 4mm (US 6) needles.

BACK
Using 3¼mm (US 3) needles and yarn A cast on 112 [124: 136: 148: 160] sts.
Row 1 (RS): K3, *P1, K2, rep from * to last st, K1.
Row 2: K1, *P2, K1, rep from * to end.
These 2 rows form rib.
Cont in rib until back meas 10 cm, dec 1 st at centre of last row and ending with RS facing for next row. 111 [123: 135: 147: 159] sts.
Place markers at both ends of last row (to denote top of side seam openings).
Change to 4mm (US 6) needles.
Beg and ending rows as indicated, using the **fairisle** technique as described on the information page and repeating the 32 row patt repeat throughout, cont in patt from chart, which is worked entirely in st st beg with a K row, as folls:
Cont straight until back meas 44 [44.5: 45: 45.5: 46] cm, ending with RS facing for next row.
Shape armholes
Keeping patt correct, cast off 5 [6: 7: 8: 9] sts at beg of next 2 rows. 101 [111: 121: 131: 141] sts.

Dec 1 st at each end of next 5 [7: 7: 9: 9] rows, then on foll 5 [5: 7: 6: 7] alt rows.
81 [87: 93: 101: 109] sts.**
Work 19 [21: 21: 25: 27] rows, ending with RS facing for next row. (Armhole should meas approx 14 [15.5: 17: 18.5: 20] cm.)
Shape back neck
Next row (RS): Patt 22 [25: 27: 31: 34] sts and turn, leaving rem sts on a holder.
Work each side of neck separately.
Keeping patt correct, dec 1 st at neck edge of next 10 rows, then on foll 2 alt rows.
10 [13: 15: 19: 22] sts.
Work 1 row, ending with RS facing for next row.
Shape shoulder
Cast off 4 [6: 7: 9: 10] sts at beg and dec 1 st at end of next row.
Work 1 row.
Cast off rem 5 [6: 7: 9: 11] sts.
With RS facing, slip centre 37 [37: 39: 39: 41] sts onto a holder (for neckband), rejoin yarns and patt to end.
Complete to match first side, reversing shapings.

FRONT
Work as given for back to **.
Work 1 [3: 1: 5: 5] rows, ending with RS facing for next row.
Shape front neck
Next row (RS): Patt 27 [30: 33: 37: 41] sts and turn, leaving rem sts on a holder.
Work each side of neck separately.

13 [14: 14.5: 15.5: 16] cm (5 [5½: 5¾: 6: 6¼] in)

32 [32: 33: 33: 33] cm (12½ [12½: 13: 13: 13] in)

65 [67: 69: 71: 73] cm (25½ [26½: 27¼: 28: 28¾] in)

46.5 [51.5: 56.5: 61.5: 66.5] cm (18¼ [20¼: 22¼: 24¼: 26¼] in)

Keeping patt correct, dec 1 st at neck edge of next 10 rows, then on foll 6 [6: 7: 7: 8] alt rows, then on 2 foll 4th rows. 9 [12: 14: 18: 21] sts. Work 3 rows, ending with RS facing for next row.

Shape shoulder

Cast off 4 [6: 7: 9: 10] sts at beg of next row. Work 1 row.

Cast off rem 5 [6: 7: 9: 11] sts.

With RS facing, slip centre 27 sts onto a holder (for neckband), rejoin yarns and patt to end. Complete to match first side, reversing shapings.

SLEEVES

Using 3¼mm (US 3) needles and yarn A cast on 58 [62: 62: 62: 66] sts.

Row 1 (RS): K2, *P2, K2, rep from * to end.

Row 2: P2, *K2, P2, rep from * to end.

These 2 rows form rib.

Cont in rib until sleeve meas 10 cm, dec [dec: inc: inc: dec] 1 st at end of last row and ending with RS facing for next row.

57 [61: 63: 63: 65] sts.

Change to 4mm (US 6) needles.

Beg and ending rows as indicated, cont in patt from chart as folls:

Inc 1 st at each end of 3rd and every foll 6th [6th: 6th: 4th: 4th] row to 67 [71: 71: 91: 91] sts, then on every foll 4th [4th: 4th: alt: alt] row until there are 81 [85: 89: 93: 97] sts, taking inc sts into patt.

Work 3 rows, ending with RS facing for next row. (Sleeve should meas approx 32 [32: 33: 3 3: 33] cm.)

Shape top

Keeping patt correct, cast off 5 [6: 7: 8: 9] sts at beg of next 2 rows. 71 [73: 75: 77: 79] sts.

Dec 1 st at each end of next 5 rows, then on every foll alt row until 43 sts rem, then on foll 9 rows, ending with RS facing for next row.

Cast off rem 25 sts.

MAKING UP

Press as described on the information page.

Join right shoulder seam using back stitch, or mattress stitch if preferred.

Neckband

With RS facing, using 3¼mm (US 3) needles and yarn A, pick up and knit 35 [35: 38: 38: 39] sts down left side of front neck, K across 27 sts on front holder, pick up and knit 35 [35: 38: 38: 39] sts up right side of front neck, and 18 sts down right side of back neck, K across 37 [37: 39: 39: 41] sts on back holder, then pick up and knit 18 sts up left side of back neck. 170 [170: 178: 178: 182] sts.

Beg with row 2, work in rib as given for sleeves for 3 cm, ending with RS facing for next row. Cast off in rib.

See information page for finishing instructions, setting in sleeves using the set-in method and leaving side seams open below markers.

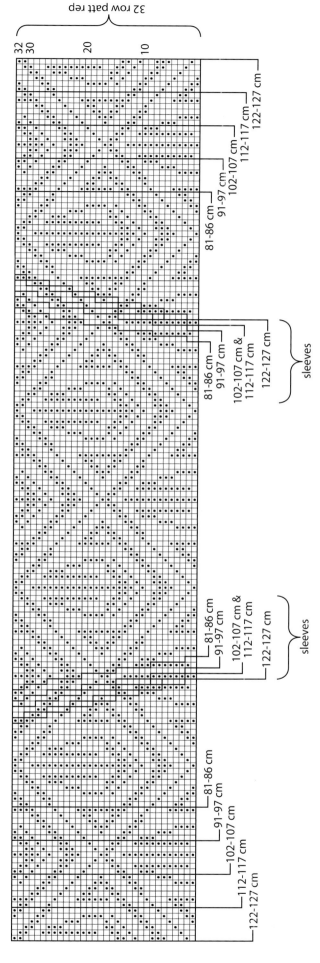

Key

A •

B □

145

BISMAR

Annika Andrea Wolke

Main image page **32, 33**

● ● ●

SIZE

To fit bust

81-86 91-97 102-107 112-117 122-127cm

32-34 36-38 40-42 44-46 48-50 in

Actual bust measurement of garment

89.5 98.5 109 119.5 129.5 cm

35¼ 38¾ 43 47 51 in

YARN

Summerlite 4ply

6 7 8 8 9 x 50gm

(photographed in Green Bay 445)

NEEDLES

1 pair 2¼mm (no 13) (US 1) needles

1 pair 3mm (no 11) (US 2/3) needles

2¼mm (no 13) (US 1) circular needle at least
120 cm long

BUTTONS – 6 x BN1624 (wrong side) from
Bedecked. Please see information page for
contact details.

TENSION

27 sts and 34 rows to 10 cm measured over patt
using 3mm (US 2/3) needles.

BACK

Using 2¼mm (US 1) needles cast on 121 [133:
147: 161: 175] sts.

Work in g st for 10 rows, ending with RS facing
for next row.

Change to 3mm (US 2/3) needles.

Now work in patt as folls:

Row 1 (RS): Knit.

Row 2: Purl.

Row 3: K2 [1: 2: 2: 3], (yfwd, K1) 2 [0: 2: 0:
2] times, (sl 1, K1, psso) 2 [0: 2: 0: 2] times, P1,
★(K2tog) twice, (yfwd, K1) 4 times, (sl 1, K1,
psso) twice, P1, rep from ★ to last 8 [1: 8: 2: 9] sts,
(K2tog) 2 [0: 2: 0: 2] times, (yfwd, K1) 2 [0: 2: 0:

2] times, K2 [1: 2: 2: 3].

Row 4: Purl.

These 4 rows form patt.

Keeping patt correct throughout, cont as folls:

Cont straight until back meas 4 [4.5: 5: 5.5: 6] cm,
ending with RS facing for next row.

Keeping patt correct, dec 1 st at each end of next
and 2 foll 8th rows, then on 3 foll 6th rows.

109 [121: 135: 149: 163] sts.

Work 17 rows, ending with RS facing for next
row.

Inc 1 st at each end of next and 2 foll 8th rows,
then on 3 foll 10th rows, taking inc sts into st st
until there are sufficient to work in patt.

121 [133: 147: 161: 175] sts.

Work 15 rows, ending with RS facing for next
row. (Back should meas approx 37.5 [38: 38.5:
39: 39.5] cm.)

Shape armholes

Keeping patt correct, cast off 6 [7: 8: 9: 10] sts at
beg of next 2 rows. 109 [119: 131: 143: 155] sts.

Dec 1 st at each end of next 5 [7: 7: 9: 9] rows,
then on foll 6 [7: 9: 8: 10] alt rows.

87 [91: 99: 109: 117] sts.

Cont straight until armhole meas 19 [20.5: 22:
23.5: 25] cm, ending with RS facing for next row.

Shape shoulders and back neck

Next row (RS): Cast off 5 [6: 7: 8: 9] sts, patt
until there are 22 [23: 25: 29: 31] sts on right
needle and turn, leaving rem sts on a holder.

Work each side of neck separately.

Keeping patt correct, dec 1 st at neck edge of
next 4 rows **and at same time** cast off 6 [6: 7:
8: 9] sts at beg of 2nd row and foll alt row.

Work 1 row.

Cast off rem 6 [7: 7: 9: 9] sts.

With RS facing, slip centre 33 [33: 35: 35: 37] sts
onto a holder (for front band), rejoin yarn and
patt to end.

Complete to match first side, reversing shapings.

LEFT FRONT

Using 2¼mm (US 1) needles cast on 61 [67: 74:
81: 88] sts.

Work in g st for 10 rows, ending with RS facing
for next row.

Change to 3mm (US 2/3) needles.

Now work in patt as folls:

Row 1 (RS): Knit.

Row 2: Purl.

Row 3: K2 [1: 2: 2: 3], (yfwd, K1) 2 [0: 2:
0: 2] times, (sl 1, K1, psso) 2 [0: 2: 0: 2] times, P1,
★(K2tog) twice, (yfwd, K1) 4 times, (sl 1, K1,
psso) twice, P1, rep from ★ to end.

Row 4: Purl.

These 4 rows form patt.

Keeping patt correct throughout, cont as folls:

Cont straight until left front meas 4 [4.5: 5:
5.5: 6] cm, ending with RS facing for next row.

Keeping patt correct, dec 1 st at beg of next and
2 foll 8th rows, then on 3 foll 6th rows.

55 [61: 68: 75: 82] sts.

Work 17 rows, ending with RS facing for next
row.

Inc 1 st at beg of next and 2 foll 8th rows, then
on 2 foll 10th rows, taking inc sts into st st until
there are sufficient to work in patt.

60 [66: 73: 80: 87] sts.

Work 7 rows, ending with RS facing for next
row.

Shape front slope

Keeping patt correct, dec 1 st at end of next and
foll 5 [2: 2: 0: 0] alt rows, then on 1 [3: 3: 4: 4] foll
4th rows **and at same time** inc 1 st at beg of
3rd row. 54 [61: 68: 76: 83] sts.

Work 3 [1: 1: 1: 1] rows, ending with RS facing
for next row.

Shape armhole

Keeping patt correct, cast off 6 [7: 8: 9: 10] sts at
beg and dec 1 [0: 0: 0: 0] st at end of next row.
47 [54: 60: 67: 73] sts.

Work 1 row.

Dec 1 st at armhole edge of next 5 [7: 7: 9: 9]
rows, then on foll 6 [7: 9: 8: 10] alt rows **and at
same time** dec 1 st at front slope edge of 3rd
[next: next: next: next] and 3 [5: 6: 6: 7] foll 4th
rows. 32 [34: 37: 43: 46] sts.

Dec 1 st at front slope edge **only** on 2nd [4th:
4th: 4th: 4th] and 7 [7: 7: 7: 6] foll 4th rows, then
on 1 [1: 1: 2: 3] foll 6th rows.

23 [25: 28: 33: 36] sts.

Cont straight until left front matches back to beg
of shoulder shaping, ending with RS facing for
next row.

Shape shoulder

Cast off 5 [6: 7: 8: 9] sts at beg of next row, then
6 [6: 7: 8: 9] sts at beg of foll 2 alt rows.

Work 1 row.

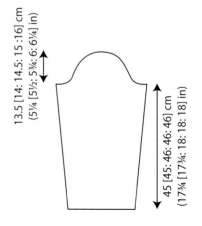

13.5 [14: 14.5: 15 :16] cm
(5¼ [5½: 5¾: 6: 6¼] in)

45 [45: 46: 46: 46] cm
(17¾ [17¾: 18: 18: 18] in)

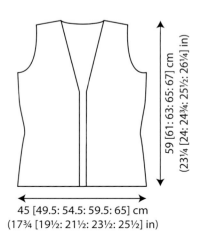

59 [61: 63: 65: 67] cm
(23¼ [24: 24¾: 25½: 26¼] in)

45 [49.5: 54.5: 59.5: 65] cm
(17¾ [19½: 21½: 23½: 25½] in)

Cast off rem 6 [7: 7: 9: 9] sts.

RIGHT FRONT

Using 2¼mm (US 1) needles cast on 61 [67: 74: 81: 88] sts.

Work in g st for 10 rows, ending with RS facing for next row.

Change to 3mm (US 2/3) needles.

Now work in patt as folls:

Row 1 (RS): Knit.

Row 2: Purl.

Row 3: P1, ★(K2tog) twice, (yfwd, K1) 4 times, (sl 1, K1, psso) twice, P1, rep from ★ to last 8 [1: 8: 2: 9] sts, (K2tog) 2 [0: 2: 0: 2] times, (yfwd, K1) 2 [0: 2: 0: 2] times, K2 [1: 2: 2: 3].

Row 4: Purl.

These 4 rows form patt.

Keeping patt correct throughout, cont as folls:

Cont straight until right front meas 4 [4.5: 5: 5.5: 6] cm, ending with RS facing for next row.

Keeping patt correct, dec 1 st at end of next and 2 foll 8th rows, then on 3 foll 6th rows. 55 [61: 68: 75: 82] sts.

Complete to match left front, reversing shapings.

SLEEVES

Using 2¼mm (US 1) needles cast on 55 [57: 59: 59: 63] sts.

Work in g st for 10 rows, ending with RS facing for next row.

Change to 3mm (US 2/3) needles.

Now work in patt as folls:

Row 1 (RS): Knit.

Row 2: Purl.

Row 3: K1 [2: 3: 3: 5], P1, ★(K2tog) twice, (yfwd, K1) 4 times, (sl 1, K1, psso) twice, P1, rep from ★ to last 1 [2: 3: 3: 5] sts, K1 [2: 3: 3: 5].

Row 4: Purl.

These 4 rows form patt.

Keeping patt correct throughout, cont as folls:

Inc 1 st at each end of 3rd [next: next: next: next] and every foll 8th [6th: 6th: 6th: 6th] row to 85 [63: 71: 87: 91] sts, then on every foll 10th [8th: 8th: 8th: 8th] row until there are 87 [91: 95: 99: 103] sts, taking inc sts into st st until there are sufficient to work in patt.

Cont straight until sleeve meas 45 [45: 46: 46: 46] cm, ending with RS facing for next row.

Shape top

Keeping patt correct, cast off 6 [7: 8: 9: 10] sts at beg of next 2 rows. 75 [77: 79: 81: 83] sts.

Dec 1 st at each end of next 5 rows, then on foll 2 alt rows, then on 4 foll 4th rows. 53 [55: 57: 59: 61] sts.

Work 1 row.

Dec 1 st at each end of next and every foll alt row until 43 sts rem, then on foll 7 rows, ending with RS facing for next row. 29 sts.

Cast off 5 sts at beg of next 2 rows.

Cast off rem 19 sts.

MAKING UP

Press as described on the information page.

Join both shoulder seams using back stitch, or mattress stitch if preferred.

Front band

With RS facing and using 2¼mm (US 1) circular needle, beg and ending at front cast-on edges, pick up and knit 96 [97: 98: 100: 101] sts up right front opening edge to beg of front slope shaping, 75 [79: 84: 88: 92] sts up right front slope, and 5 sts down right side of back neck, K across 33 [33: 35: 35: 37] sts on back holder, then pick up and knit 5 sts up left side of back neck, 75 [79: 84: 88: 92] sts down left front slope to beg of front slope shaping, and 96 [97: 98: 100: 101] sts down left front opening edge. 385 [395: 409: 421: 433] sts.

Work in g st for 3 rows, ending with RS facing for next row.

Row 4 (RS): K3 [4: 5: 2: 3], ★K2tog, yfwd (to make a buttonhole), K16 [16: 16: 17: 17], rep from ★ 4 times more, K2tog, yfwd (to make 6th buttonhole), K to end.

Work in g st for a further 4 rows, ending with **WS** facing for next row.

Cast off knitwise (on **WS**).

See information page for finishing instructions, setting in sleeves using the set-in method.

ROTHKO

Kaffe Fassett

Main image page **88, 89**

YARN

Kidsilk Haze

A Wicked 599	1	x 25gm
B Steel 664	1	x 25gm
C Cream 634	1	x 25gm

NEEDLES

1 pair 4½mm (no 7) (US 7) needles
1 pair 5mm (no 6) (US 8) needles

TENSION

18 sts and 23 rows to 10 cm measured over st st using 5mm (US 8) needles.

FINISHED SIZE

Completed scarf is 22 cm (8¾ in) wide and 190 cm (74¾ in) long.

SCARF

Using 4½mm (US 7) needles and yarn A cast on 40 sts.

Work in g st for 4 rows, ending with RS facing for next row.

Change to 5mm (US 8) needles.

Joining in and breaking off colours as required, cont as folls:

Row 1 (RS): Using yarn B, knit.

Row 2: Using yarn B, K2, P to last 2 sts, K2.

Rows 3 and 4: As rows 1 and 2.

Row 5: Using yarn C, knit.

Row 6: Using yarn C, K2, P to last 2 sts, K2.

Rows 7 to 10: As rows 5 and 6, twice.

Row 11: Using yarn A, knit.

Row 12: Using yarn A, K2, P to last 2 sts, K2.

These 12 rows form patt.

Cont in patt until scarf meas approx 189 cm, ending after patt row 10 and with RS facing for next row.

Break off yarns B and C and cont using yarn A **only**.

Change to 4½mm (US 7) needles.

Work in g st for 4 rows, ending with RS facing for next row.

Cast off.

MAKING UP

Press as described on the information page.

See information page for finishing instructions.

ELEMENTARY

Martin Storey

Main image page **40, 41**

● ●

SIZE

To fit bust

81-86 91-97 102-107 112-117 122-127cm

32-34 36-38 40-42 44-46 48-50 in

Actual bust measurement of garment

115.5 126.5 135.5 146.5 155.5 cm

45½ 49¾ 53¼ 57¾ 61¼ in

YARN

Softyak DK

10 11 12 14 15 x 50gm

(photographed in Taupe 245)

NEEDLES

1 pair 3¼mm (no 10) (US 3) needles

1 pair 4mm (no 8) (US 6) needles

3¼mm (no 10) (US 3) circular needle at least 120 cm long

TENSION

22 sts and 31 rows to 10 cm measured over patt using 4mm (US 6) needles.

BACK

Using 3¼mm (US 3) needles cast on 127 [139: 149: 161: 171] sts.

Work in g st for 6 rows, ending with RS facing for next row.

Change to 4mm (US 6) needles.

Now work in patt as folls:

Row 1 (RS): K1, *P1, K1, rep from * to end.

Row 2: As row 1.

Row 3: P1, *K1, P1, rep from * to end.

Row 4: As row 3.

These 4 rows form patt.

Cont in patt until back meas 34 [34.5: 35: 35.5: 36] cm, ending with RS facing for next row.

Shape for sleeve extensions

Inc 1 st at each end of next and 2 foll 4th rows, then on foll 4 alt rows, then on foll 15 rows, taking inc sts into patt and ending with RS

facing for next row.

171 [183: 193: 205: 215] sts.

Cast on 5 [5: 7: 7: 7] sts at beg of next 2 rows.

181 [193: 207: 219: 229] sts.

Work 42 [46: 50: 56: 60] rows, ending with RS facing for next row.

Shape shoulders

Keeping patt correct, cast off 3 [3: 4: 4: 4] sts at beg of next 18 [6: 32: 22: 14] rows, then 4 [4: –: 5: 5] sts at beg of foll 14 [26: –: 10: 18] rows.

71 [71: 79: 81: 83] sts.

Shape back neck

Next row (RS): Cast off 4 [4: 4: 5: 5] sts, patt until there are 17 [17: 20: 20: 20] sts on right needle and turn, leaving rem sts on a holder.

Work each side of neck separately.

Dec 1 st at neck edge of next 5 rows, ending with RS facing for next row, **and at same time** cast off 4 [4: 5: 5: 5] sts at beg of 2nd and foll alt row.

Cast off rem 4 [4: 5: 5: 5] sts.

With RS facing, slip centre 29 [29: 31: 31: 33] sts onto a holder (for front band), rejoin yarn and patt to end.

Complete to match first side, reversing shapings.

POCKET LININGS (make 2)

Using 4mm (US 6) needles cast on 33 [33: 35: 35: 37] sts.

Beg with row 1, work in patt as given for back for 46 [46: 48: 48: 50] rows, ending with RS facing for next row.

Break yarn and leave sts on a holder.

LEFT FRONT

Using 3¼mm (US 3) needles cast on 63 [69: 74: 80: 85] sts.

Work in g st for 6 rows, ending with RS facing for next row.

Change to 4mm (US 6) needles.

Now work in patt as folls:

Row 1 (RS): *K1, P1, rep from * to last 1 [1: 0: 0: 1] st, K1 [1: 0: 0: 1].

Row 2: K1 [1: 0: 0: 1], *P1, K1, rep from * to end.

Row 3: *P1, K1, rep from * to last 1 [1: 0: 0: 1] st, P1 [1: 0: 0: 1].

Row 4: P1 [1: 0: 0: 1], *K1, P1, rep from * to end.

These 4 rows form patt.

Cont in patt for a further 42 [42: 44: 44: 46] rows, ending with RS facing for next row.

Place pocket

Next row (RS): Patt 12 [14: 16: 18: 20] sts, slip next 33 [33: 35: 35: 37] sts onto a holder (for pocket top) and, in their place, patt across 33 [33: 35: 35: 37] sts of first pocket lining, patt rem 18 [22: 23: 27: 28] sts.

Cont straight until 6 rows less have been worked than on back to beg of sleeve extension shaping, ending with RS facing for next row.

Shape front slope

Keeping patt correct, dec 1 st at end of next row.

62 [68: 73: 79: 84] sts.

Work 5 rows, ending with RS facing for next row.

Shape for sleeve extension

Inc 1 st at beg of next and 2 foll 4th rows, then on foll 4 alt rows, then at same edge on foll 15 rows, taking inc sts into patt and ending with RS facing for next row, **and at same time** dec 1 st at front slope edge of next and 5 foll 6th rows.

78 [84: 89: 95: 100] sts.

Cast on 5 [5: 7: 7: 7] sts at beg of next row.

83 [89: 96: 102: 107] sts.

Keeping patt correct, dec 1 st at front slope edge of 4th and 6 [7: 7: 7: 9] foll 6th rows, then on 0 [0: 0: 1: 0] foll 8th row. 76 [81: 88: 93: 97] sts.

Work 3 [1: 5: 3: 3] rows, ending with RS facing for next row.

Shape shoulder

Keeping patt correct, cast off 3 [3: 4: 4: 4] sts at beg of next and foll 8 [2: 16: 10: 6] alt rows, then 4 [4: 5: 5: 5] sts at beg of foll 10 [16: 2: 8: 12] alt rows **and at same time** dec 1 st at front slope edge of 3rd [5th: next: 5th: 5th] and 3 [0: 2: 0: 0] foll 6th rows, then on 1 [3: 2: 3: 3] foll 8th rows.

Work 1 row.

Cast off rem 4 [4: 5: 5: 5] sts.

RIGHT FRONT

Using 3¼mm (US 3) needles cast on 63 [69: 74: 80: 85] sts.

Work in g st for 6 rows, ending with RS facing for next row.

Change to 4mm (US 6) needles.

Now work in patt as folls:

Row 1 (RS): K1 [1: 0: 0: 1], *P1, K1, rep from * to end.

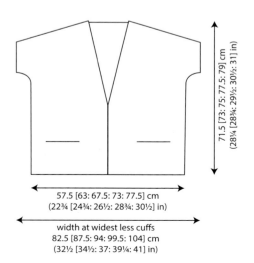

71.5 [73: 75: 77.5: 79] cm
(28¼ [28¾: 29½: 30½: 31] in)

57.5 [63: 67.5: 73: 77.5] cm
(22¾ [24¾: 26½: 28¾: 30½] in)

width at widest less cuffs
82.5 [87.5: 94: 99.5: 104] cm
(32½ [34½: 37: 39¼: 41] in)

Row 2: ★K1, P1, rep from ★ to last 1 [1: 0: 0: 1] st, K1 [1: 0: 0: 1].
Row 3: P1 [1: 0: 0: 1], ★K1, P1, rep from ★ to end.
Row 4: ★P1, K1, rep from ★ to last 1 [1: 0: 0: 1] st, P1 [1: 0: 0: 1].
These 4 rows form patt.
Cont in patt for a further 42 [42: 44: 44: 46] rows, ending with RS facing for next row.
Place pocket
Next row (RS): Patt 18 [22: 23: 27: 28] sts, slip next 33 [33: 35: 35: 37] sts onto a holder (for pocket top) and, in their place, patt across 33 [33: 35: 35: 37] sts of second pocket lining, patt rem 12 [14: 16: 18: 20] sts.
Cont straight until 6 rows less have been worked than on back to beg of sleeve extension shaping, ending with RS facing for next row.
Shape front slope
Keeping patt correct, dec 1 st at beg of next row.
62 [68: 73: 79: 84] sts.
Complete to match left front, reversing shapings.

MAKING UP
Press as described on the information page.

Join both shoulder seams using back stitch, or mattress stitch if preferred.
Front band
With RS facing and using 3¼mm (US 3) circular needle, beg and ending at front cast-on edges, pick up and knit 76 [77: 78: 79: 80] sts up right front opening edge to beg of front slope shaping, 94 [97: 101: 108: 112] sts up right front slope, and 5 sts down right side of back neck, K across 29 [29: 31: 31: 33] sts on back holder inc 1 st at centre, then pick up and knit 5 sts up left side of back neck, 94 [97: 101: 108: 112] sts down left front slope to beg of front slope shaping, and 76 [77: 78: 79: 80] sts down left front opening edge. 380 [388: 400: 416: 428] sts.
Row 1 (WS): K1, P2, ★K2, P2, rep from ★ to last st, K1.
Row 2: K3, ★P2, K2, rep from ★ to last st, K1.
These 2 rows form rib.
Cont in rib for a further 12 rows, ending with **WS** facing for next row.
Row 15 (WS): K1, P3 [2: 3: 1: 2], P2tog, (P8, P2tog) 37 [38: 39: 41: 42] times, P3 [2: 3: 1: 2], K1. 342 [349: 360: 374: 385] sts.
Row 16: Knit.

Row 17: K1, P to last st, K1.
Rep last 2 rows twice more, ending with RS facing for next row.
Cast off.
Cuffs (both alike)
With RS facing and using 3¼mm (US 3) needles, pick up and knit 66 [74: 78: 86: 94] sts evenly along armhole opening row-end edge.
Row 1 (WS): P2, ★K2, P2, rep from ★ to end.
Row 2: K2, ★P2, K2, rep from ★ to end.
These 2 rows form rib.
Cont in rib until cuff meas 8 cm, ending with RS facing for next row.
Cast off in rib.
Pocket tops (both alike)
Slip 33 [33: 35: 35: 37] sts on pocket top holder onto 3¼mm (US 3) needles and rejoin yarn with RS facing.
K 1 row, inc 3 [3: 1: 1: 3] sts evenly.
36 [36: 36: 36: 40] sts.
Beg with row 1, work in rib as given for front band for 5 rows, ending with RS facing for next row.
Cast off in rib.
See information page for finishing instructions.

CORNELIA
Martin Storey
Main image page **76**
● ● ●

YARN
Kidsilk Haze and Fine Lace

A	KSH Cream 634	3	x 25gm
B	Lace White 944	2	x 50gm
C	KSH Wicked 599	3	x 25gm
D	Lace Noir 934	2	x 50gm

NEEDLES
1 pair 3¼mm (no 10) (US 3) needles

TENSION
27 sts and 49 rows to 10 cm measured over border patt, 20 sts and 43 rows to 10 cm measured over main patt, both using 3¼mm (US 3) needles and one strand each of Kidsilk Haze and Fine lace held together

FINISHED SIZE
Completed wrap is 46 cm (18 in) wide and 210 cm (82½ in) long.

SPECIAL ABBREVIATION
sl 2 = slip 2 sts purlwise with yarn held at **WS** of work – see pattern note.

Pattern note: All slipped sts should be worked with yarn held at **WS** of work – this is back of work on RS rows, and front of work on WS rows.

WRAP
First section
Using 3¼mm (US 3) needles and one strand each of yarns C and D held together cast on 124 sts.
Work in g st for 6 rows, ending with RS facing for next row.
Join in yarns A and B and work in border patt as folls:
Row 1 (RS): Using one strand each of yarns A and B held together, K1, ★sl 2 – see pattern note, K4, rep from ★ to last 3 sts, sl 2, K1.
Row 2: Using one strand each of yarns A and B held together, P1, ★sl 2 – see pattern note, P4, rep from ★ to last 3 sts, sl 2, P1.
Row 3: Using one strand each of yarns C and D held together, K1, ★K4, (sl 2, K4, sl 2, K2) twice, rep from ★ to last 3 sts, K3.
Row 4: Using one strand each of yarns C and

D held together, P1, ★P4, (sl 2, P4, sl 2, P2) twice, rep from ★ to last 3 sts, P3.
Row 5: Using one strand each of yarns A and B held together, K1, ★K2, sl 2, K4, sl 2, K6, sl 2, K4, sl 2, rep from ★ to last 3 sts, K3.
Row 6: Using one strand each of yarns A and B held together, P1, ★P2, sl 2, P4, sl 2, P6, sl 2, P4, sl 2, rep from ★ to last 3 sts, P3.
Row 7: Using one strand each of yarns C and D held together, K1, ★sl 2, K4, rep from ★ to last 3 sts, sl 2, K1.
Row 8: Using one strand each of yarns C and D held together, P1, ★sl 2, P4, rep from ★ to last 3 sts, sl 2, P1.
Row 9: Using one strand each of yarns A and B held together, K1, ★K4, (sl 2, K4, sl 2, K2) twice, rep from ★ to last 3 sts, K3.
Row 10: Using one strand each of yarns A and B held together, P1, ★P4, (sl 2, P4, sl 2, P2) twice, rep from ★ to last 3 sts, P3.
Row 11: Using one strand each of yarns C and D held together, K1, ★K2, sl 2, K4, sl 2, K6, sl 2, K4, sl 2, rep from ★ to last 3 sts, K3.
Row 12: Using one strand each of yarns C and D held together, P1, ★P2, sl 2, P4, sl 2, P6, sl 2, P4, sl 2, rep from ★ to last 3 sts, P3.
These 12 rows form border patt.
Cont in border patt until work meas approx 38.5 cm, ending after patt row 4 and with RS facing for next row.
Next row (RS): Using one strand each of yarns C and D held together, K5, K2tog, (K1, K2tog, K2, K2tog) 16 times, K5. 91 sts.
Now work in main patt as folls:
Row 1 (WS): Using one strand each of yarns C and D held together, knit.
Row 2: Using one strand each of yarns A and B held together, knit.
Row 3: Using one strand each of yarns A and B

149

held together, P1, ★yrn, P2tog, rep from ★ to end.
Row 4: As row 1.
These 4 rows form main patt.
Cont in main patt until work meas 105 cm, ending with RS facing for next row.★★
Break yarn and leave sts on a holder.

Second section
Work as given for first section to ★★.
Join sections
Slip sts of first section onto a spare 3¼mm (US 3) needle and, holding first and second sections with their RS together, cast off both sets

of sts at same time, taking one st from first section with corresponding st from second section.

MAKING UP
Press as described on the information page.
See information page for finishing instructions.

PENGA
Emma Wright
Main image page **20, 21**
● ● ●

SIZE
To fit bust
81-86 91-97 102-107 112-117 122-127cm
32-34 36-38 40-42 44-46 48-50 in
Actual bust measurement of garment

| 102 | 111.5 | 121 | 130.5 | 142 | cm |
| 40¼ | 44 | 47½ | 51½ | 56 | in |

YARN
Creative Linen

A Mustard 647					
3	3	3	4	4	x 100gm
B Stormy 635					
1	1	1	1	1	x 100gm
C Natural 621					
3	3	3	3	4	x 100gm
D Teal 625					
1	1	1	1	1	x 100gm
E Raspberry 631					
1	1	1	1	1	x 100gm

NEEDLES
1 pair 4½mm (no 7) (US 7) needles
4½mm (no 7) (US 7) circular needle at least
110 cm long

TENSION
21 sts and 28 rows to 10 cm measured over plain st st, 25 sts and 24 rows to 10 cm measured over patterned st st, both using 4½mm (US 7) needles.

BACK
Using 4½mm (US 7) needles and yarn A cast on 106 [118: 126: 138: 150] sts.
Row 1 (RS): K2, ★P2, K2, rep from ★ to end.
Row 2: P2, ★K2, P2, rep from ★ to end.
These 2 rows form rib.
Work in rib for a further 14 rows, inc [dec: inc: dec: dec] 1 st at end of last row and ending with RS facing for next row.
107 [117: 127: 137: 149] sts.
Beg with a K row, now work in st st as folls:
Cont straight until back meas 22.5 [23.5: 24.5: 25.5: 26.5] cm, ending with **WS** facing for next row.
Next row (WS): P6 [6: 6: 6: 7], M1P, (P5, M1P) 19 [21: 23: 25: 27] times, P6 [6: 6: 6: 7].
127 [139: 151: 163: 177] sts.
Beg and ending rows as indicated and using a combination of the **fairisle** and **intarsia** techniques as described on the information page, cont in patt from chart for body, which is worked entirely in st st beg with a K row, as folls:
Work all 22 rows of chart, ending with RS facing for next row.
Break off contrasts and cont using yarn C **only**.
Next row (RS): K6 [6: 6: 6: 7], K2tog, (K4, K2tog) 19 [21: 23: 25: 27] times, K5 [5: 5: 5: 6].
107 [117: 127: 137: 149] sts.
Beg with a P row, cont in st st until back meas 56 [58: 60: 62: 64] cm, ending with RS facing for next row.

Shape shoulders
Cast off all sts, placing a marker on centre st.

LEFT FRONT
Using 4½mm (US 7) needles and yarn A cast on 55 [59: 67: 71: 75] sts.
Row 1 (RS): K2, ★P2, K2, rep from ★ to last st, K1.
Row 2: K1, P2, ★K2, P2, rep from ★ to end.
These 2 rows form rib.
Work in rib for a further 14 rows, dec 1 [0: 3: 2: 0] sts evenly across last row and ending with RS facing for next row. 54 [59: 64: 69: 75] sts.
Beg with a K row, now work in st st as folls:
Cont straight until left front meas 22.5 [23.5: 24.5: 25.5: 26.5] cm, ending with **WS** facing for next row.
Next row (WS): P4 [4: 4: 4: 5], (M1P, P5) 10 [11: 12: 13: 14] times. 64 [70: 76: 82: 89] sts.
Beg and ending rows as indicated, cont in patt from chart for body as folls:
Work all 22 rows of chart, ending with RS facing for next row.
Break off contrasts and cont using yarn C **only**.
Next row (RS): K4 [4: 4: 4: 5], (K2tog, K4) 10 [11: 12: 13: 14] times. 54 [59: 64: 69: 75] sts.
Beg with a P row, cont in st st until left front matches back to shoulder cast-off, ending with RS facing for next row.
Shape shoulder
Cast off.

RIGHT FRONT
Using 4½mm (US 7) needles and yarn A cast on 55 [59: 67: 71: 75] sts.
Row 1 (RS): K3, ★P2, K2, rep from ★ to end.

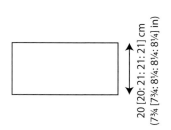
20 [20: 21: 21: 21] cm
(7¾ [7¾: 8¼: 8¼: 8¼] in)

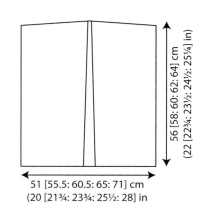
56 [58: 60: 62: 64] cm
(22 [22¾: 23½: 24½: 25¼] in)
51 [55.5: 60.5: 65: 71] cm
(20 [21¾: 23¾: 25½: 28] in)

Row 2: P2, ★K2, P2, rep from ★ to last st, K1.
These 2 rows form rib.

Work in rib for a further 14 rows, dec 1 [0: 3: 2: 0] sts evenly across last row and ending with RS facing for next row. 54 [59: 64: 69: 75] sts.
Complete to match left front, reversing shapings.

SLEEVES

Using 4½mm (US 7) needles and yarn A cast on 78 [86: 94: 98: 106] sts.
Work in rib as given for back for 16 rows, inc [inc: dec: inc: dec] 1 st at end of last row and ending with RS facing for next row.
79 [87: 93: 99: 105] sts.
Beg with a K row, now work in st st as folls:
Work 3 rows, ending with **WS** facing for next row.
Next row (WS): P2 [6: 4: 7: 5], M1P, (P5, M1P) 15 [15: 17: 17: 19] times, P2 [6: 4: 7: 5].
95 [103: 111: 117: 125] sts.
Beg and ending rows as indicated and using the **fairisle** technique as described on the information page, cont in patt from chart for sleeve, which is worked entirely in st st beg with a K row, as folls:
Work all 5 rows of chart, ending with **WS** facing for next row.
Break off contrasts and cont using yarn C **only**.
Next row (WS): P1 [5: 3: 6: 4], P2tog, (P4, P2tog) 15 [15: 17: 17: 19] times, P2 [6: 4: 7: 5].
79 [87: 93: 99: 105] sts.
Beg with a K row, cont in st st until sleeve meas 20 [20: 21: 21: 21] cm, ending with RS facing for next row.
Cast off.

MAKING UP

Press as described on the information page.
Positioning front opening edges so they meet at marked centre back neck st, join both shoulder seams using back stitch, or mattress stitch if preferred.
Front band
With RS facing, using 4½mm (US 7) circular needle and yarn A, beg and ending at front cast-on edges, pick up and knit 118 [122: 126: 130: 134] sts evenly up entire right front opening edge, then 118 [122: 126: 130: 134] sts evenly down entire left front opening edge.
236 [244: 252: 260: 268] sts.
Row 1 (WS): K1, P2, ★K2, P2, rep from ★ to last st, K1.
Row 2: K3, ★P2, K2, rep from ★ to last st, K1.
These 2 rows form rib.
Work in rib for a further 13 rows, ending with RS facing for next row.
Cast off in rib.
Mark points along side seam edges 20 [21.5: 23: 24.5: 26] cm either side of shoulder seams (to denote base of armhole openings). See information page for finishing instructions, setting in sleeves using the straight cast-off method.

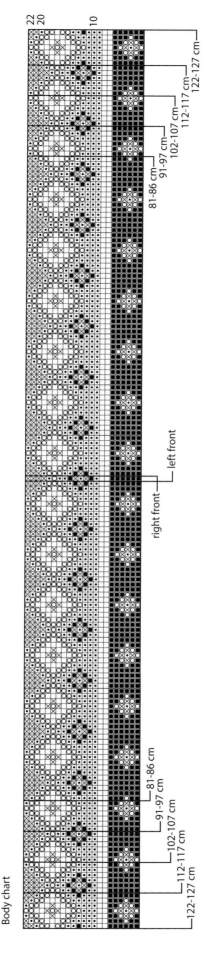

Body chart

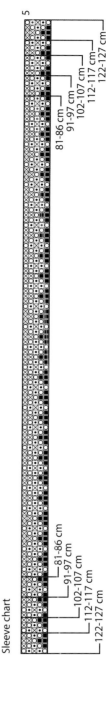

Sleeve chart

Key
A
B
C
D
E

CUGGLE

Lisa Richardson

Main image page **28, 29**

● ● ●

SIZE

To fit bust
81-86 91-97 102-107 112-117 122-127cm
32-34 36-38 40-42 44-46 48-50 in
Actual bust measurement of garment
94.5 103.5 114.5 123.5 134.5 cm
37¼ 40¾ 45 48½ 53 in

YARN

Creative Linen

6 6 7 8 8 x 100gm

(photographed in Apple 629)

NEEDLES

1 pair 4½mm (no 7) (US 7) needles
4mm (no 8) (US 6) circular needle no more than
40 cm long
Cable needle

TENSION

22 sts and 30 rows to 10 cm measured over
textured patt using 4½mm (US 7) needles. Cable
panel (15 sts) measures 4.5 cm.

SPECIAL ABBREVIATIONS

C6B = slip next 3 sts onto cable needle and
leave at back of work, K3, then K3 from cable
needle; **C6F** = slip next 3 sts onto cable needle
and leave at front of work, K3, then K3 from
cable needle.

BACK

Using 4½mm (US 7) needles cast on 107 [117:
129: 139: 151] sts.

Row 1 (RS): K0 [0: 0: 0: 1], P1 [2: 0: 1: 2], (K2,
P2) 4 [5: 7: 8: 9] times, *P1, K1, P1, inc once
knitwise in each of next 2 sts, K1, inc once
knitwise in each of next 2 sts, P1, K1, P1*, (K2,
P2) 5 times, rep from * to * once more, (K2, P2)
5 times, rep from * to * once more, (K2, P2)
4 [5: 7: 8: 9] times, P1 [2: 0: 1: 2], K0 [0: 0: 0: 1].

119 [129: 141: 151: 163] sts.
Now work in patt as folls:

Row 1 (WS): P0 [0: 0: 0: 1], K1 [2: 0: 1: 2], (P2,
K2) 4 [5: 7: 8: 9] times, *K1, P1, K1, P9, K1,
P1, K1*, (P2, K2) 5 times, rep from * to * once
more, (K2, P2) 5 times, rep from * to * once
more, (K2, P2) 4 [5: 7: 8: 9] times, K1 [2: 0: 1: 2],
P0 [0: 0: 0: 1].

Row 2: P0 [0: 0: 0: 1], K1 [2: 0: 1: 2], (P2, K2)
4 [5: 7: 8: 9] times, *P1, K1, P1, K3, C6F, P1,
K1, P1*, (P2, K2) 5 times, rep from * to * once
more, (K2, P2) 5 times, rep from * to * once
more, (K2, P2) 4 [5: 7: 8: 9] times, K1 [2: 0: 1: 2],
P0 [0: 0: 0: 1].

Row 3: K0 [0: 0: 0: 1], P1 [2: 0: 1: 2], (K2, P2)
4 [5: 7: 8: 9] times, *K1, P1, K1, P9, K1, P1, K1*,
(K2, P2) 5 times, rep from * to * once more, (P2,
K2) 5 times, rep from * to * once more, (P2, K2)
4 [5: 7: 8: 9] times, P1 [2: 0: 1: 2], K0 [0: 0: 0: 1].

Row 4: K0 [0: 0: 0: 1], P1 [2: 0: 1: 2], (K2, P2)
4 [5: 7: 8: 9] times, *P1, K1, P1, C6B, K3, P1,
K1, P1*, (K2, P2) 5 times, rep from * to * once
more, (P2, K2) 5 times, rep from * to * once
more, (P2, K2) 4 [5: 7: 8: 9] times, P1 [2: 0: 1: 2],
K0 [0: 0: 0: 1].

These 4 rows set the sts − 3 cable panels and all
other sts in textured patt.
Keeping patt correct throughout, cont as folls:
Work 1 row, ending with RS facing for next row.
Counting in from both ends of last row, place a
marker after 17th [22nd: 28th: 33rd: 39th] st, miss
next 14 sts and place another marker after st just
missed − 4 markers in total, and 57 sts at centre
of row between markers.

Next row (RS): Patt to first marker, M1, slip
marker onto right needle, patt to next marker,
slip marker onto right needle, P2tog, patt to
within 2 sts of next marker, P2tog tbl, slip marker
onto right needle, patt to next marker, slip
marker onto right needle, M1, patt to end.
This row moves side cable panels one st closer to
centre of row.
Taking all inc sts into textured patt, cont in this
way, moving side cable panels one st closer to
centre of rows on 2nd and foll 19 alt rows **and
at same time** dec 1 st at each end of 14th and
foll 12th row. 115 [125: 137: 147: 159] sts, and
15 sts at centre of row between markers.

Work 9 rows, ending with RS facing for next
row.
Move all 4 markers one st closer to centre of row
– 13 sts now between markers at centre of row,
and 14 sts between each pair of markers.
Now start to move side cable back towards side
seam edges as folls:

Next row (RS): Patt to within 2 sts of first
marker, P2tog tbl, slip marker onto right needle,
patt to next marker, slip marker onto right
needle, M1, patt to next marker, M1, slip marker
onto right needle, patt to next marker, slip
marker onto right needle, P2tog, patt to end.
This row moves side cable panels one st closer to
ends of row.
Taking all inc sts into textured patt, cont in this
way, moving side cable panels one st closer to
ends of rows on 6th and 2 foll 6th rows **and at
same time** inc 1 st at each end of 2nd and foll
18th row. 119 [129: 141: 151: 163] sts.
Now moving cable panels one st closer to
ends of row on 4th and every foll 6th row
throughout, cont straight until back meas
34 [34.5: 35: 35.5: 36] cm, ending with RS
facing for next row.

Shape armholes

Keeping patt correct (and still moving side cables
on every 6th row as set), cast off 4 [5: 6: 7: 8] sts
at beg of next 2 rows.
111 [119: 129: 137: 147] sts.
Dec 1 st at each end of next 5 [7: 7: 9: 9] rows,
then on foll 5 [5: 7: 6: 7] alt rows.
91 [95: 101: 107: 115] sts.
Cont straight (but still moving side cables on
every 6th row as set) until armhole meas
19 [20.5: 22: 23.5: 25] cm, ending with RS
facing for next row.

Shape shoulders and back neck

Cast off 6 [6: 7: 8: 8] sts at beg of next 2 rows.
79 [83: 87: 91: 99] sts.

Next row (RS): Cast off 6 [7: 7: 8: 9] sts, patt
until there are 16 [17: 18: 19: 21] sts on right
needle and turn, leaving rem sts on a holder.
Work each side of neck separately.
Keeping patt correct, dec 1 st at neck edge of
next 3 rows **and at same time** cast off 6 [7: 7:
8: 9] sts at beg of 2nd row.
Cast off rem 7 [7: 8: 8: 9] sts.

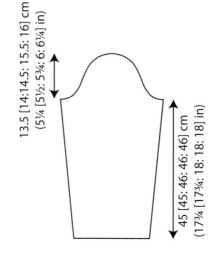

13.5 [14:14.5: 15.5: 16] cm
(5¼ [5½: 5¾: 6: 6¼] in)

45 [45: 46: 46: 46] cm
(17¾ [17¾: 18: 18: 18] in)

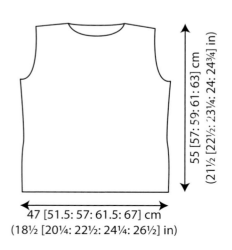

55 [57: 59: 61: 63] cm
(21½ [22½: 23¼: 24: 24¾] in)

47 [51.5: 57: 61.5: 67] cm
(18½ [20¼: 22½: 24¼: 26½] in)

With RS facing, slip centre 35 [35: 37: 37: 39] sts onto a holder (for neckband), rejoin yarn and patt to end.
Complete to match first side, reversing shapings.

FRONT

Work as given for back until 22 [22: 24: 24: 26] rows less have been worked than on back to beg of shoulder shaping, ending with RS facing for next row.

Shape front neck

Next row (RS): Patt 36 [38: 41: 44: 48] sts and turn, leaving rem sts on a holder.
Work each side of neck separately.
Keeping patt correct (and still moving side cables on every 6th row as set), dec 1 st at neck edge of next 6 rows, then on foll 4 [4: 5: 5: 6] alt rows, then on foll 4th row. 25 [27: 29: 32: 35] sts.
Work 3 rows, ending with RS facing for next row.

Shape shoulder

Cast off 6 [6: 7: 8: 8] sts at beg of next row, then 6 [7: 7: 8: 9] sts at beg of foll 2 alt rows.
Work 1 row.
Cast off rem 7 [7: 8: 8: 9] sts.
With RS facing, slip centre 19 sts onto a holder (for neckband), rejoin yarn and patt to end.
Complete to match first side, reversing shapings.

SLEEVES

Using 4½mm (US 7) needles cast on 48 [50: 52: 52: 54] sts.
Row 1 (RS): K0 [0: 1: 1: 0], P1 [2: 2: 2: 0], *K2, P2, rep from * to last 3 [0: 1: 1: 2] sts, K2 [0: 1: 1: 2], P1 [0: 0: 0: 0].
Row 2: P0 [0: 1: 1: 0], K1 [2: 2: 2: 0], *P2, K2, rep from * to last 3 [0: 1: 1: 2] sts, P2 [0: 1: 1: 2], K1 [0: 0: 0: 0].
Row 3: As row 2.
Row 4: As row 1.
These 4 rows form textured patt.
Cont in patt, shaping sides by inc 1 st at each end of 5th [5th: 3rd: 3rd: next] and every foll 10th [10th: 8th: 8th: 6th] row to 60 [74: 58: 78: 58] sts, then on every foll 12th [-: 10th: 10th: 8th] row until there are 70 [-: 78: 82: 86] sts, taking inc sts into patt.
Cont straight until sleeve meas 45 [45: 46: 46: 46] cm, ending with RS facing for next row.

Shape top

Keeping patt correct, cast off 4 [5: 6: 7: 8] sts at beg of next 2 rows. 62 [64: 66: 68: 70] sts.
Dec 1 st at each end of next 3 rows, then on foll 3 alt rows, then on 3 foll 4th rows. 44 [46: 48: 50: 52] sts.
Work 1 row.
Dec 1 st at each end of next and every foll alt row until 38 sts rem, then on foll 11 rows, ending with RS facing for next row.
Cast off rem 16 sts.

MAKING UP

Press as described on the information page.
Join both shoulder seams using back stitch, or mattress stitch if preferred.

Neckband

With RS facing and using 4mm (US 6) circular needle, pick up and knit 24 [24: 25: 25: 28] sts down left side of front neck, work across 19 sts on front holder as folls: K5, K2tog, sl 1, K1, psso, K1, K2tog, sl 1, K1, psso, K5, pick up and knit 24 [24: 25: 25: 28] sts up right side of front neck, and 3 sts down right side of back neck, work across 35 [35: 37: 37: 39] sts on back holder as folls: K13 [13: 14: 14: 15], K2tog, sl 1, K1, psso, K1, K2tog, sl 1, K1, psso, K13 [13: 14: 14: 15], then pick up and knit 3 sts up left side of back neck.
100 [100: 104: 104: 112] sts.
Round 1 (RS): *K2, P2, rep from * to end.
Rep last round until neckband meas 9 cm from pick-up round.
Cast off in rib.
See information page for finishing instructions, setting in sleeves using the set-in method.

DALI

Lisa Richardson

Main image page **77**

● ●

YARN

Cotton Cashmere
         9   x 50gm
(photographed in Paper 210)

Alternatively you could use Rowan Handknit Cotton in the following shade(s):
Bleached 263   14   x 50gm

NEEDLES

1 pair 4mm (no 8) (US 6) needles
1 pair 4½mm (no 7) (US 7) needles
Cable needle

TENSION

19 sts and 28 rows to 10 cm measured over patt using 4½mm (US 7) needles.

FINISHED SIZE

Completed shawl is 60 cm (23½ in) wide and 190 cm (74¾ in) long.

SPECIAL ABBREVIATION

C2F = slip next st onto cable needle and leave at front of work, K1, then K1 from cable needle.

SHAWL

Using 4mm (US 6) needles cast on 114 sts.
Work in g st for 2 rows, ending with RS facing for next row.
Change to 4½mm (US 7) needles.
Now work in patt as folls:

Row 1 (RS): K1, P1, *C2F, P2, rep from * to last 4 sts, C2F, P1, K1.
Row 2: K2, *P2, K2, rep from * to end.
Row 3: K1, *K2tog, (yfwd) twice, sl 1, K1, psso, rep from * to last st, K1.
Row 4: K1, P1, *K into front and back of double yfwd of previous row, P2, rep from * to last 4 sts, K into front and back of double yfwd of previous row, P1, K1.
Row 5: K2, P2, *C2F, P2, rep from * to last 2 sts, K2.
Row 6: K1, P1, *K2, P2, rep from * to last 4 sts, K2, P1, K1.
Row 7: K1, yfwd, sl 1, K1, psso, *K2tog, (yfwd) twice, sl 1, K1, psso, rep from * to last 3 sts, K2tog, yfwd, K1.
Row 8: K2, P2, *K into front and back of double yfwd of previous row, P2, rep from * to last 2 sts, K2.
These 8 rows form patt.
Cont in patt until shawl meas approx 189 cm, ending after patt row 2 or 6 and with RS facing for next row.
Change to 4mm (US 6) needles.
Work in g st for 2 rows, ending with RS facing for next row.
Cast off.

MAKING UP

Press as described on the information page.
See information page for finishing instructions.

TOORIE

Martin Storey

Main image page **23, 24, 25**

● ● ●

SIZE

To fit bust

81–86 91–97 102–107 112–117 122–127cm
32–34 36–38 40–42 44–46 48–50 in

Actual bust measurement of garment

90 101 110 121 130 cm
35½ 39¾ 43¼ 47½ 51¼ in

YARN

Felted Tweed

A Alabaster 197

   5   6   6   7   7   x 50gm

B Avocado 161

   1   1   1   1   2   x 50gm

C Mineral 181

   1   1   1   1   1   x 50gm

D Ginger 154

   1   1   1   1   1   x 50gm

E Delft 194

   2   2   2   2   2   x 50gm

NEEDLES

1 pair 3¼mm (no 10) (US 3) needles
1 pair 3¾mm (no 9) (US 5) needles

BUTTONS – 7 x BN1979 from Bedecked.
Please see information page for contact details.

TENSION

26 sts and 27 rows to 10 cm measured over
patterned st st using 3¾mm (US 5) needles.

BACK

Using 3¼mm (US 3) needles and yarn A cast on
118 [130: 142: 158: 170] sts.
Row 1 (RS): K2, ★P2, K2, rep from ★ to end.
Row 2: P2, ★K2, P2, rep from ★ to end.
These 2 rows form rib.
Work in rib for a further 20 rows, dec [inc: inc:
dec: dec] 1 st at end of last row and ending with
RS facing for next row.

117 [131: 143: 157: 169] sts.
Change to 3¾mm (US 5) needles.
Beg and ending rows as indicated, using
the **fairisle** technique as described on the
information page and repeating the 64 row patt
repeat throughout, cont in patt from chart, which
is worked entirely in st st beg with a K row, as
folls:
Work 62 [62: 64: 64: 64] rows, ending after chart
row 62 [62: 64: 64: 64] and with RS facing for
next row. (Back should meas approx 29 [29: 30:
30: 30] cm.)
Shape armholes
Keeping patt correct, cast off 5 [6: 7: 8: 9] sts at
beg of next 2 rows. 107 [119: 129: 141: 151] sts.
Dec 1 st at each end of next 5 [7: 7: 9: 9] rows,
then on foll 6 [7: 8: 8: 9] alt rows.
85 [91: 99: 107: 115] sts.
Cont straight until armhole meas 19 [20.5: 22:
23.5: 25] cm, ending with RS facing for next row.
Shape shoulders and back neck
Next row (RS): Cast off 5 [6: 7: 8: 9] sts, patt
until there are 22 [24: 26: 29: 31] sts on right
needle and turn, leaving rem sts on a holder.
Work each side of neck separately.
Keeping patt correct, dec 1 st at neck edge of
next 4 rows **and at same time** cast off 6 [6: 7:
8: 9] sts at beg of 2nd row and 6 [7: 7: 8: 9] sts at
beg of foll alt row.
Work 1 row.
Cast off rem 6 [7: 8: 9: 9] sts.
With RS facing, slip centre 31 [31: 33: 33: 35] sts
onto a holder (for neckband), rejoin yarns and
patt to end.
Complete to match first side, reversing shapings.

LEFT FRONT
Using 3¼mm (US 3) needles and yarn A cast on
67 [75: 79: 87: 95] sts.
Row 1 (RS): K2, ★P2, K2, rep from ★ to last
9 sts, (P1, K1) 4 times, K1.
Row 2: K1, (P1, K1) 4 times, P2, ★K2, P2, rep
from ★ to end.
These 2 rows form rib.
Work in rib for a further 19 rows, ending with
WS facing for next row.
Row 22 (WS): Rib 9 and slip these 9 sts onto
a holder (for button band), M1, rib to end dec
1 [2: 0: 1: 3] sts evenly. 58 [65: 71: 78: 84] sts.
Change to 3¾mm (US 5) needles.

Beg and ending rows as indicated, cont in patt
from chart as folls:
Work 62 [62: 64: 64: 64] rows, ending after chart
row 62 [62: 64: 64: 64] and with RS facing for
next row.
Shape armhole
Keeping patt correct, cast off 5 [6: 7: 8: 9] sts at
beg of next row. 53 [59: 64: 70: 75] sts.
Work 1 row.
Dec 1 st at armhole edge of next 5 [7: 7: 9: 9]
rows, then on foll 6 [7: 8: 8: 9] alt rows.
42 [45: 49: 53: 57] sts.
Cont straight until 16 [16: 18: 18: 20] rows
less have been worked than on back to beg of
shoulder shaping, ending with RS facing for next
row.
Shape front neck
Next row (RS): Patt 34 [37: 41: 45: 49] sts
and turn, leaving rem 8 sts on a holder (for
neckband).
Keeping patt correct, dec 1 st at neck edge of
next 8 rows, then on foll 3 [3: 4: 4: 5] alt rows.
23 [26: 29: 33: 36] sts.
Work 1 row, ending with RS facing for next row.
Shape shoulder
Cast off 5 [6: 7: 8: 9] sts at beg of next and foll
0 [1: 2: 2: 2] alt rows, then 6 [7: –: –: –] sts at beg
of foll 2 [1: –: –: –] alt rows.
Work 1 row.
Cast off rem 6 [7: 8: 9: 9] sts.

RIGHT FRONT
Using 3¼mm (US 3) needles and yarn A cast on
67 [75: 79: 87: 95] sts.
Row 1 (RS): K1, (K1, P1) 4 times, K2, ★P2, K2,
rep from ★ to end.
Row 2: P2, ★K2, P2, rep from ★ to last 9 sts, (K1,
P1) 4 times, K1.
These 2 rows form rib.
Work in rib for a further 6 rows, ending with RS
facing for next row.
Row 9 (RS): K2, P1, sl 1, K1, psso, yfwd (to
make first buttonhole), rib to end.
Work in rib for a further 12 rows, ending with
WS facing for next row.
Row 22 (WS): Rib to last 9 sts dec 1 [2: 0: 1:
3] sts evenly, M1 and turn, leaving rem 9 sts on a
holder (for buttonhole band).
58 [65: 71: 78: 84] sts.
Complete to match left front, reversing shapings

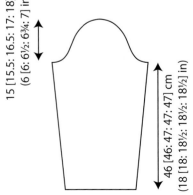
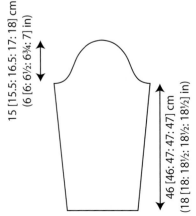

15 [15.5: 16.5: 17: 18] cm
(6 [6: 6½: 6¾: 7] in)

46 [46: 47: 47: 47] cm
(18 [18: 18½: 18½: 18½] in)

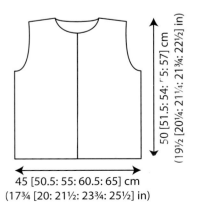

50 [51.5: 54: ¯5: 57] cm
(19½ [20¼: 21¼: 21¾: 22½] in)

45 [50.5: 55: 60.5: 65] cm
(17¾ [20: 21½: 23¾: 25½] in)

and working first row of neck shaping as folls:

Shape front neck

Next row (RS): Break yarns. Slip first 8 sts onto a holder (for neckband), rejoin yarns and patt to end. 34 [37: 41: 45: 49] sts.

SLEEVES

Using 3¼mm (US 3) needles and yarn A cast on 58 [58: 62: 62: 66] sts.

Work in rib as given for back for 22 rows, dec [inc: inc: inc: dec] 1 st at end of last row and ending with RS facing for next row.
57 [59: 63: 63: 65] sts.

Change to 3¾mm (US 5) needles.

Beg and ending rows as indicated and **beg with chart row 19**, cont in patt from chart as folls:

Inc 1 st at each end of 5th [5th: 5th: 3rd: 3rd] and every foll 6th [6th: 6th: 4th: 4th] row to 75 [85: 85: 67: 75] sts, then on every foll 8th [8th: 8th: 6th: 6th] row until there are 85 [89: 93: 97: 101] sts, taking inc sts into patt.

Cont straight until sleeve meas approx 46 [46: 47: 47: 47] cm, ending after chart row 62 [62: 64: 64: 64] and with RS facing for next row.

Shape top

Keeping patt correct, cast off 5 [6: 7: 8: 9] sts at beg of next 2 rows. 75 [77: 79: 81: 83] sts.

Dec 1 st at each end of next 5 rows, then on every foll alt row until 43 sts rem, then on foll 9 rows, ending with RS facing for next row. 25 sts.

Cast off 4 sts at beg of next 2 rows.

Cast off rem 17 sts.

MAKING UP

Press as described on the information page.

Join both shoulder seams using back stitch, or mattress stitch if preferred.

Button band

Slip 9 sts on left front holder onto 3¼mm (US 3) needles and rejoin yarn A with RS facing.

Row 1 (RS): K2, *P1, K1, rep from * to last st, K1.

Row 2: K1, *P1, K1, rep from * to end.

These 2 rows form rib.

Cont in rib until button band, when slightly stretched, fits up left front opening edge to neck shaping, sewing in place as you go along and ending with RS facing for next row.

Break yarn and leave sts on a holder.

Mark positions for 7 buttons on this band – first to come level with buttonhole already worked in right front, last to come just above neck shaping and rem 5 buttons evenly spaced between.

Buttonhole band

Slip 9 sts on right front holder onto 3¼mm (US 3) needles and rejoin yarn A with **WS** facing.

Beg with row 2, complete to match button band with the addition of a further 5 buttonholes worked to correspond with positions marked for buttons as folls:

Buttonhole row (RS): K2, P1, sl 1, K1, psso, yfwd (to make a buttonhole), K1, P1, K2.

When buttonhole band is complete, ending with RS facing for next row, do NOT break yarn.

Neckband

With RS facing, using 3¼mm (US 3) needles and yarn A (still attached to buttonhole band), rib across 9 sts of buttonhole band as folls: K1, (K1, P1) 4 times, K across 8 sts on right front holder,

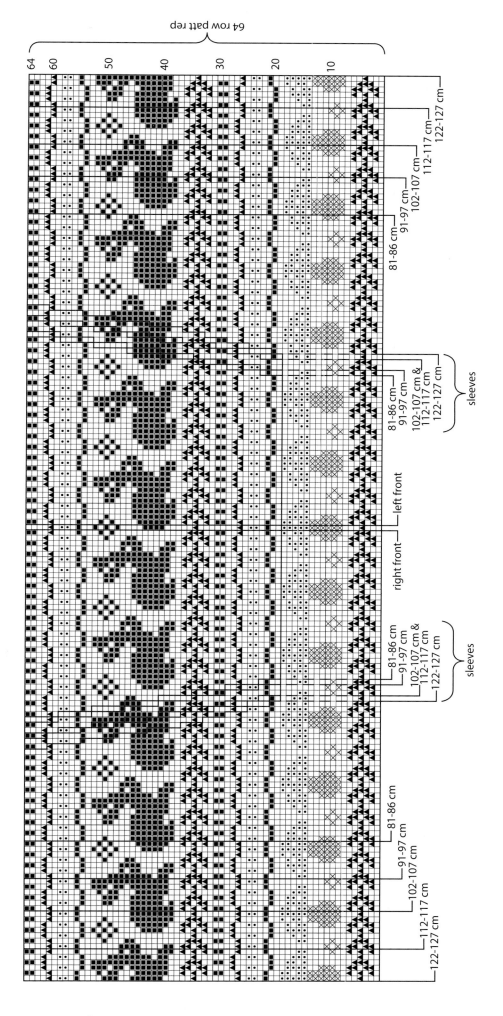

pick up and knit 22 [22: 24: 24: 26] sts up right side of front neck, and 5 sts down right side of back neck, K across 31 [31: 33: 33: 35] sts on back holder, pick up and knit 5 sts up left side of back neck, and 22 [22: 24: 24: 26] sts down left side of front neck, K across 8 sts on left front holder, then work across 9 sts on button band

holder as folls: (P1, K1) 4 times, K1.
119 [119: 125: 125: 131] sts.
Beg with row 2, work in rib as given for button band for 3 rows, ending with RS facing for next row.
Row 4 (RS): K2, P1, sl 1, K1, psso, yfwd (to make 7th buttonhole), rib to end.

Work in rib for a further 4 rows, ending with **WS** facing for next row.
Cast off in rib (on **WS**).
See information page for finishing instructions, setting in sleeves using the set-in method.

ESSENTIAL

Lisa Richardson

Main image page **42, 43**

● ●

SIZE
To fit bust
81-86 91-97 102-107 112-117 122-127cm

32-34 36-38 40-42 44-46 48-50 in
Actual bust measurement of garment

91.5 101.5 112.5 122 131.5 cm
36 40 44¼ 48 51¾ in

YARN
Fine Lace
2 3 3 3 3 x 50gm
(photographed in Cobweb 922)

NEEDLES
1 pair 3mm (no 11) (US 2/3) needles

TENSION
29 sts and 41 rows to 10 cm measured over st st using 3mm (US 2/3) needles.

BACK and FRONT (both alike)
Using 3mm (US 2/3) needles cast on as folls:
cast on 5 sts, ★cast off 2 sts, slip st on right needle back onto left needle★★, cast on 3 sts, rep from ★ until there are 80 [87: 95: 102: 109] sts on left needle (ending last rep at ★★), cast on 1 st.
81 [88: 96: 103: 110] sts.
Row 1 (RS): K2, ★yfwd, K1, rep from ★ to last st,

K1. 159 [173: 189: 203: 217] sts.
Beg with a P row, now work in st st throughout as folls:
Cont straight until work meas 7 [7.5: 8: 8.5: 9] cm, ending with RS facing for next row.
Dec 1 st at each end of next and 15 foll 6th rows.
127 [141: 157: 171: 185] sts.
Work 19 rows, ending with RS facing for next row.
Inc 1 st at each end of next and 2 foll 20th rows.
133 [147: 163: 177: 191] sts.
Cont straight until work meas 48.5 [49: 49.5: 50: 50.5] cm, ending with RS facing for next row.
Shape armholes
Cast off 10 [11: 12: 13: 14] sts at beg of next 2 rows. 113 [125: 139: 151: 163] sts.
Next row (RS): K2, sl 1, K1, psso, K to last 4 sts, K2tog, K2.
Next row: P2, P2tog, P to last 4 sts, P2tog tbl, P2.
Working all armhole decreases as set by last 2 rows, cont as folls:
Dec 1 st at each end of next 9 [11: 11: 13: 13] rows, then on foll 1 [3: 4: 6: 7] alt rows.
89 [93: 105: 109: 119] sts.
Work 1 row, ending with RS facing for next row.
Shape neck
Next row (RS): K2, sl 1, K1, psso, K27 [29: 35: 37: 42] and turn, leaving rem sts on a holder.
30 [32: 38: 40: 45] sts.
Work each side of neck separately.
Working all neck and armhole decreases as set by armhole decreases, dec 1 st at neck edge of next 8 rows, then on foll 3 alt rows, then on 3 [3: 4: 4: 5] foll 4th rows, then on foll 6th row, then on foll 8th row, then on foll 10th row **and at same time** dec 1 st at armhole edge of 2nd and foll 6 [5: 7: 5: 5] alt rows. 6 [9: 12: 16: 20] sts.
Cont straight until armhole meas 22 [23.5: 25:

26.5: 28] cm, ending with RS facing for next row.
Shape shoulder
Cast off 3 [4: 6: 8: 10] sts at beg of next row.
Work 1 row.
Cast off rem 3 [5: 6: 8: 10] sts.
With RS facing, slip centre 27 sts onto a holder (for neckband), rejoin yarn and K to last 4 sts, K2tog, K2.
Complete to match first side, reversing shapings.

MAKING UP
Press as described on the information page.
Join right shoulder seam using back stitch, or mattress stitch if preferred.
Neckband
With RS facing and using 3mm (US 2/3) needles, pick up and knit 56 [56: 59: 59: 62] sts down left side of front neck, K across 27 sts on front holder, pick up and knit 56 [56: 59: 59: 62] sts up right side of front neck, and 56 [56: 59: 59: 62] sts down right side of back neck, K across 27 sts on back holder, then pick up and knit 56 [56: 59: 59: 62] sts up left side of back neck.
278 [278: 290: 290: 302] sts.
Work in g st for 2 rows, ending with **WS** facing for next row.
Cast off knitwise (on **WS**).
Join left shoulder and neckband seam.
Armhole borders (both alike)
With RS facing and using 3mm (US 2/3) needles, pick up and knit 148 [158: 170: 180: 190] sts evenly all round armhole edge.
Work in g st for 2 rows, ending with **WS** facing for next row.
Cast off knitwise (on **WS**).
See information page for finishing instructions.

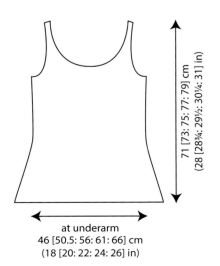

71 [73: 75: 77: 79] cm
(28 [28¾: 29½: 30¼: 31] in)

at underarm
46 [50.5: 56: 61: 66] cm
(18 [20: 22: 24: 26] in)

JONI

Dee Hardwicke

Main image page **82, 83**

● ● ●

YARN

Cotton Cashmere

A	Stormy Sky 225	3	x 50gm
B	Paper 210	2	x 50gm

Alternatively you could use Rowan Handknit
Cotton in the following shade(s):

A	Slate 347	5	x 50gm
B	Bleached 263	4	x 50gm

NEEDLES

1 pair 4mm (no 8) (US 6) needles
1 pair 4½mm (no 7) (US 7) needles

TENSION

20 sts and 28 rows to 10 cm measured over st st
using 4mm (US 6) needles.

FINISHED SIZE

Completed shawl is 43.5 cm (17¼ in) deep and
meas 120.5 cm (47½ in) along upper edge.

SHAWL
Using 4mm (US 8) needles and yarn B cast on
241 sts **loosely**.
Row 1 (RS): Knit.
Row 2: K1, P to last st, K1.
These 2 rows set the sts – first and last st of every
row worked as a K st and all other sts worked in
st st.
Keeping sts correct as now set throughout and
joining in and breaking off colours as required,
cont as folls:
Work 2 rows.
Join in yarn A.
Using yarn A, work 2 rows, ending with RS
facing for next row.
Change to 4½mm (US 7) needles.
Beg and ending rows as indicated, using
the **fairisle** technique as described on the

information page and repeating the 10 st patt
repeat 23 times across each row, cont in patt from
chart A, which is worked mainly in st st, as folls:
Work chart rows 1 to 16.
Change to 4mm (US 6) needles.
Row 23 (RS): Using yarn A, K1, sl 1, K1, psso,
K to last 3 sts, K2tog, K1. 239 sts.
Using yarn A, work 1 row, ending with RS
facing for next row.
Using yarn B, work 2 rows.
Working all decreases as set by row 23, cont as
folls:
Using yarn A, work 16 rows, dec 1 st at each end
of 3rd and 3 foll 4th rows. 231 sts.
Using yarn B, work 2 rows.
Using yarn A, work 16 rows, dec 1 st at each end
of next and foll 7 alt rows. 215 sts.
Using yarn B, work 2 rows, dec 1 st at each end
of first of these rows. 213 sts.
Using yarn A, work 2 rows, dec 1 st at each end
of first of these rows. 211 sts.
Change to 4½mm (US 7) needles.
Beg and ending rows as indicated, using
the **fairisle** technique as described on the
information page and repeating the 10 st patt
repeat 18 times across each row, cont in patt from
chart B, which is worked mainly in st st, as folls:
Dec 1 st at each end of next and foll 7 alt rows.
195 sts.
Work 1 row, ending after chart row 16 and with
RS facing for next row.
Change to 4mm (US 6) needles.
Using yarn A, work 2 rows, dec 1 st at each end
of first of these rows. 193 sts.

Using yarn B, work 2 rows, dec 1 st at each end
of first of these rows. 191 sts.
Using yarn A, work 4 rows, dec 1 st at each end
of next and foll alt row and ending with RS
facing for next row. 187 sts.
Row 89 (RS): Using yarn A, K1, sl 1, psso,
K to last 3 sts, K2tog, K1.
Row 90: Using yarn A, K1, P2tog, P to last 3 sts,
P2tog tbl, K1. 183 sts.
Now working all decreases as set by last 2 rows,
cont as folls:
Using yarn A, work a further 10 rows, dec 1 st at
each end of every row. 163 sts.
Using yarn B, work 2 rows, dec 1 st at each end
of both rows. 159 sts.
Using yarn A, work 8 rows, dec 1 st at each end
of every row. 143 sts.
Row 111 (RS): Using yarn A, K1, sl 1, K2tog,
psso, K to last 4 sts, K3tog, K1.
Row 112: Using yarn A, K1, P3tog, P to last
4 sts, P3tog tbl, K1. 135 sts.
Now working all decreases as set by last 2 rows,
cont as folls:
Using yarn A, work 6 rows, dec 2 sts at each end
of every row. 111 sts.
Using yarn B, work 4 rows, dec 2 sts at each end
of every row and ending with RS facing for next
row. 95 sts.
Using yarn B, cast off.

MAKING UP
Press as described on the information page.
See information page for finishing instructions.

Chart A

10 st patt rep

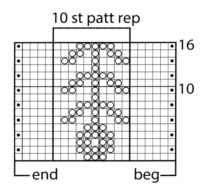

16

10

end   beg

Key

□	A
Ⓞ	B
⊡	K on WS with yarn A
▨	K2tog
◺	Sl1, K1, psso

Chart B

10 st patt rep

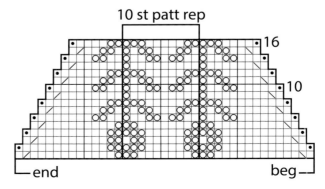

16

10

end   beg

KATZ
Grace Jones

Main image page **84, 85**

● ● ●

SIZE
To fit bust
81–86 91–97 102–107 112–117 122–127cm
32–34 36–38 40–42 44–46 48–50 in
Actual bust measurement of garment
88	97.5	108	117.5	128	cm
34½	38½	42½	46¼	50½	in

YARN
Kidsilk Haze
A White 612
4	4	5	5	6	x 25gm

B Wicked 599
1	1	1	1	1	x 25gm

NEEDLES
1 pair 4mm (no 8) (US 6) needles
4mm (no 8) (US 6) circular needle no more than
60 cm long

TENSION
22 sts and 30 rows to 10 cm measured over st st
using 4mm (US 6) needles.

FRONT
Using 4mm (US 6) needles and yarn B cast on
97 [107: 119: 129: 141] sts **loosely**.
Break off yarn B and join in yarn A.
Beg with a K row, work in st st until front meas
5 [5.5: 6: 6.5: 7] cm, ending with RS facing for
next row.
Dec 1 st at each end of next and 6 foll 6th rows.
83 [93: 105: 115: 127] sts.
Work 15 rows, ending with RS facing for next
row.★★
Inc 1 st at each end of next and 6 foll 6th rows.
97 [107: 119: 129: 141] sts.
Work 15 rows, ending with RS facing for next
row. (Front should meas approx 39.5 [40: 40.5:
41: 41.5] cm.)
Shape armholes
Cast off 3 [4: 5: 6: 7] sts at beg of next 2 rows.
91 [99: 109: 117: 127] sts.
Dec 1 st at each end of next 5 [5: 7: 7: 9] rows,
then on foll 3 [5: 5: 5: 4] alt rows.
75 [79: 85: 93: 101] sts.
Work 29 [29: 31: 35: 37] rows, ending with RS
facing for next row.
Shape front neck
Next row (RS): K24 [26: 29: 33: 37] and turn,
leaving rem sts on a holder.
Work each side of neck separately.
Dec 1 st at neck edge of next 8 rows, then on
foll 4 [4: 5: 5: 6] alt rows. 12 [14: 16: 20: 23] sts.
Work 1 row, ending with RS facing for next row.
(Armhole should meas approx 20 [21.5: 23: 24.5:
26] cm.)
Shape shoulder
Cast off 6 [7: 8: 10: 11] sts at beg of next row.
Work 1 row.
Cast off rem 6 [7: 8: 10: 12] sts.
With RS facing, slip centre 27 sts onto a holder
(for neckband), rejoin yarn and K to end.
Complete to match first side, reversing shapings.

BACK
Work as given for front to ★★.
Inc 1 st at each end of next and 5 foll 6th rows.

95 [105: 117: 127: 139] sts.
Work 1 row, ending with RS facing for next row.
Divide for back opening
Next row (RS): K47 [52: 58: 63: 69] and turn,
leaving rem sts on a holder.
Work each side of back separately.
Dec 1 st at back opening edge of 2nd and foll
alt row **and at same time** inc 1 st at side seam
edge of 4th row.
46 [51: 57: 62: 68] sts.
Work 5 rows, ending with RS facing for next
row.
Inc 1 st at back opening edge of next and foll
4th row. 48 [53: 59: 64: 70] sts.
Work 1 row, ending with RS facing for next row.
Place marker at beg of last row (to denote top of
back opening and beg of back neck shaping).
Shape back neck
Dec 1 st at end of next and foll alt row.
46 [51: 57: 62: 68] sts.
Work 1 row, ending with RS facing for next row.
Shape armhole
Cast off 3 [4: 5: 6: 7] sts at beg and dec 1 st at end
of next row.
42 [46: 51: 55: 60] sts.
Work 1 row.
Dec 1 st at armhole edge of next 5 [5: 7: 7: 9]
rows, then on foll 3 [5: 5: 5: 4] alt rows **and at
same time** dec 1 st at back neck edge of next
and foll 5 [7: 8: 8: 8] alt rows.
28 [28: 30: 34: 38] sts.
Dec 1 st at neck edge **only** on 2nd and foll 11
[7: 5: 3: 3] alt rows, then on 3 [5: 7: 9: 10] foll 4th
rows, then on foll 6th row. 12 [14: 16: 20: 23] sts.
Work 5 rows, ending with RS facing for next
row.
Shape shoulder
Cast off 6 [7: 8: 10: 11] sts at beg of next row.
Work 1 row.
Cast off rem 6 [7: 8: 10: 12] sts.
With RS facing, slip centre st onto a holder (for
back opening trim), rejoin yarn and K to end.
Complete to match first side, reversing shapings.

SLEEVES
Using 4mm (US 6) needles and yarn B cast on
36 [38: 40: 40: 42] sts **loosely**.
Break off yarn B and join in yarn A.

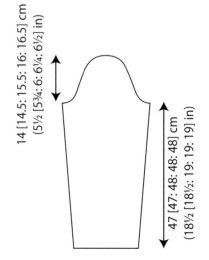

14 [14.5: 15.5: 16: 16.5] cm
(5½ [5¾: 6: 6¼: 6½] in)

47 [47: 48: 48: 48] cm
(18½ [18½: 19: 19: 19] in)

Front

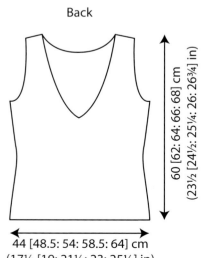

Back

60 [62: 64: 66: 68] cm
(23½ [24½: 25¼: 26: 26¾] in)

44 [48.5: 54: 58.5: 64] cm
(17¼ [19: 21¼: 23: 25¼] in)

Beg with a K row, work in st st throughout as folls:
Inc 1 st at each end of 7th [7th: 7th: 5th: 5th] and every foll 8th [8th: 8th: 6th: 6th] row to 50 [62: 70: 54: 64] sts, then on every foll 10th [10th: 10th: 8th: 8th] row until there are 64 [68: 72: 76: 80] sts.
Cont straight until sleeve meas 47 [47: 48: 48: 48] cm, ending with RS facing for next row.
Shape top
Cast off 3 [4: 5: 6: 7] sts at beg of next 2 rows.
58 [60: 62: 64: 66] sts.
Dec 1 st at each end of next 3 rows, then on foll 2 alt rows, then on 3 foll 4th rows.
42 [44: 46: 48: 50] sts.
Work 1 row.
Dec 1 st at each end of next and every foll alt row until 30 sts rem, then on foll 9 rows, ending with RS facing for next row.
Cast off rem 12 sts.

MAKING UP
Press as described on the information page.
Join both shoulder seams using back stitch, or mattress stitch if preferred.
Back opening trim
With RS facing, using 4mm (US 6) needles and yarn B, beg and ending at markers denoting beg of back neck shaping, pick up and knit 12 sts down right side of back opening, K st on holder at base of opening, then pick up and knit 12 sts up left side of back opening. 25 sts.
Cast off knitwise (on **WS**).

Neckband
With RS facing, using 4mm (US 6) circular needle and yarn B, cast on 50 sts (to form first tie), turn and pick up and knit 53 [56: 59: 62: 65] sts up left side of back neck from cast-off edge of back opening trim to shoulder seam, and 19 [19: 21: 21: 23] sts down left side of front neck, K across 27 sts on front holder, then pick up and knit 19 [19: 21: 21: 23] sts up right side of front neck, and 53 [56: 59: 62: 65] sts down right side of back neck to cast-off edge of back opening trim, turn and cast on 50 sts (to form second tie). 271 [277: 287: 293: 303] sts.
Cast off knitwise (on **WS**).
See information page for finishing instructions, setting in sleeves using the set-in method.

FONTANA
ARNE & CARLOS
Main image page **90, 91**
● ● ●

YARN
Cotton Cashmere

A	Stormy Sky 225	3	x 50gm
B	Silver Lining 224	3	x 50gm
C	Paper 210	2	x 50gm

Alternatively you could use Rowan Handknit Cotton in the following shade(s):

A	Slate 347	5	x 50gm
B	Feather 373	5	x 50gm
C	Bleached 263	4	x 50gm

NEEDLES
4mm (no 8) (US 6) circular needle at least 120 cm long

TENSION
21 sts and 32 rows to 10 cm measured over patt using 4mm (US 6) needles.

FINISHED SIZE
Completed wrap is 33 cm (13 in) wide and 192 cm (75½ in) long.

WRAP (knitted sideways)
Using 4mm (US 6) circular needle and yarn A cast on 403 sts **loosely**. (**Note:** To ensure cast-on edge is correct length, it is advisable to cast on using the thumb method.)
Work in g st for 2 rows, ending with RS facing for next row.
Cont as folls:
Row 1 (RS): Using yarn A, K3, ★P3, sl 1, K3tog, psso, (yfwd, K1) 5 times, yfwd, K4tog, P2, rep from ★ to last 4 sts, P1, K3.
Row 2: Using yarn A, K4, ★K2, P13, K3, rep from ★ to last 3 sts, K3.
Row 3: Using yarn A, K3, ★P3, K13, P2, rep from ★ to last 4 sts, P1, K3.

Row 4: As row 2.
Rows 5 to 7: As rows 1 to 3.
Joining in and breaking off colours as required, now work in patt as folls:
Row 1 (WS): Using yarn B, K4, ★K2, P13, K3, rep from ★ to last 3 sts, K3.
Row 2: Using yarn B, K3, ★(K1, yfwd) 3 times, K4tog, P5, sl 1, K3tog, psso, yfwd, (K1, yfwd) twice, rep from ★ to last 4 sts, K4.
Row 3: Using yarn B, K3, P1, ★P6, K5, P7, rep from ★ to last 3 sts, K3.
Row 4: Using yarn B, K3, ★K7, P5, K6, rep from ★ to last 4 sts, K4.
Row 5: As row 3.
Rows 6 to 8: As rows 2 to 4.
Row 9: Using yarn C, K3, P1, ★P6, K5, P7, rep from ★ to last 3 sts, K3.
Row 10: Using yarn C, K3, ★P3, sl 1, K3tog, psso, (yfwd, K1) 5 times, yfwd, K4tog, P2, rep from ★ to last 4 sts, P1, K3.
Row 11: Using yarn C, K4, ★K2, P13, K3, rep from ★ to last 3 sts, K3.
Row 12: Using yarn C, K3, ★P3, K13, P2, rep from ★ to last 4 sts, P1, K3.
Row 13: As row 11.
Rows 14 to 16: As rows 10 to 12.
Rows 17 to 24: As rows 1 to 8.
Rows 25 to 32: As rows 9 to 16 **but using yarn A.**
These 32 rows form patt.
Rep these 32 rows twice more, ending with **WS** facing for next row.
Using yarn A, work in g st for 2 rows.
Cast off **loosely** knitwise (on **WS**).

MAKING UP
Press as described on the information page.
See information page for finishing instructions.

WITTER

Martin Storey

Main image page **18, 19**

● ●

SIZE

To fit bust

81-86 91-97 102-107 112-117 122-127cm
32-34 36-38 40-42 44-46 48-50 in

Actual bust measurement of garment

| 101 | 110 | 121 | 130 | 141 | cm |
| 39¾ | 43¼ | 47½ | 51¼ | 55½ | in |

YARN

Softyak DK

| 11 | 12 | 13 | 14 | 15 | x 50gm |

(photographed in Prairie 233)

NEEDLES

1 pair 3¼mm (no 10) (US 3) needles
1 pair 4mm (no 8) (US 6) needles
Cable needle

TENSION

22 sts and 30 rows to 10 cm measured over st
st using 4mm (US 6) needles. Body cable panel
(103 sts) measures 39.5 cm. Sleeve panel (41 sts)
measures 15.5 cm.

SPECIAL ABBREVIATIONS

C6B = slip next 3 sts onto cable needle and
leave at back of work, K3, then K3 from cable
needle; **C6F** = slip next 3 sts onto cable needle
and leave at front of work, K3, then K3 from
cable needle.

BACK

Using 3¼mm (US 3) needles cast on 127 [137:
149: 159: 171] sts.
Row 1 (RS): P1, ★K1 tbl, P1, rep from ★ to end.
Row 2: K1, ★P1, K1, rep from ★ to end.
These 2 rows form rib.
Work in rib for a further 18 rows, ending with
RS facing for next row.
Change to 4mm (US 6) needles.

Now work in patt, placing body panel chart as
folls:
Row 1 (RS): K12 [17: 23: 28: 34], work next
103 sts as row 1 of chart for body panel, K12 [17:
23: 28: 34].
Row 2: P12 [17: 23: 28: 34], work next 103 sts
as row 2 of chart for body panel, P12 [17: 23:
28: 34].
These 2 rows set the sts – central section in patt
from chart for body panel and st st at each side.
Keeping sts correct as now set and repeating the
20 row patt panel repeat throughout, cont as folls:
Cont straight until back meas 41 [41.5: 42: 42.5:
43] cm, ending with RS facing for next row.
Shape raglan armholes
Keeping patt correct, cast off 3 sts at beg of next
2 rows. 121 [131: 143: 153: 165] sts.
Next row (RS): K2, sl 1, K1, psso, patt to last
4 sts, K2tog, K2.
Next row: P2, P2tog, patt to last 4 sts, P2tog tbl,
P2.
Rep last 2 rows 8 [11: 14: 17: 19] times more.
85 [83: 83: 81: 85] sts.
Next row (RS): K2, sl 1, K1, psso, patt to last
4 sts, K2tog, K2.
Next row: P3, patt to last 3 sts, P3.
Rep last 2 rows 21 [20: 19: 18: 19] times more,
ending with RS facing for next row.
41 [41: 43: 43: 45] sts.
Break yarn and leave sts on a holder (for
neckband).

FRONT

Work as given for back until 53 [53: 57: 57: 61] sts
rem in raglan armhole shaping.
Work 1 row, ending with RS facing for next row.
Shape front neck
Next row (RS): K2, sl 1, K1, psso, patt 12 [12:
14: 14: 16] sts and turn, leaving rem sts on a
holder. 15 [15: 17: 17: 19] sts.
Work each side of neck separately.
Keeping patt correct and working all raglan
armhole decreases as set, dec 1 st at neck edge
of next 6 rows, then on foll 1 [1: 2: 2: 3] alt rows
and at same time dec 1 st at raglan armhole
edge of 2nd and foll 3 [3: 4: 4: 5] alt rows. 4 sts.
Work 1 row.
Next row (RS): K1, sl 1, K2tog, psso.
Next row: P2.
Next row: K2tog and fasten off.

With RS facing, slip centre 21 sts onto a holder
(for neckband), rejoin yarn and patt to last 4 sts,
K2tog, K2.
Complete to match first side, reversing shapings.

SLEEVES

Using 3¼mm (US 3) needles cast on 59 [61: 65:
65: 67] sts.
Work in rib as given for back for 20 rows, ending
with RS facing for next row.
Change to 4mm (US 6) needles.
Now work in patt, placing sleeve panel chart as
folls:
Row 1 (RS): K9 [10: 12: 12: 13], work next
41 sts as row 1 of chart for sleeve panel, K9 [10:
12: 12: 13].
Row 2: P9 [10: 12: 12: 13], work next 41 sts
as row 2 of chart for sleeve panel, P9 [10: 12:
12: 13].
These 2 rows set the sts – central section in patt
from chart for sleeve panel and st st at each side.
Keeping sts correct as now set and repeating the
20 row patt panel repeat throughout, cont as folls:
Inc 1 st at each end of 3rd [3rd: 3rd: 3rd: next]
and every foll 6th [6th: 6th: 6th: 4th] row to
69 [79: 79: 95: 75] sts, then on every foll 8th [8th:
8th: 8th: 6th] row until there are 87 [91: 95:
99: 105] sts, taking inc sts into st st.
Cont straight until sleeve meas 45 [45: 46:
46: 46] cm, ending with RS facing for next row.
Shape raglan
Keeping patt correct, cast off 3 sts at beg of next
2 rows. 81 [85: 89: 93: 99] sts.
Working all raglan decreases in same way as
raglan armhole decreases, dec 1 st at each end of
next and 4 foll 4th rows, then on every foll alt
row until 27 sts rem.
Work 1 row, ending with RS facing for next row.
Break yarn and leave sts on a holder (for
neckband).

MAKING UP

Press as described on the information page.
Join both front and right back raglan seams using
back stitch, or mattress stitch if preferred.
Neckband
With RS facing and using 3¼mm (US 3)
needles, K across 27 sts on left sleeve holder, pick
up and knit 10 [10: 12: 12: 14] sts down left side
of front neck, K across 21 sts on front holder,

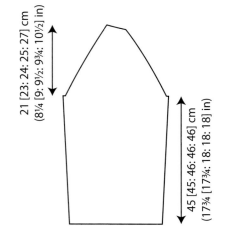

21 [23: 24: 25: 27] cm
(8¼ [9: 9½: 9¾: 10½] in)

45 [45: 46: 46: 46] cm
(17¾ [17¾: 18: 18: 18] in)

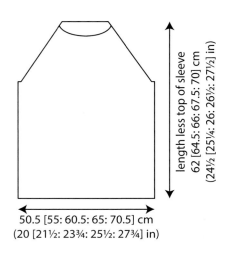

length less top of sleeve
62 [64.5: 66: 67.5: 70] cm
(24½ [25¼: 26: 26½: 27½] in)

50.5 [55: 60.5: 65: 70.5] cm
(20 [21½: 23¾: 25½: 27¾] in)

Body panel

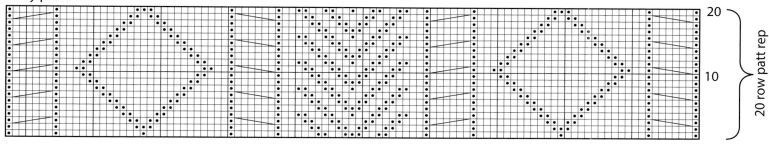

20 row patt rep

Sleeve panel

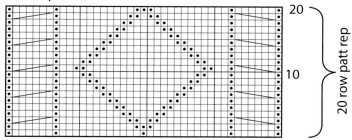

20 row patt rep

Key

☐	K on RS, P on WS
⊡	P on RS, K on WS
⟋ C6F	C6F
⟍ C6B	C6B

pick up and knit 10 [10: 12: 12: 14] sts up right side of front neck, then K across 27 sts on right sleeve holder, and 41 [41: 43: 43: 45] sts on back

holder dec 1 st at centre.
135 [135: 141: 141: 147] sts.
Beg with row 2, work in rib as given for back for

7 rows, ending with RS facing for next row.
Cast off in rib.
See information page for finishing instructions.

REGAIN

Martin Storey

Main image page **54, 55**

● ●

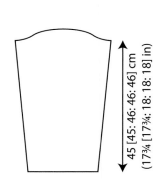

SIZE
To fit bust

81-86	91-97	102-107	112-117	122-127	cm
32-34	36-38	40-42	44-46	48-50	in

Actual bust measurement of garment

110.5	121	129.5	140	150.5	cm
43½	47½	51	55	59¼	in

YARN
Kidsilk Haze

14	15	17	18	19	x 25gm

(photographed in Aura 676)

NEEDLES
1 pair 3¼mm (no 10) (US 3) needles
1 pair 3¾mm (no 9) (US 5) needles

TENSION
23 sts and 32 rows to 10 cm measured over st st using 3¾mm (US 5) needles and yarn DOUBLE.

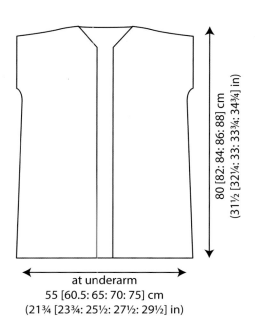

45 [45: 46: 46: 46] cm
(17¾ [17¾: 18: 18: 18] in)

80 [82: 84: 86: 88] cm
(31½ [32¼: 33: 33¾: 34¾] in)

at underarm
55 [60.5: 65: 70: 75] cm
(21¾ [23¾: 25½: 27½: 29½] in)

BACK

Using 3¼mm (US 3) needles and yarn DOUBLE cast on 150 [162: 174: 186: 198] sts.
Row 1 (RS): K2, ★P2, K2, rep from ★ to end.
Row 2: P2, ★K2, P2, rep from ★ to end.
These 2 rows form rib.
Cont in rib for a further 17 rows, ending with **WS** facing for next row.
Row 20 (WS): Rib 2 [2: 2: 1: 0], work 2 tog, (rib 10 [11: 10: 11: 12], work 2 tog) 12 [12: 14: 14: 14] times, rib 2 [2: 2: 1: 0].
137 [149: 159: 171: 183] sts.
Change to 3¾mm (US 5) needles.
Beg with a K row, now work in st st throughout as folls:
Work 32 rows, ending with RS facing for next row.
Dec 1 st at each end of next and 4 foll 22nd rows. 127 [139: 149: 161: 173] sts.
Cont straight until back meas 52.5 [53: 53.5: 54: 54.5] cm, ending with RS facing for next row.
Inc 1 st at each end of next and foll 6th row, then on foll 4th row, then on foll 2 alt rows.
137 [149: 159: 171: 183] sts.
Place markers at both ends of last row (to denote base of armhole openings).
Cont straight until work meas 18 [19.5: 21: 22.5: 24] cm from markers, ending with RS facing for next row.
Shape shoulders and back neck
Cast off 5 [6: 6: 7: 7] sts at beg of next 12 [12: 10: 12: 6] rows, then − [−: 7: −: 8] sts at beg of foll − [−: 2: −: 6] rows. 77 [77: 85: 87: 93] sts.
Next row (RS): Cast off 6 [6: 7: 7: 8] sts, K until there are 15 [15: 17: 18: 19] sts on right needle and turn, leaving rem sts on a holder.
Work each side of neck separately.
Dec 1 st at neck edge of next 3 rows, ending with RS facing for next row, **and at same time** cast off 6 [6: 7: 7: 8] sts at beg of 2nd row.
Cast off rem 6 [6: 7: 8: 8] sts.
With RS facing, slip centre 35 [35: 37: 37: 39] sts onto a holder (for neckband), rejoin yarn and K to end.
Complete to match first side, reversing shapings.

LEFT FRONT

Using 3¼mm (US 3) needles and yarn DOUBLE cast on 67 [71: 79: 83: 91] sts.
Row 1 (RS): K2, ★P2, K2, rep from ★ to last st, K1.
Row 2: K1, P2, ★K2, P2, rep from ★ to end.
These 2 rows form rib.
Cont in rib for a further 17 rows, ending with **WS** facing for next row.
Row 20 (WS): Rib 2 [7: 2: 6: 5], work 2 tog, (rib 10 [16: 10: 15: 11], work 2 tog) 5 [3: 6: 4: 6] times, rib 3 [8: 3: 7: 6]. 61 [67: 72: 78: 84] sts.
Change to 3¾mm (US 5) needles.
Now work in patt as folls:
Row 1 (RS): K to last 12 sts, yfwd, sl 1, K1, psso, K10.
Row 2 and every foll alt row: Purl.
Row 3: K to last 14 sts, K2tog, yfwd, K1, yfwd, sl 1, K1, psso, K9.
Row 5: K to last 15 sts, K2tog, yfwd, K3, yfwd, sl 1, K1, psso, K8.
Row 7: K to last 16 sts, K2tog, yfwd, K5, yfwd, sl 1, K1, psso, K7.

Row 9: K to last 17 sts, K2tog, yfwd, K7, yfwd, sl 1, K1, psso, K6.
Row 11: K to last 18 sts, K2tog, yfwd, K9, yfwd, sl 1, K1, psso, K5.
Row 13: K to last 19 sts, K2tog, yfwd, K11, yfwd, sl 1, K1, psso, K4.
Row 15: K to last 20 sts, K2tog, yfwd, K13, yfwd, sl 1, K1, psso, K3.
Row 17: K to last 20 sts, yfwd, sl 1, K1, psso, K13, K2tog, yfwd, K3.
Row 19: K to last 19 sts, yfwd, sl 1, K1, psso, K11, K2tog, yfwd, K4.
Row 21: K to last 18 sts, yfwd, sl 1, K1, psso, K9, K2tog, yfwd, K5.
Row 23: K to last 17 sts, yfwd, sl 1, K1, psso, K7, K2tog, yfwd, K6.
Row 25: K to last 16 sts, yfwd, sl 1, K1, psso, K5, K2tog, yfwd, K7.
Row 27: K to last 15 sts, yfwd, sl 1, K1, psso, K3, K2tog, yfwd, K8.
Row 29: K to last 14 sts, yfwd, sl 1, K1, psso, K1, K2tog, yfwd, K9.
Row 31: K to last 13 sts, yfwd, sl 1, K2tog, psso, yfwd, K10.
Row 32: Purl.
These 32 rows form patt.
Keeping patt correct, cont as folls:
Dec 1 st at beg of next and 4 foll 22nd rows. 56 [62: 67: 73: 79] sts.
Cont straight until left front meas 52.5 [53: 53.5: 54: 54.5] cm, ending with RS facing for next row.
Inc 1 st at beg of next and foll 6th row, then on foll 4th row, then on foll 2 alt rows.
61 [67: 72: 78: 84] sts.
Place marker at beg of last row (to denote base of armhole opening).
Cont straight until 30 [30: 34: 34: 36] rows less have been worked than on back to beg of shoulder shaping, ending with RS facing for next row.
Shape front slope
Place marker at beg of last row (to denote beg of front slope shaping).
Next row (RS): K to last 25 sts, K2tog, patt 23 sts.
Working all front slope decreases as set by last row, dec 1 st at front slope edge of 2nd and foll 4 [4: 4: 4: 5] alt rows, then on 4 [4: 5: 5: 5] foll 4th rows. 51 [57: 61: 67: 72] sts.
Work 3 rows, ending with RS facing for next row.
Shape shoulder
Cast off 5 [6: 6: 7: 7] sts at beg of next and foll 5 [7: 4: 7: 2] alt rows, then 6 [−: 7: −: 8] sts at beg of foll 2 [−: 3: −: 5] alt rows **and at same time** dec 1 st at front slope edge of next and 2 foll 4th rows.
Work 1 row.
Cast off rem 6 [6: 7: 8: 8] sts.

RIGHT FRONT

Using 3¼mm (US 3) needles and yarn DOUBLE cast on 67 [71: 79: 83: 91] sts.
Row 1 (RS): K3, ★P2, K2, rep from ★ to end.
Row 2: P2, ★K2, P2, rep from ★ to last st, K1.
These 2 rows form rib.
Cont in rib for a further 17 rows, ending with **WS** facing for next row.
Row 20 (WS): Rib 2 [7: 2: 6: 5], work 2 tog, (rib 10 [16: 10: 15: 11], work 2 tog) 5 [3: 6: 4: 6] times, rib 3 [8: 3: 7: 6]. 61 [67: 72: 78: 84] sts.

Change to 3¾mm (US 5) needles.
Now work in patt as folls:
Row 1 (RS): K11, yfwd, sl 1, K1, psso, K to end.
Row 2 and every foll alt row: Purl.
Row 3: K9, K2tog, yfwd, K1, yfwd, sl 1, K1, psso, K to end.
Row 5: K8, K2tog, yfwd, K3, yfwd, sl 1, K1, psso, K to end.
Row 7: K7, K2tog, yfwd, K5, yfwd, sl 1, K1, psso, K to end.
Row 9: K6, K2tog, yfwd, K7, yfwd, sl 1, K1, psso, K to end.
Row 11: K5, K2tog, yfwd, K9, yfwd, sl 1, K1, psso, K to end.
Row 13: K4, K2tog, yfwd, K11, yfwd, sl 1, K1, psso, K to end.
Row 15: K3, K2tog, yfwd, K13, yfwd, sl 1, K1, psso, K to end.
Row 17: K3, yfwd, sl 1, K1, psso, K13, K2tog, yfwd, K to end.
Row 19: K4, yfwd, sl 1, K1, psso, K11, K2tog, yfwd, K to end.
Row 21: K5, yfwd, sl 1, K1, psso, K9, K2tog, yfwd, K to end.
Row 23: K6, yfwd, sl 1, K1, psso, K7, K2tog, yfwd, K to end.
Row 25: K7, yfwd, sl 1, K1, psso, K5, K2tog, yfwd, K to end.
Row 27: K8, yfwd, sl 1, K1, psso, K3, K2tog, yfwd, K to end.
Row 29: K9, yfwd, sl 1, K1, psso, K1, K2tog, yfwd, K to end.
Row 31: K10, yfwd, sl 1, K2tog, psso, yfwd, K to end.
Row 32: Purl.
These 32 rows form patt.
Keeping patt correct, cont as folls:
Dec 1 st at end of next and 4 foll 22nd rows. 56 [62: 67: 73: 79] sts.
Cont straight until right front meas 52.5 [53: 53.5: 54: 54.5] cm, ending with RS facing for next row.
Inc 1 st at end of next and foll 6th row, then on foll 4th row, then on foll 2 alt rows.
61 [67: 72: 78: 84] sts.
Place marker at end of last row (to denote base of armhole opening).
Cont straight until 30 [30: 34: 34: 36] rows less have been worked than on back to beg of shoulder shaping, ending with RS facing for next row.
Shape front slope
Place marker at end of last row (to denote beg of front slope shaping).
Next row (RS): Patt 23 sts, sl 1, K1, psso, K to end.
Working all front slope decreases as set by last row, complete to match left front, reversing shapings.

SLEEVES

Using 3¼mm (US 3) needles and yarn DOUBLE cast on 54 [54: 58: 58: 58] sts.
Work in rib as given for back for 20 rows, dec [inc: dec: dec: inc] 1 st at end of last row and ending with RS facing for next row.
53 [55: 57: 57: 59] sts.
Change to 3¾mm (US 5) needles.
Beg with a K row, now work in st st throughout as folls:

Inc 1 st at each end of 5th [5th: 3rd: 3rd: 3rd] and every foll 6th [6th: 6th: 4th: 4th] row to 57 [75: 95: 77: 97] sts, then on every foll 8th [8th: –: 6th: 6th] row until there are 81 [87: –: 101: 109] sts. Cont straight until sleeve meas 45 [45: 46: 46: 46] cm, ending with RS facing for next row.

Shape top

Cast off 5 [5: 6: 6: 7] sts at beg of next 6 [2: 6: 2: 6] rows, then 6 [6: 7: 7: 8] sts at beg of foll 4 [8: 4: 8: 4] rows.

Cast off rem 27 [29: 31: 33: 35] sts.

MAKING UP

Press as described on the information page. Join both shoulder seams using back stitch, or mattress stitch if preferred.

Neckband

With RS facing, using 3¼mm (US 3) needles and yarn DOUBLE, beg and ending at markers denoting beg of front slope shaping, pick up and knit 41 [41: 44: 44: 47] sts up right front slope, and 3 sts down right side of back neck, K across 35 [35: 37: 37: 39] sts on back holder inc 1 st at centre, then pick up and knit 3 sts up left side of back neck, and 41 [41: 44: 44: 47] sts down left front slope. 124 [124: 132: 132: 140] sts.

Row 1 (WS): K1, P2, *K2, P2, rep from * to last st, K1.

Row 2: K3, *P2, K2, rep from * to last st, K1.

These 2 rows form rib.

Cont in rib for a further 17 rows, ending with RS facing for next row.

Cast off in rib.

Front bands (both alike)

With RS facing, using 3¼mm (US 3) needles and yarn DOUBLE, pick up and knit 160 [164: 168: 172: 176] sts evenly along front opening edge, between cast-on edge and marker denoting beg of front slope shaping.

Beg with row 1, work in rib as given for neckband for 19 rows, ending with RS facing for next row.

Cast off in rib.

See information page for finishing instructions, setting in sleeves using the straight cast-off method.

TOREY

Martin Storey

Main image page **74, 75**

● ● ●

YARN

Cotton Cashmere and Kidsilk Haze

A CC Silver Lining 224					
5	6	6	7	7	x 50gm
B *KSH Cream 634					
3	3	3	4	4	x 25gm
C CC Stormy Sky 225					
2	2	3	3	3	x 50gm
D CC Paper 210					
3	3	3	3	3	x 50gm

*Use **THREE** strands of Kidsilk Haze held together throughout

Alternatively, you could use Rowan Handknit Cotton in the following shade(s):

A HK Feather 373					
8	10	10	11	11	x 50gm
B *KSH Cream 634					
3	3	3	4	4	x 25gm
C HK Slate 347					
4	4	5	5	5	x 50gm
D HK Bleached 263					
5	5	5	5	5	x 50gm

*Use **THREE** strands of Kidsilk Haze held together throughout

SIZE

To fit bust

81–86 91–97 102–107 112–117 122–127cm
32–34 36–38 40–42 44–46 48–50 in

Actual bust measurement of garment

145.5 155 166.5 176 185.5 cm
57¼ 61 65½ 69¼ 73 in

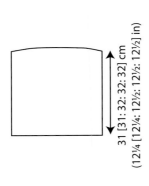

31 [31: 32: 32: 32] cm
(12¼ [12¼: 12½: 12½: 12½] in)

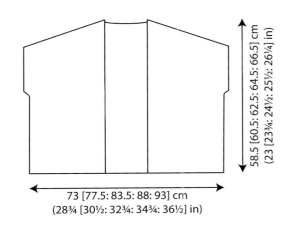

58.5 [60.5: 62.5: 64.5: 66.5] cm
(23 [23¾: 24½: 25½: 26¼] in)

73 [77.5: 83.5: 88: 93] cm
(28¾ [30½: 32¾: 34¾: 36½] in)

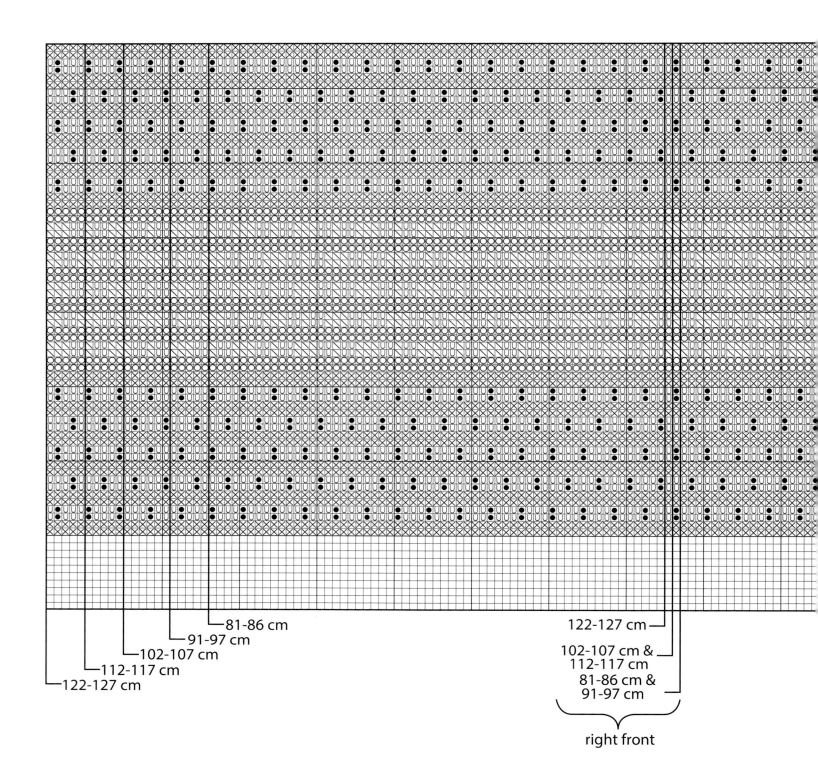

—81-86 cm
—91-97 cm
—102-107 cm
—112-117 cm
—122-127 cm

122-127 cm—
102-107 cm &
112-117 cm
81-86 cm &
91-97 cm

right front

Key

☐ K on RS, P on WS in B

☒ K on RS, P on WS in C

Ⓤ Slip st with yarn on WS

◱ K on RS and WS in C

◎ K on RS, P on WS in D

● K on RS and WS in D

NEEDLES

1 pair 3¼mm (no 10) (US 3) needles
1 pair 4mm (no 8) (US 6) needles
3¼mm (no 10) (US 3) circular needle at least
160 cm long

TENSION

21 sts and 27 rows to 10 cm measured over st st
using 3 strands of yarn B held together, 21 sts and
40 rows to 10 cm measured over dot patt (chart
rows 11 to 32, and 55 to 76), 21 sts and 37 rows
to 10 cm measured over dash patt (chart rows 33
to 54), all using 4mm (US 6) needles.

Pattern notes: Complete patt repeat is 152

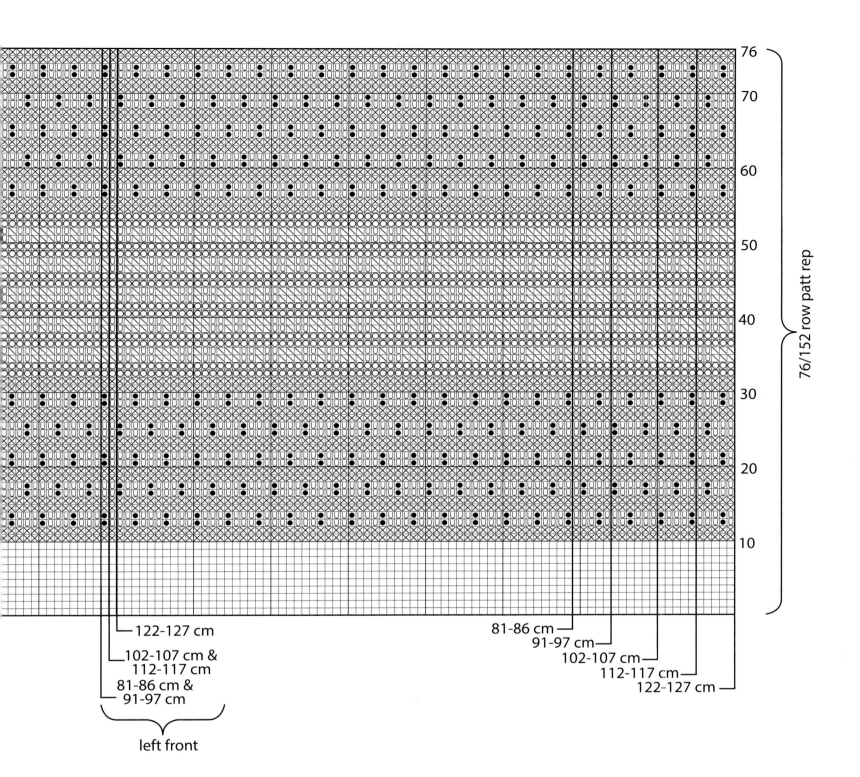

76

70

60

50

40

30

20

10

76/152 row patt rep

122-127 cm

102-107 cm &
112-117 cm

81-86 cm &
91-97 cm

left front

81-86 cm
91-97 cm
102-107 cm
112-117 cm
122-127 cm

---

rows, but only the first 76 of these rows are shown on chart. Once these 76 rows have been worked, repeat them **BUT**, for this repeat, using yarn A in place of yarn C. (Note all other colours remain as for first repeat.) Once this second rep of chart rows 1 to 76 has been worked, start again working chart rows 1 to 76 using colours as shown on chart.

When working chart rows 13 to 74, all slipped sts should be worked with yarn held at **WS** of work – this is back of work on RS rows, and front of work on WS rows.

BACK
Using 3¼mm (US 3) needles and yarn A cast on 153 [165: 177: 189: 195] sts.

Row 1 (RS): K3, ★P3, K3, rep from ★ to end.
Row 2: P3, ★K3, P3, rep from ★ to end.
These 2 rows form rib.
Work in rib for a further 10 rows, dec 0 [2: 2: 4: 0] sts evenly across last row and ending with RS facing for next row. 153 [163: 175: 185: 195] sts.
Change to 4mm (US 6) needles.
Beg and ending rows as indicated and taking time to read pattern note (above) thoroughly, cont in patt from chart, which is worked mainly in st st beg with a K row, as folls:
Remembering to use **THREE** strands of yarn B held together, work chart rows 1 to 76.
Working next 76 rows using colours as detailed in pattern note and then repeating all 152 rows of the full repeat, now cont in patt as now set as

folls:
Cont straight until back meas 30 [30.5: 31: 31.5: 32] cm, ending with RS facing for next row.
Shape for sleeve extension
Keeping patt correct, inc 1 st at each end of next and foll 8th row, then on foll 6th row, then on foll 4th row, then on foll alt row, taking inc sts into patt and ending with **WS** facing for next row. 163 [173: 185: 195: 205] sts.
Place markers at both ends of last row (to denote base of armhole openings).
Cont straight until work meas 16 [17.5: 19: 20.5: 22] cm from markers, ending with RS facing for next row.
Shape shoulders
Keeping patt correct, cast off 3 [3: 4: 4: 4] sts at

beg of next 12 [2: 28: 18: 10] rows, then 4 [4: –: 5: 5] sts at beg of foll 16 [26: –: 10: 18] rows.
63 [63: 73: 73: 75] sts.

Shape back neck

Next row (RS): Cast off 4 [4: 5: 5: 5] sts, patt until there are 16 [16: 19: 19: 19] sts on right needle and turn, leaving rem sts on a holder.
Work each side of neck separately.
Dec 1 st at neck edge of next 4 rows **and at same time** cast off 4 [4: 5: 5: 5] sts at beg of 2nd and foll alt row.
Work 1 row.
Cast off rem 4 [4: 5: 5: 5] sts.
With RS facing, slip centre 23 [23: 25: 25: 27] sts onto a holder (for front band), rejoin yarns and patt to end.
Complete to match first side, reversing shapings.

LEFT FRONT

Using 3¼mm (US 3) needles and yarn A cast on 64 [70: 76: 76: 82] sts.
Row 1 (RS): K3, *P3, K3, rep from * to last st, K1.
Row 2: K1, P3, *K3, P3, rep from * to end.
These 2 rows form rib.
Work in rib for a further 10 rows, dec 3 [4: 5: 0: 2] sts evenly across last row and ending with RS facing for next row. 61 [66: 71: 76: 80] sts.
Change to 4mm (US 6) needles.
Beg and ending rows as indicated, cont in patt from chart as folls:
Cont straight until left front matches back to beg of sleeve extension shaping, ending with RS facing for next row.

Shape for sleeve extension

Keeping patt correct, inc 1 st at beg of next and foll 8th row, then on foll 6th row, then on foll 4th row, then on foll alt row, taking inc sts into patt and ending with **WS** facing for next row.
66 [71: 76: 81: 85] sts.
Place marker at beg of last row (to denote base of armhole opening).
Cont straight until left front matches back to beg of shoulder shaping, ending with RS facing for next row.

Shape shoulder

Keeping patt correct, cast off 3 [3: 4: 4: 4] sts at beg of next and foll 5 [0: 13: 8: 4] alt rows, then 4 [4: 5: 5: 5] sts at beg of foll 11 [16: 3: 8: 12] alt rows.
Work 1 row.
Cast off rem 4 [4: 5: 5: 5] sts.

RIGHT FRONT

Using 3¼mm (US 3) needles and yarn A cast on 64 [70: 76: 76: 82] sts.
Row 1 (RS): K4, *P3, K3, rep from * to end.
Row 2: P3, *K3, P3, rep from * to last st, K1.
These 2 rows form rib.
Complete to match left front, reversing shapings.

SLEEVES

Using 3¼mm (US 3) needles and yarn A cast on 69 [75: 81: 87: 93] sts.
Beg with row 1, work in rib as given for back as folls:
Work 6 rows, ending with RS facing for next row.

Change to 4mm (US 6) needles.
Cont in rib until sleeve meas 31 [31: 32: 32: 32] cm, ending with RS facing for next row.

Shape top

Cast off 7 [8: 9: 9: 10] sts at beg of next 2 [4: 6: 2: 4] rows, then 8 [9: –: 10: 11] sts at beg of foll 4 [2: –: 4: 2] rows.
Cast off rem 23 [25: 27: 29: 31] sts.

MAKING UP

Press as described on the information page.
Join both shoulder seams using back stitch, or mattress stitch if preferred.

Front band

With RS facing, using 3¼mm (US 3) circular needle and yarn A, beg and ending at front cast-on edges, pick up and knit 130 [136: 141: 144: 149] sts up entire right front opening edge, and 5 sts down right side of back neck, K across 23 [23: 25: 25: 27] sts on back holder, then pick up and knit 5 sts up left side of back neck, and 130 [136: 141: 144: 149] sts down entire left front opening edge. 293 [305: 317: 323: 335] sts.
Row 1 (WS): K1, P3, *K3, P3, rep from * to last st, K1.
Row 2: K4, *P3, K3, rep from * to last st, K1.
These 2 rows form rib.
Cont in rib until front band meas 4 cm, ending with RS facing for next row.
Cast off in rib.
See information page for finishing instructions, setting in sleeves using the straight cast-off method.

·············

SIZING GUIDE

·············

ROWAN

When you knit and wear a Rowan design we want you to look and feel fabulous. This all starts with the size and fit of the design you choose. To help you to achieve a great knitting experience we have looked at the sizing of our womens and menswear patterns.

The menswear designs are now available to knit in a wider range of sizes from 81 cm (32") chest to a 137 cm (54") chest.

Dimensions in the charts below are body measurements, not garment dimensions, therefore

please refer to the measuring guide to help you to determine which is the best size for you to knit. We also now give full garment measurements around chest/bust at the beginning of each pattern so that you can see how much ease there will be for your size.

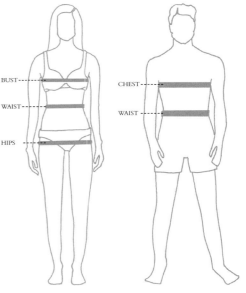

STANDARD WOMENS SIZING GUIDE
The sizing within this chart is also based on the larger size within the range.

To fit bust	32 – 34	36 – 38	40 – 42	44 – 46	48 – 50	inches
	81 – 86	91 - 97	102 – 107	112 – 117	122 – 127	cm
To fit waist	24 – 26	28 – 30	32 – 34	36 – 38	40 – 42	inches
	61 – 66	71 – 76	81 – 86	91 – 97	102 – 107	cm
To fit hips	34 – 36	38 – 40	42 – 44	46 – 48	50 – 52	inches
	86 – 91	97 – 102	107 – 112	117 – 122	127 – 132	cm

STANDARD MENS AND UNISEX SIZING GUIDE
The sizing within this chart is also based on the larger size within the range.

To fit Chest	32-34	36-38	40-42	44-46	48-50	52-54	inches
	81-86	91-97	102-107	112-117	122-127	132-137	cm
To fit waist	24-26	28-30	32-34	36-38	40-42	44-46	inches
	61-66	71-76	81-86	91-97	102-107	112-117	cm

SIZING & SIZE DIAGRAM NOTE
The instructions are given for the smallest size. Where they vary, work the figures in brackets for the larger sizes. **One set of figures refers to all sizes.** Included with most patterns in this magazine is a '**size diagram**' - see image on the right, of the finished garment and its dimensions. The measurement shown at the bottom of each '**size diagram**' shows the garment width 2.5cm below the armhole shaping. To help you choose the size of garment to knit please refer to the sizing guide. Generally in the majority of designs the welt width (at the cast on edge of the garment) is the same width as the chest. However, some designs are 'A-Line' in shape or have a flared edge and in these cases the welt width will be wider than the chest width.

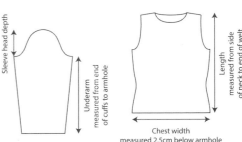

MEASURING GUIDE
For maximum comfort and to ensure the correct fit when choosing a size to knit, please follow the tips below when checking your size.

Measure yourself close to your body, over your underwear and don't pull the tape measure too tight!

Bust/chest – measure around the fullest part of the bust/chest and across the shoulder blades.

Waist – measure around the natural waistline.

Hips – measure around the fullest part of the bottom.

To be extra sure, measure your favourite jumper and then compare these measurements with the Rowan size diagram given at the end of the individual instructions.

Finally, once you have decided which size is best for you, please ensure that you achieve the tension required for the design you wish to knit.

Remember if your tension is too loose, your garment will be bigger than the pattern size. If your tension is too tight, your garment could be smaller than the pattern size both of which will alter the amount of yarn used to that stated in the pattern.

Furthermore if your tension is incorrect, the handle of your fabric will be too stiff or floppy and will not fit properly. It really does make sense to check your tension before starting every project.

INFORMATION

TENSION

Obtaining the correct tension is perhaps the single factor which can make the difference between a successful garment and a disastrous one. It controls both the shape and size of an article, so any variation, however slight, can distort the finished garment. Different designers feature in our books and it is **their** tension, given at the **start** of each pattern, which you must match. We recommend that you knit a square in pattern and/or stocking stitch (depending on the pattern instructions) of perhaps 5 - 10 more stitches and 5 - 10 more rows than those given in the tension note. Mark out the central 10cm square with pins. If you have too many stitches to 10cm try again using thicker needles, if you have too few stitches to 10cm try again using finer needles. Once you have achieved the correct tension your garment will be knitted to the measurements indicated in the size diagram shown at the end of the pattern.

CHART NOTE

Many of the patterns in the book are worked from charts. Each square on a chart represents a stitch and each line of squares a row of knitting. Each colour used is given a different letter and these are shown in the **materials** section, or in the **key** alongside the chart of each pattern. When working from the charts, read odd rows (K) from right to left and even rows (P) from left to right, unless otherwise stated. When working lace from a chart it is important to note that all but the largest size may have to alter the first and last few stitches in order not to lose or gain stitches over the row.

WORKING A LACE PATTERN

When working a lace pattern it is important to remember that if you are unable to work both the increase and corresponding decrease and vica versa, the stitches should be worked in stocking stitch.

KNITTING WITH COLOUR

There are two main methods of working colour into a knitted fabric: **Intarsia** and **Fairisle** techniques. The first method produces a single thickness of fabric and is usually used where a colour is only required in a particular area of a row and does not form a repeating pattern across the row, as in the fairisle technique.

Fairisle type knitting: When two or three colours are worked repeatedly across a row, strand the yarn **not** in use loosely behind the stitches being worked. If you are working with more than two colours, treat the "floating" yarns as if they were one yarn and always spread the stitches to their correct width to keep them elastic. It is advisable not to carry the stranded or "floating" yarns over more than three stitches at a time, but to weave them under and over the colour you are working. The "floating" yarns are therefore caught at the back of the work.

Intarsia: The simplest way to do this is to cut short lengths of yarn for each motif or block of colour used in a row. Then joining in the various colours at the appropriate point on the row, link one colour to the next by twisting them around each other where they meet on the wrong side to avoid gaps. All ends can then either be darned along the colour join lines, as each motif is completed or then can be "knitted-in" to the fabric of the knitting as each colour is worked into the pattern. This is done in much the same way as "weaving- in" yarns when working the Fairisle technique and does save time darning-in ends. It is essential that the tension is noted for intarsia as this may vary from the stocking stitch if both are used in the same pattern.

FINISHING INSTRUCTIONS

After working for hours knitting a garment, it seems a great pity that many garments are spoiled because such little care is taken in the pressing and finishing process. Follow the text below for a truly professional-looking garment.

PRESSING

Block out each piece of knitting and following the instructions on the ball band press the garment pieces, omitting the ribs. Tip: Take special care to press the edges, as this will make sewing up both easier and neater. If the ball band indicates that the fabric is not to be pressed, then covering the blocked out fabric with a damp white cotton cloth and leaving it to stand will have the desired effect. Darn in all ends neatly along the selvage edge or a colour join, as appropriate.

STITCHING

When stitching the pieces together, remember to match areas of colour and texture very carefully where they meet. Use a seam stitch such as back stitch or mattress stitch for all main knitting seams and join all ribs and neckband with mattress stitch, unless otherwise stated.

CONSTRUCTION

Having completed the pattern instructions, join left shoulder and neckband seams as detailed above. Sew the top of the sleeve to the body of the garment using the method detailed in the pattern, referring to the appropriate guide:

Straight cast-off sleeves: Place centre of cast-off edge of sleeve to shoulder seam. Sew top of sleeve to body, using markers as guidelines where applicable.

Square set-in sleeves: Place centre of cast-off edge of sleeve to shoulder seam. Set sleeve head into armhole, the straight sides at top of sleeve to form a neat right-angle to cast-off sts at armhole on back and front.

Shallow set-in sleeves: Place centre of cast off edge of sleeve to shoulder seam. Match decreases at beg of armhole shaping to decreases at top of sleeve. Sew sleeve head into armhole, easing in shapings.

Set-in sleeves: Place centre of cast-off edge of sleeve to shoulder seam. Set in sleeve, easing sleeve head into armhole.

Join side and sleeve seams.

Slip stitch pocket edgings and linings into place. Sew on buttons to correspond with buttonholes. Ribbed welts and neckbands and any areas of garter stitch should not be pressed.

ABBREVIATIONS

K	knit
P	purl
st(s)	stitch(es)
inc	increas(e)(ing)
dec	decreas(e)(ing)
st st	stocking stitch (1 row K , 1 row P)
g st	garter stitch (K every row)
beg	begin(ning)
foll	following
rem	remain(ing)
rev st st	reverse stocking stitch (1 row K , 1 row P)
rep	repeat
alt	alternate
cont	continue
patt	pattern
tog	together
mm	millimetres
cm	centimetres
in(s)	inch(es)
RS	right side
WS	wrong side
sl 1	slip one stitch
psso	pass slipped stitch over
p2sso	pass 2 slipped stitches over
tbl	through back of loop
M1	make one stitch by picking up horizontal loop before next stitch and knitting into back of it
M1P	make one stitch by picking up horizontal loop before next stitch and purling into back of it
yfwd	yarn forward
yrn	yarn round needle
meas	measures
0	no stitches, times or rows
-	no stitches, times or rows for that size
yon	yarn over needle
yfrn	yarn forward round needle
wyib	with yarn at back

CROCHET TERMS

UK crochet terms and abbreviations have been used throughout. The list below gives the US equivalent where they vary.

ABBREV.	UK	US
dc (sc)	double crochet	(single crochet)
htr (hdc)	half treble	(half double crochet)
tr (dc)	treble	(double crochet)
dtr (tr)	double treble	(treble)

EXPERIENCE RATING - for guidance only

● Beginner Techniques
For the beginner knitter, basic garment shaping and straight forward stitch technique.

● ● Simple Techniques
Simple straight forward knitting, introducing various, shaping techniques and garments.

● ● ● Experienced Techniques
For the more experienced knitter, using more advanced shaping techniques at the same time as colourwork or more advanced stitch techniques.

● ● ● ● Advanced Techniques
Advanced techniques used, using advanced stitches and garment shaping along with more challenging techniques

BUTTONS, BEADS AND RIBBONS USED IN THIS MAGAZINE ARE SOURCED FROM:

Bedecked Haberdashery
The Coach House
Barningham Park
Richmond
DL11 7DW

Tel: +44 (0)1833 621 451
Email:Judith.lewis@bedecked.co.uk
Web: www.bedecked.co.uk

Groves
Eastern Bypass
Thame, Oxfordshire
OX9 3FU
Email: groves@stockistenquiries.co.uk
Web: www.grovesltd.co.uk

Debbie Abrahams Beads
26 Church Drive
Nottingham
NG5 2BA
Tel: 0115 960 7991
Email: beads@debbieabrahams.com
Web: www.debbieabrahamsbeads.co.uk

WASH CARE INFORMATION

To help you to care for your knitting and crochet more easily below are the symbols you are likely to find on our ball bands and shade cards and a brief explanation of each.

MACHINE WASH SYMBOLS

Machine Wash, Cold	Machine Wash, Cold, Gentle	Machine Wash, Warn	Machine Wash, Warm, Gentle

HAND WASH SYMBOLS

Do Not Wash	Hand Wash, Normal	Hand Wash, Cold	Hand Wash, Warm

DRY CLEAN SYMBOLS

Do Not Dry Clean	Dry Clean	Dry Clean, in Certain Solvents, Consult Cleaner	Dry Clean, Any Solvent

IRONING SYMBOLS

Do Not Iron	Iron Low Heat	Iron Medium Heat

DO NOT BLEACH SYMBOL

Do Not Bleach

DRYING SYMBOLS

Do Not Tumble Dry	Tumble Dry, Gentle, Low Heat	Dry Flat in Shade	Do Not Wring

STOCKISTS

For more information on overseas stockists and mail order details, please contact the Rowan distributor listed under each country. 'FLAGSHIP ....' stockists, carry the full range of Rowan Yarns.

ROWAN

County	Town / City	Stockist	Address	Postcode	Email	Website	Telephone	Yarn	Fabric	Online	Instore
			AUSTRALIA								
NSW	*Sydney*	*Morris and Sons (Distributor)*	*50 York Street*	*2000*		*morrisandsons.com.au*	*(02) 92998588*	•			•
VIC	*Melbourne*	*Morris and Sons (Distributor)*	*Level 1, 234 Collins Street*	*3000*		*morrisandsons.com.au*	*(03) 9654 0888*	•			•
ACT	Mawson	Stitch N Time	P O BOX 145	2607	dalenalan@bigpond.com		(02) 6282 8383	•			•
NSW	Avalon Beach	Avalon Fabrics & Crafts	Shop 4, 24 Avalon Parade	2107	info@avalonfabrics.com		(02) 99182978	•			•
NSW	Orange	Caboodle of Orange Gifts	186a Anson Street	2800	greenbrook@bigpond.com		(02) 6362 6310	•			•
NSW	Tweed Heads	Fantazia Fabricland	P O BOX 6113	2486	raso@netspace.net.au		(07) 5523 2220	•			•
NSW	Holbrook	Grandma's Closet	128 Albury Street	2644	grandmascloset@southernphone.com.au		(02) 6036 2322	•			•
NSW	Hornsby	Hornsby Wool & Craft Nook	Shop 3-3A, 25-31 Florence St	2077	hornsbywoolcraft@optusnet.com		(02) 9482 4924	•			•
NSW	Mosman	Mosman Needlecraft	Shop 3, 529 Military Road	2088	mosmanneedlecraft@bigpond.com		(02) 9969 5105	•			•
NSW	MERIMBULA	Pins & Needles	P O BOX 758	2548	tara.birdinatree@gmail.com		(02) 6495 3646	•			•
NSW	Pennant Hills	Sue's Cherryhills	Shop 7, 354 Pennant Hills Road	2120	cherryhills@live.com.au		(02) 9484 0212	•			•
NSW	Smeaton Grange	Tijuana	Unit 1/8 Blackmore Road	2567	sharon@tijuana-alpacas.com.au		(02) 4647 1155	•			•
NSW	Wollombi	Wollombi Wool Store	2883 Wollombi Road	2325	enquiries@wollombiwoolstore.com		(02) 4998 3154	•			•
NSW	Bowral	Wool Addiction	Shop 4, 31 Station Street	2576	jill@wooladdiction.com.au		(02) 4862 4799	•			•
NSW	Penrith	The Wool Inn	Shop 14 N & K Centre, 450 High Street	2750	penrith@the-wool-inn.com.au		(02) 4732 2201	•			•
NSW	Beecroft	Yarns & Gifts	Shop 8a 16-24 Hannah St	2119	yarns_and_gifts@optusnet.com.au		(02) 8407 9512	•			•
QLD	Booval	John Watts Sewing Machines	168 Brisbane Street	4304	info@johnwattssewing.com.au		(07) 3282 4711	•			•
SA	Gelenelg	Barb's Sew & Knits	2 Byron Street	5045	barb@barbssewandknits.com.au		(08)8294 7441	•			•
TAS	Moonah	The Wool Shop	P O Box 394	7009	woolsuppliers@bigpond.com		(03) 6278 1800	•			•
VIC	Brunswick	Clegs	P O BOX 185	3057	clegsbrunswick@clegs.com.au		(03) 9654 7677	•			•
VIC	LWR Templestowe	Wollybutt PTY Ltd	P O BOX 2493	3107	lorraine@woolybutt.com.au		(03) 9458 3101	•			•
VIC	Mansfield	Country Folk	P O BOX 233	3724	lafolk@bigpond.com		(03) 5775 2044	•			•
VIC	Oakleigh	Craftee Cottage	Shop 5 52-54 Atherton Road	3166	info@crafteecottage.com.au		(03) 9568 3606	•			•
VIC	Healesville	Crumbz Craft	P O BOX 1714	3777	shop@crumbz.com.au		0412 389192	•			•
VIC	Sassafras	Dalcheri Sassafras	Shop 2, 372 Mt. Dandenong Tourist Road	3787	dalcheri2@bigpond.com		(03) 9755 2510	•			•
VIC	Warrandyte	Needles And Pins	102 Melbourne Hill Road	3113	kayjay15@bigpond.com		(03) 9844 1720	•			•
VIC	Kyneton	Pick Up Stitches Pty Ltd	30 Piper Street	3444	sharon@pickupstitches.com.au		(03) 5422 6614	•			•
VIC	Blackburn	Sunspun	15 Myrtle Grove	3130	amy.doran@sunspun.com.au		(03) 9830 1609	•			•
VIC	Croydon	Threads of Nature	Shop 8, 30-32 Mcadam Square	3136	office@threadsofnature.com.au		(03) 9723 9242	•			•
VIC	Geelong	Twisted Threads	106 Ryrie Street	3220	mandy@twistedthreads.com.au		(03) 5221 0099	•			•
VIC	Mount Eliza	Windmills & Roses	36-38 Ranelagh Drive	3930	windmillsandroses@bigpond.com		(03) 9787 4949	•			•
VIC	Albert Park	Albert Park Wool Baa	124 Bridport Street	3206	sales@woolbaa.com		(03) 9690 6633	•			•
VIC	Northcote	Woolarium	211 A High Street	3070	sharron@woolarium.com		(03) 9486 5275	•			•
VIC	Surrey Hills	Wool Shop	486 Whitehorse Road	3127	woolshop@thewoolshop.com		(03) 9836 9614	•			•
WA	Mosman Park	Calico and Ivy	10 Glyde Street	6012	info@calicoandivy.com.		(08) 9383 3794	•			•
WA	Subiaco	Crossways Wool & Fabrics	Shop 15, Crossways S/CTR	6008	sales@crosswayswoolandfabrics.com.aucom.au		(08) 9381 4286	•			•
			AUSTRIA								
	Wien	*MEZ Harlander GmbH (Distributor)*	*Schulhof 6, 1. Stock, 1010*		*verkauf.harlander@mezcrafts.com*	*www.mezcrafts.at*	*0800 262 72 8 00*				
	Kitzbuehel	Kitzbuehel Handarbeiten	Im Gries Nr. 23	6370	kbhandarbeiten@networld.at		05356?2646	•			•
	Kolsass	Wolle + Staune (Sabine Schatz)	Auweg 2a	6114	kahn@wolleundstaune.at	www.wolleundstaune.at	0522467198	•			•
	Melk	Frau Wolle	Haupstr.11	3390			06604641203	•			•
	Wien	Laniato - das Wiener Wollcafe	Beatrixgasse 4	1030	wolle@laniato.com	www.laniato.com	069915249911	•			•
	Wien	Stick + Strick	Simmeringer Haupstrasse 86	1110	susanne.hasieber@stickundstrick.at	www.stickundstrick.at	69917494268	•			•
	Wien	Wollboutique Pinguin	Alserstrasse 21	1080	pingouin.wolle@yahoo.de	www.pingouinwolle.at	014080010	•			•
	Wien	Wolle fuer Mode Fleischmann	Neubaugasse 59/3	1070	evafleischmann@aon.at		015233394	•			•
	Mödling	Krawany GmbH	Hauptstrasse 83	2340	handarbeit@krawany.com	www.krawany.com	0223641500	•	•		•
	Wiener Neustadt	Wollerei Onlineshop	Grazer Strasse 90/1	2700	shop@wollerei.at	www.wollerei.at	069910330775	•		•	•
			BELGIUM								
		MEZ crafts Belgium NV (Distributor)	*MEZ GmbH Herbolzheim, Haupstasse, 79336*		*sales.be-nl@mezcrafts.com*	*www.mezcrafts.com*					
Oost-Vlaanderen	Lede	Petit Bear	Kasteeldreef 34	9340	kathba@hotmail.com		0486 31.37.94	•			•
	Antwerpen	Veritas	Nationalestraat 47	2000	aankoopcreatief@veritas.be	www.veritas.eu	03 361 06 61	•		•	•
	Antwerpen	**FLAGSHIP Lana**	**Anselmostraat 92**	**2018**	**info@lana-antwerpen.be**	**www.lana-antwerpen.be**	**03/ 238 70 17**	•		•	•
	Arlon	Veritas	Parc de l'hydrion, unité 8	6700	aankoopcreatief@veritas.be	www.veritas.eu	063 22 11 68	•		•	•
	Arlon	Brin De Soi	Rue des Faubourg 19	6700	brindesoi@skynet.be		063/ 445 680	•		•	•
	Assenede	Kashmire	Kloosterstraat 46	9960	info@kashmire.be		09 343 05 93	•		•	•
	Auvelais	Veritas	Rue du Bois Sainte Marie 124 Unit 14	5060	aankoopcreatief@veritas.be	www.veritas.eu	071 72 83 72	•		•	•
	Boortmeerbeek	Veritas	Leuvensesteenweg 381 - 383	3190	aankoopcreatief@veritas.be	www.veritas.eu	016/35.36.34	•		•	•
	Brasschaat	Genious	Augustijnslei 99	2930	greet@wollebolleke.be		0468 11 81 51	•		•	•
	Bredene	Veritas	Brugsesteenweg 9-35, 19 - Lokaal 19	8450	aankoopcreatief@veritas.be	www.veritas.eu	059 50 10 27	•		•	•
	Brugge	Veritas	Steenstraat 20	8000	aankoopcreatief@veritas.be	www.veritas.eu	050.33.77.90	•		•	•
	Brugge	Cathie's breiboetiek	Karel De Stoutelaan 22	8000	info@cathiesbreiboetiek.be	www.cathiesbreiboetiek.be	050/31.87.87	•		•	•
	Brussel	Veritas	Wolvengracht 14-16	1000	aankoopcreatief@veritas.be	www.veritas.eu	02 486 13 50	•		•	•
	Brussel	**FLAGSHIP Be creative by schleiper**	**63 Rue de l'Etang**	**1040**	**becreative@schleiper.be**	**www.becreativebyschleiper.com**	**02.541.05.12**	•	•	•	•
	Chênée	Rêve de quilts	Rue d'Embourg 29	4032	quiltsdream@skynet.be	www.revedequilts.be	0475 66 76 61	•	•	•	•
	Deinze	Perfecta	Markt 123	9800	info@perfectadeinze.be		09 386 71 74	•	•	•	•
	Eeklo	Hobbyfarm	Pastoor Bontestraat, 37	9900	hobbyfarm@pandora.be	www.hobbyfarm.be	09/3786664	•		•	•
	Eupen	Veritas	rue Mitoyenne 11/D	4837	aankoopcreatief@veritas.be	www.veritas.eu	087/461561	•		•	•
	Fleron	Veritas	Avenue des Marthyrs 269a-271-273	4620	aankoopcreatief@veritas.be	www.veritas.eu	04/3694861	•		•	•
	Gembloux	La boite au boutons	Rue Léopold 2	5030	info@buromatix.net		081 61 18 10			•	•
	Gent	Stoffenidee	Burgstraat 38A	9000	stoffenidee@skynet.be	www.stoffenidee.net	09/233.37.48	•		•	•
	Geraardsbergen	Maxime's Hobby	Guilleminlaan 237	9500	info@maximeshobby.com	www.maximeshobby.com	054/411145	•		•	•
	Hamme	Guy's Naaicentrum	Roodkruisstraat 98	9220	info@guysnaaicentrum.be	www.guysnaaicentrum.be	052/ 47 18 05	•	•	•	•
	Hasselt	Veritas	Koning albertstraat 5	3500	aankoopcreatief@veritas.be	www.veritas.eu	011.23.62.93	•		•	•
	Huy	Au Fil Des Laines	Rue du Pont 8	4500	roche.nathalie.34@gmail.com		085 84 64 32	•		•	•
	Kalken	Calcken	Brugstraat 12	9270	info@calcken.be	www.calcken.be	0494.37.56.35	•	•		•
	Keerbergen	Linnenmandje	Mechelsebaan 3	3140	linnenmand@hotmail.com		015 515 753	•			•
	Kraainem	Atelier de la passion	Avenue des Tarins 24	1950			02 731 85 83	•			•
	Landen	Nodo	Stationstraat 93	3400	info@nodo-mercerie.be		011.83.18.00	•	•		•
	Leper	Origami	Jules Capronstraat 10	8900	nicolie.origami@scarlet.be	www.hobbyshop-origami@skynet.be	057/216022	•	•	•	•
	Leuven	**FLAGSHIP Wolwinkeltje**	**Parijsstraat 25**	**3000**	**deforcerosemie@hotmail.com**	**www.twolwinkeltje.be**	**016 22 75 48**	•	•		•
	Leuven	Veritas	Brusselsestraat 26-30	3000	aankoopcreatief@veritas.be	www.veritas.eu	016.23.90.65	•		•	•
	LIEGE	TRICOTEA	Rue du Laveu 30	4000	info@valeureux.be		0477.91.25.02	•			•
	Lochristi	Veritas	Antwerpsesteenweg 91	9080	aankoopcreatief@veritas.be	www.veritas.eu	09/3420633	•		•	•
	Lokeren	Veritas	Zelebaan 75	9160	aankoopcreatief@veritas.be	www.veritas.eu	09/360.50.26	•		•	•
	Lokeren	De Wolkamer	Gentsesteenweg 477	9160	therese.coens@telenet.be		09/355 20 55	•			•
	Leuven	Veritas	Brusselsestraat 26-30	3000	aankoopcreatief@veritas.be	www.veritas.eu	016/23.90.65	•		•	•
	Mechelen	Veritas	Ijzerenleen 40-42	2800	aankoopcreatief@veritas.be	www.veritas.eu	015/20.10.33	•		•	•
	Mechelen	Huis Inge Goderis	O.L.V. straat 131-133	2800	info@dehandwerkwinkel.be	www.dehandwerkwinkel.be	015.41.40.54	•			•
	Merksem	Veritas	Bredabaan 970	2170	aankoopcreatief@veritas.be	www.veritas.eu	03 644 06 01	•		•	•
	Olen	Veritas	Lammerdries Winkelstraat 4 unit B6a	2250	aankoopcreatief@veritas.be	www.veritas.eu	014 22 91 68	•		•	•
	Ronse	Creasis VOF	Jan van Nassaustraat 10	9600	creasis@telenet.be	www.creasis.be	0495 70 81 90	•	•	•	•
	Roeselare	Veritas	Brugsesteenweg 343 Unit 12	8800	aankoopcreatief@veritas.be	www.veritas.eu	051 22 95 50	•		•	•
	ROESELARE	CLARA'S WOL	Lepersestraat 199	8800	info@claraswol.be						•
	Schelle	Veritas	Boomsesteenweg 37	2627	aankoopcreatief@veritas.be	www.veritas.eu	03 449 36 29	•		•	•
	Sint-Denijs-Westrem	Veritas	Kortrijksesteenweg 1118	9051	aankoopcreatief@veritas.be	www.veritas.eu	09 221 64 79	•		•	•
	Sint Truiden	mercerie GOVAERTS bvba	Markt 61	3800		www.merceriegovaerts.be	011/682288	•	•	•	•
	Sint-Genesius-Rode	The Cosy Cottage	Lindestraat 16	1640	thecosycottage@skynet.be		02 361 70 72		•		•
	Sint-Niklaas	Baele Naaicentrum	Ankerstraat 53	9100	info@baelenaaicentrum.be	www.baelenaaicentrum.be	03.776.16.26				
	Sint-Pieters-Leeuw	Veritas	Bergensesteenweg 65	1600	aankoopcreatief@veritas.be	www.veritas.eu	02 331 19 15	•		•	•
	Stabroek	Dolce Lana	Laageind 3B	2940	info@dolcelana.be	www.dolcelana.be	03/689 24 88				
	Torhout	Lana Exclusief	Oostendestraat 88A	8820	retrans@skynet.be	www.lana-exclusief.be	050/213632	•		•	•
	Tournai	Paprika Cotton	Rue Saint-Martin 62	7500		www.paprikacotton.be	069/235383	•			•
	Turnhout	Veritas	Gasthuisstraat 40	2300	aankoopcreatief@veritas.be	www.veritas.eu	014/41.22.95	•		•	•
	Waanrode	Vlijtig Bijtje	Dorp 12	3473	het.vlijtig.bijtje@skynet.be		016.49.00.16	•	•		•
	Werchter	Vlijtig Bijtje	Hoge Weg 1	3118	het.vlijtig.bijtje@skynet.be		016.53.16.16	•	•		•
	Westerlo	Atelier Salgarollo	Koning Leopoldlaan 16	2260	kristel.salgarollo@telenet.be	www.salgarollo.be	014 264 393	•			•
	Wevelgem	Veritas	Kortrijkstraat 337	8560	aankoopcreatief@veritas.be	www.veritas.eu	09 262 03 47	•		•	•
	Willebroek	Mooi Gemaakt	Mooi Gemaakt	2830	info@mooigemaakt.be		O3 336 27 59	•	•		•
	Wilsele	D.Yarns	P.Van Langendoncklaan 17	3012	d_van_nueten@hotmail.com		(016) 20 13 81	•			•
			BULGARIA								
	Sofia	*MEZ Crafts Bulgaria EOOD (Distributor)*	*25A, Rozhen Blvd.*	*1220*	*office.bg@mezcrafts.com*	*www.mezcrafts.com*	*+359 2 439 24 24*	•	•		
			CANADA								
North Carolina	*Hickory*	*Sirdar USA Inc (Distributor)*	*406 20th Street SE*	*28602*	*sirdarusa@sirdar.co.uk*		*828 404 3705*	•	•	•	•
AB	Canmore	Yarn & Company	#105 717 9th Street	T1W 2V7	yarncanmore@gmail.com		(403) 675-9276	•			•
AB	**Calgary**	**FLAGSHIP Pudding Yarn**	**1516 6th Street SW**	**T2R 0Z8**	**sschuld@puddingyarn.com**		**(403) 244-2996**	•			•
AB	**Edmonton**	**FLAGSHIP River City Yarns, Ltd**	**16956-111 Ave**	**T5M 4C9**	**barb@rivercityyarns.com**		**(780) 477-9276**	•			•
AL	Lethbridge	Knitting Time	1240 2nd Avenue A North	T1H 0E4	sales@knittingtime.com		(403) 320-5648	•			•
BC	Vancouver	Three Bags Full Knit Shop	4458 Main Street	V5V 3R3	francesca@threebagsfull.ca		(604) 874-9665	•			•
BC	Vancouver	Pretty Good Ideas Ltd		V5L 1B1	nicole@prettygoodideas.ca		(604) 807-8865	•			
BC	Victoria	Beehive Wool Shop	1700 Douglas Street	V8W 2G7	beehivewoolshop@telus.net		(250)385-2727	•			•
BC	Surrey	Valley Yarn Ltd.	#192 6758 188 Street	V4N 6K2	info@valleyyarn.com		(604) 576-4222	•			•
BC	Port Moody	Black Sheep Yarns LTD	88 Grant Street	V3H 0B6	helen@blacksheepyarns.ca		(778) 355-9665	•			•
BC	**Vancouver**	**FLAGSHIP Urban Yarns Ventures**	**4437 West 10th Avenue**	**V6R 2H8**	**knitting@urbanyarns.com**		**(604) 228-1122**	•			•
BC	Kamloops	Knit 2 Yarns	40-1967 Trans Canada Hwy East	V2C 4A4	contact@knit2yarns.com		(250) 314-027[illegible]	•			•
BC	Vernon	A Twist of Yarn	3915 31 Street	V1T 5J7	info@atwistofyarn.com		(250) 549-42[illegible]	•			•
BC	Prince George	Top Drawer Yarn Studio	#203 1685 Third Avenue	V2L 3G5	topdraweryarn@yahoo.com		(250) 596-4276	•			•
BC	Comox	Village Yarn Shoppe	103A - 1705 Comox Ave	V9M 3N1	jacquie@villageyarnshoppe.ca		(250) 339-2474	•			•
BC	Armstrong	The Twisted Purl	2451 Pleasant Valley Rd	V1T 6M6	thetwistedpurlyarnstuido@shaw.ca		(250) 542-7432	•			•
BC	Richmond	Wool & Wicker Sales Ltd	130-12051 Second Ave	V7E 3L6	dianedebray@shaw.ca		(604) 275-1239	•			•
MB	**Winnipeg**	**FLAGSHIP Wolseley Wool Ltd.**	**889 Westminster Avenue**	**R3G 1B4**	**info@wolseleywool.com**		**(204) 772-5648**	•			•
NS	Wolfville	Gaspereau Valley Fibres	830 Gaspereau River Rd.	B4P 2N5	brenda@gasperequvalleyfibres.ca		(902) 542-2656	•			•
ON	**Orleans**	**FLAGSHIP Wool N' Things**	**1439 Youville Drive**	**K1C 4M8**	**gisele@woolnthings.com**		**(613) 841-8689**	•			•
ON	McGregor	Sue2Knits	12045 Ducharme Lane	N0R 1J0	sue2knits@gmail.com		(519) 726-4226	•			•
ON	Port Elgin	Dockknits	Box 2140 651 Goderich Street	N0H 2C0	dockknits@eastlink.ca		(226) 453-5648	•			•

County	Town / City	Stockist	Address	Postcode	Email	Website	Telephone	Yarn	Fabric	Online	Instore
ON	Carleton Place	The Real Wool Shop	142 Franktown Road	K7C 3P3	woolshop@wool.ca		(613) 257-2714	•			•
ON	Toronto	Eweknit	875 Bloor Street W	M6G 1M2	claudia@eweknit.ca		(416) 530-4438	•			•
ON	Perth	Unraveled	53 Wilson Street E		beckie@unraveled.ca		(613) 565-1505	•			•
ON	Lindsay	Aberdeen's Wool Company	228 Kent Street West	K9V 2Z2	heather@aberdeenswool.com		(705) 928-5417	•			•
ON	**Ancaster**	**FLAGSHIP The Needle Emporium**	**420 Wilson Street East**	**L9G 2C3**	**julie@needleemporium.com**		**(905) 648-1994**	•			•
ON	**Toronto**	**FLAGSHIP Romni Wools**	**658 Queen Street W**	**M6J 1E5**	**jonathon@romniwools.com**		**(416) 703-0202**	•			•
QC	Owen Sound	Riverside Yarns	928 2nd Aye E	N4K 2H6	willow@riversideyarns.ca		(519) 371-4311	•			•
QC	Montreal	Espace Tricot Inc	6050 Monkland Avenue	H4A 1H2	info@espacetricot.com		(514) 486-2648	•			•
QC	Sutton	Mont Tricot	50-K Principale North	J0E 2K0	monttricot@gmail.com		(450) 538-8040	•			•
QC	Quebec	Boutique Point Mousse	3146 de Versailles	G1X 1E4	pointmousse.ca@gmail.com		(418) 651-2352	•			•
QC	St. Eustache	Tricotine et cie	112 B Rue St. Laurent	J7P 5H1	bianca@tricotine.ca		(450) 974-1313	•			•
QC	L'Ile Perrot	Marie Mode Tricot	200 Grand Boulevard	J7V 4X1	mariemodetricot.ca		(514) 453-1708	•			•
QC	Gatineau	Magifil	317 Boul St. Joseph	J8Y 3Z1	lorra@hotmail.com		(819) 595-3694	•			•
QC	St-Jn-S-Richlieu	Tricolane	231 Rue Saint-Jacques	J3B 2K6	info@tricolane.com		(450) 346-0990	•			•
SK	Saskatoon	Prairie Lily Knitting	7-1730 Quebec Avenue	S7K 1V9	prairielilyknitting@saskatool.com		(306)665-2771	•			•
SK	Humboldt	Humboldt Haus of Stitches	626 Main Street	S0K 2A0	haus.stitches@sasktel.net		(306) 682-0772	•			•

CHINA

County	Town / City	Stockist	Address	Postcode	Email	Website	Telephone	Yarn	Fabric	Online	Instore
China	Shanghai	Shanghai Yujun CO. LTD (Distributor)	Room 701 Wangjiao Plaza, No.175 Yan'an Road	200002	jessechang@vip.163.com		86-21-63739785	•			
Germany		Mr Victor Li (Commercial agent)	c/o MEZ GmbH Hauptstasse, Herbolzheim, Germany		victor.li@mezcrafts.com		+86 13816681825				
China	Shanghai	Ning Tian international Trading CO.LTD		200002	tangning95@outlook.com		82-21-31220391				
China	ZhengZhou	Ru Yi Cultural Development CO.LTD		450000	2585742685@qq.com		86-371-65770660				

CYPRUS

County	Town / City	Stockist	Address	Postcode	Email	Website	Telephone	Yarn	Fabric	Online	Instore
	Sofia	MEZ Crafts Bulgaria EOOD (Distributor)	7 Magnaurska Shkola Str., BG-1784		office.bg@mezcrafts.com	www.mezcrafts.com	+359 2 439 24 24	•	•		

CZECH REPUBLIC

County	Town / City	Stockist	Address	Postcode	Email	Website	Telephone	Yarn	Fabric	Online	Instore
	Praha	MEZ Crafts Czech Republic, s.r.o. (Distributor)	Na poříčí 1079/3a, Praha	110 00	info@mezcrafts-cz.cz	info@mezcrafts-cz.cz		•	•		
	Ceske Budejovice	Tvoriva Ovecka	Obchod Tvoriva Ovecka, Plachého 299/22	370 01	welcome@dextera.cz	www.tvoriva-ovecka.cz	420607949059				

DENMARK

County	Town / City	Stockist	Address	Postcode	Email	Website	Telephone	Yarn	Fabric	Online	Instore
	Rodovre	Carl J. Permin A/S (Distributor)	Egegårdsvej 28	2610	permin@permin.dk	www.permin.dk	45 36 36 89 89	•			
	Alborg	Design Værkstedet	Boulevarden 9	8000	butik@design-vaerkstedet.dk		45 98 12 07 13				
	Århus	City Stoffer	Park Alle 9	8000	mail@citystoffer.dk	www.citystoffer.dk	45 86 19 03 93				
	Århus	Garnkisten	Volden 19	8000	kontakt@garnkisten.dk	www.garnkisten.dk	45 86 19 40 44				
	Bogense	Garngut	Adelgade 40 A	5400	mail@garngut.dk	www.garngut.dk	45 64 81 11 88				
	Blåvand	Ho Strik	Hovej 21	6857	info@hostrik.dk	www.hostrik.dk	45 75 27 54 03				
	Esbjerg	Esbjerg Garn	Østre Gjesingvej 13	6715	info@esbjerggarn.dk	www.esbjerggarn.dk	45 53 38 45 38				
	Fanø	Kutstladen	Postvejen 29	6720	kunstladenfano@gmail.com		45 75 16 35 04				
	Frederikshavn	Living By Vanja	H.C. Ørstedsvej 18	9900	info@livingbyvanja.dk	livingbyvanja.dk/by-vanja	4525824757				
	Give	Min Garnbutik Givskud	Vejlevej 65, Givskud	7323	0509497@minkobmand.dk		45 22 52 29 69				
	Haderslev	Garnache	Nørregade 7 St.	6100	connyboysentreddersen@gmail.com		45 75 85 87 57				
	Haslev	Knithouse Denmark ApS	Hesede Hovedgård 3	4690	oliver@isabellasmith.com	www.knithouse.dk	45 55 94 14 85				
	Hjørring	Knudegarn	Strandvejen 94	9800	tina@knudegarn.dk	www.knudegarn.dk	45 40 98 13 37				
	Hornslet	Uldfisken	Tingvej 7B	8543	fischer-tilt@mail.dk	www.fischer-tilt.dk	45 86 97 51 33				
	Horsholm	Engle Stof	Usserod Kongevej 10 A	2970	englestof@mail.dk		45 45 86 33 78				
	Kgs. Lyngby	Uldstedet	Gl. Jernbanevej 2	2800	uldstedet@uldstedet.dk	www.uldstedet.dk	45 45 88 10 88				
	Kobenhavn K	Sommerfuglen	Vandkunsten 3, Kbh.K	1467	mail@sommerfuglen.dk	www.sommerfuglen.dk	45 33 32 82 90				
	Kobenhavn K	Uldstedet	Vendersgade 3	1363	uldstedet@uldstedet.dk	www.uldstedet.dk	45 33 91 17 71				
	Kolding	Cashmere Company	Skovlokkevej 11	6000	lisa.repner@post.cybercity.dk	www.symaskineland.dk	45 20 32 08 22				
	Ribe	Ribes Broderi & Garn	Dagmarsgade 4	6760	symaskineland@symaskineland.dk		45 75 42 16 37				
	Ringsted	S.P Garn	Søgade 28	4100	spgarn@hotmail.com		45 57 61 56 37				
	Roskilde	Garnhokeren	Karen Olsdatterstræde 9	4000	annette@wilson.dk	www.onskegarn.dk	45 46 37 20 63				
	Søby Ærø	Tjes Strik	Albertsvkke 10	5985	bch.tisvilde@mail.dk		45 40 29 16 83				
	Silkeborg	Onskegarn	Nygade 7	8600	sus.garnstricken@gmail.com	www.onskegarn.dk	45 86 81 05 07				
	Skanderborg	Stof og Sy	Adelgade 123	8660	info@stofogsy.dk	www.stofogsy.dk	45 86 52 02 45				
	Slangerup	Paradisets Bamser, Tøj og Brugskunst	Kvindørupvej 17	3550	pia.freck@mail.tele.dk	www.butikparadiset.dk	45 47 33 58 60				
	Steje	Sy og Strik	Storegade 70	4780	j.naur@mail.dk		45 55 81 41 31				
	Tarm	Uldgarden	Herbækvej 12 Vostrup	6880	uldgaarden@uldgaarden.dk	www.uldgaarden.dk	97 37 42 73				

EIRE

County	Town / City	Stockist	Address	Postcode	Email	Website	Telephone	Yarn	Fabric	Online	Instore
Co. Clare	Tulla	Saoire	Tulla Stables Studio				353876496040	•			•
Co. Cork	Kinsale	Vivi's Trading Company	16 Main Street	P17VX83			353 21 470 0000	•			•

ESTONIA

County	Town / City	Stockist	Address	Postcode	Email	Website	Telephone	Yarn	Fabric	Online	Instore
Harjumaa	Tallinn	Mez Crafts Estonia OÜ (Distributor)	Helgi tee 2, Peetri alevik	75312	info.ee@mezcrafts.com	www.mezcrafts.ee	+372 6 306 759	•	•		
Harjumaa	Tallinn	Kaubamaja kodumaailm	Gonsiori 2	10143							
Harjumaa	Tallinn	Karnaluks	K.A Hermanni 1	10121							
Harjumaa	Tallinn	Kasitoojaam	Pärnu mnt 238	11624							
Harjumaa	Tallinn	Kosmose Lõngapood	Pärnu mnt 46	10119		www.pood.kasitoojaam.ee					
Viimsi	Viimsi	Kauplus Piste	Randvere tee 6	74001							
Parnumaa	Pärnu	Kauplus "Nidid, Nöobid"	Turihe 3	80011							
Tartumaa	Tartu	Vikkel Kasitöötarbed	Rüütee 76	51014		www.vikkel.ee					
Saaremaa	Kuressaare	Lõngapood	Tallinna tn 9	93813							

FAROE ISLANDS

County	Town / City	Stockist	Address	Postcode	Email	Website	Telephone	Yarn	Fabric	Online	Instore
	Klaksvik	Búnin	Nolsgarpálsgota 18, Box 282	700	bunin2010@hotmail.com		298 455210	•			•

FINLAND

County	Town / City	Stockist	Address	Postcode	Email	Website	Telephone	Yarn	Fabric	Online	Instore
	Kerava	Prym Consumer Finland Oy (Distributor)	Huhtimontie 6	FI-04200			358 9 274871	•			
	Espoo	Menita Outlet	Ylakartanontie 26	5360		www.fiinneule.fi	358 9 250/7536				
	Helsinki	Titinneule	Isonniitynkatu 5	100	helsinki@menita.fi		358 9 47890065				
	Helsinki	Oy Menita Ab	Korkeavuorenkatu 20	120			358 9 6343 844				
	Järvenpää	Lentävä Lapanen	Mannilantie 30	4200	info@lentavalapanen.fi		358 50 434 2374				
	Joensuu	Joensuun Käsityovakka	Kauppakatu 30	80100	myyriti@kasityovakka.fi	www.kasityovakka.fi	358 400 602 908				
	Kirkkonummi	Mannran Tupa	Torihe 3	2400			358 45 2311470				
	Kuopio	Kuopion Nauha ja Nappi	Vuorikatu 23	70100			358 44 5575545				
	Oulu	Nappi Kikka Design Atelieé Oy	Pakkahuoneenkatu 18	90100	nappikikka@gmail.com		358 17 2165756				
	Pantine	Tapio E. Neyanpaa	Oikotie 4	61980	info@tapionkauppa.net	www.lankatalo.net	358400362416				
	Sastamala	Silmu & Solmu	Marttilankatu 16	38200	info@silmusolmu.fi	www.silmusolmu.fi	358 50 407 5758				

FRANCE

County	Town / City	Stockist	Address	Postcode	Email	Website	Telephone	Yarn	Fabric	Online	Instore
	Toulouse	3hcom (Distributor)	35 avenue de Larrieu	31094	Commercial@3h-com.com		0033 (0) 562 202 096	•			
	Angers	Nos Ouvrages	12 Rue Chapernomare	49010			02 41 88 37 66				
	Azày Le Rideau	Theophile	11 Rue Nationale	37190	theophile37@hotmail.fr		02 48 28 19 80				
	Besançon	La Boîte a Laine	15 Rue Xavier Marnier	25000	contact@laboitealaine-besancon.fr		06 07 23 25 37				
	Bordeaux	**FLAGSHIP La Lainerie**	**22 rue des Ayres**	**33000**	**la.lainerie@orange.fr**	**www.lalainerie.com**	**05 56 81 43 92**				
	Briançon	L'Atelier de la laine	2 Rue Pasteur	5100	ruthphilip@email.com		04 92 20 45 60				
	Cesson	ABC laines	1068 Route de Lucats	77240	abclaines@orange.fr		06 69 52 11 28				
	Colmar	Ambiance Laine	5 Rue Des Pretres	68000	info@ambiance-laine.fr	www.ambiance-laine.fr	03 89 41 82 71				
	Gerardmer	Rosavril	43 rue Charles De Gaulle	88400	rosavril@laposte.net		03 29 41 35 49				
	Gisors	Pretty Laine	29 Rue Louis Pasteur	27140	contact@prettylaine.com	www.prettylaine.com					
	Grenoble	Jus d'carottes	5 Rue de Genissieu	38000	jusdcarottes@gmail.com		04 80 38 27 41				
	Joigny	Lady Laine	47 bis rue Gambetta	89300	ladylaine.joigny@wapadoo.fr	www.ladylaine.fr	03 86 62 23 61				
	La Réunion (ile de)	ce a nwin	Sainte Clothilde	97490	cahoarca@orange.fr	www.ceanwin.re	2620697 30 39 08				
	Levallois-Perret	Laines en Vogue	36 rue Gabriel Peri	923000	contact@milllemillersdemailles.fr	www.millemillersdemailles.fr	01 47 57 58 64				
	Montpellier	Anne Ouvrages	28 Rue Paul Brousse	34000	anneouvrages@bbox.fr		04 67 92 50 92				
	Nancy	2 Aiguilles dans la Cafetière	5 rue Gustave Simon	54000	www.annexpays.fr		03 83 39 46 70				
	Oyoninax	La roulotte des laines		01100	contact@laroulottedeslaines.fr	www.leslaines.com	06 33 43 33 40				
	Parents en Borne	Sur la rive coté laine	1068 Route de Lucats	40160	robelmvirgmne@gmail.com	www.surlarivecotelaine.fr	06 33 43 32 40				
	Paris	Le Minor	5 Rue du Sabot	75006	sandra.kremmer@neuf.fr		07 78 69 12 92				
	Paris (6)	LIL WEASEL	1 passage du grand cerf	75008	contact@lilweasel.com	www.lilweasel.com	01 73 71 70 48				•
	Paris (9)	Le Comptoir	26 rue Cadet	75009			01 42 46 20 75				
	Ploeren	1000 et 1 mailles	38 Rue de 2 moulins	56880	1000et1mailles@gmail.com	1000et1mailles@gmail.com	09 86 16 10 18			•	
	Poitiers	La Mercerie	9 rue Lebascles	86000	boutiquelecomptoir@gmail.com	www.lapetiteboutiqueducomptoir.fr	05 49 52 52 62				
	Rennes	LTM	1 Rue Hoal001 Duparc	35000	ltm.hobby@wanadoo.fr		05 44 78 15 95				
	Sarzeau	Les chemins buissonniers	1 place Marie Le Franc	56370			02 97 48 08 30				
	Thonon les Bains	Au vieux rouet	7 rue Ferdinand Dubouloz	74200	auvieuxrouet@orange.fr		04 50 71 07 33				
	Toulouse	Jeu de mailles	18 J. Perrin, Le Chapitre Actisud, Bat	31100	contact@jeudemailles.com	www.jeudemailles.com	05 34 27 62 31			•	
	Tours	La Boîte a Laine	37, rue du Grand Marché	37000	laboitealaine@orange.fr	http://milb-div.com/	02 47 75 42 02				
	Vichy	MIHI / Argan Agnes	14 Rue du Lery	03200	agnes@maillesshop.fr	www.maillesshop.fr	04 70 31 37 02				

GERMANY

County	Town / City	Stockist	Address	Postcode	Email	Website	Telephone	Yarn	Fabric	Online	Instore
	Herbolzheim	MEZ GmbH (Distributor)	Hauptstrasse 78	79336	endverbraucherservice@mezcrafts.com	www.mezcrafts.com	+49 (0) 7643 33 30 288	•			
	Aachen	StrickStück	Harscampstraße 81	52062	info@strickstueck.de	www.strickstueck.de	0151 64414900				
	Arnsten	Jutta Heurung	Markstr. 5	97450			09363 6975				
	Augsburg	Augsburger Restehaus	Vorderer Lech 39	86150	augsburger@der-stoff.de		0821 519019				
	Bad Hindelang	Schlaterladen	Am Bauernmarkt 2	87541	info@schaeferladen.de	www.schaeferladen.de	08324 8620				
	Bad Iburg	Outlet Wollecke Bad Iburg	Fuchbreite 17a	49186	outlet-wollecke@t-online.de						
	Bad Neuenahr-Ahrweiler	Dat Lädche	Niederhutstr. 17	53474	dat-laedche_adams@t-online.de	www.dat-laedche.de	02641 1464				
	Bad Segeberg	Woll-Idgen	Kirchstraße 34	23795	wollidgen@web.de		04551 80953348				
	Bamberg	Wollstudio Pfund	Promenade 4	96047	wollstudio@fritzi.pfund.de	www.wollstudio-pfund.de	0951 2022173				
	Berlin	Knit Knit	Lnienstr. 154	10115	mail@knitknit.de	www.knitknit.de	030 98366430				
	Berlin	Simply Stitch	Dietzgenstraße 88	13156	info@simplystitch.de	www.simplystitch.de	030 47489698				
	Betzdorf	Herzstücke	Wilhelmstr. 13	57518	angelikahfedrich@gmail.com	www.denheherzstuecke.de	02741 9494209				
	Bielefeld	Haken & Stricken nach Maaß	Westerfeldstr. 22	33611	info@haken-stricken.de	www.haken-stricken.de	0521 3842043				
	Bocholt	Neue Masche	Nordstrasse 49	46399	info@neuemasche.de	www.neuemasche.de	02871 2373601				
	Bremen	Wollpar A. Heyn	Bruggeweg 40-42	28309			0421 413869				
	Bremen	Woolbar	Hindenburgstr. 39	28205	info@woolbar.de	www.woolbar.de	0421 63925133				
	Buchloe	Rosine	Bahnhofstr. 50	86807	info@rosine-stoffe.de		08241 966033				
	Coburg	**FLAGSHIP umGarnt**	**Judengasse 1 a**	**96450**	**info@umgarnt.de**	**www.umgarnt.de**	**09561 7958133**				
	Creuzburg	Wollmaus-Wolle	Adelbert-Kühmstädt-Str. 2	99831			036926 90411				
	Dachau	Cotton Club	Konrad-Adenauer-Str. 20	85221	info@cotton-club-dachau.com	www.cotton-club-dachau.com	08131 736859				
	Dannenberg	Annette Gierow	Lange Str. 32	29451	roterfaden@arcor.de		05861 970050				
	Dornhan	Regi's Wollstube	Rossgartenstr. 14	72175			07455 2785				
	Dresden	nach Strick und Faden	Rothenburger Str. 14	01099	nachstrickundfaden@web.de		87104086				
	Dresden	Woll-Kontor	Friedrich-Wieck-Str. 4	1326	info@wollkontor-dresden.de	www.wollkontor-dresden.de	0351 4007040130				
	Emmering	Luise stricken nähen schenken	Kirchplatz 7	82275	info@luise-online.net	www.luise-online.net	08141 3634839				
	Eslingen	Schergerei	Markplatz 2	73728	info@schergerei.de		0711 35151111				
	Felsberg-Gensungen	Wolle 7	Bahnhofstr. 8	34587	info@wolle7.de	www.wolle7.de	05662 4005350				
	Felsburg	Wollsucht	Rote Str. 16	24937	info@wollsucht.de	www.wollsucht.de	0461 3183454				
	Frankfurt am Main	Wolle-Boutique Elffein	Eckenheimer Landstr. 34	60318	k-elffein@web.de		069 95909164				
	Frankfurt am Main	Maschenwerke	Marburger Str. 4	60487	maschenwerke@t-online.de	www.maschenwerke.de	069 71 58 89 80				
	Freiburg	Welt der Handarbeit	Salzstr. 57-59	79098	info@welt-der-handarbeit.de		0761 2 75201				
	Garmisch-Partenkirchen	Edith Vogel	Ludwigstr. 87	82467			08821 72761				
	Hagen	Der Wollwichtel	Im Mühlenwert 20	58135	info@derwollwichtel.de		02331 7379433				
	Hamburg	Karstadt Warenhaus GmbH	Mönckebergstraße 16	20095							
	Hamburg	Purpur-Wolle	Heußweg 41b.	20255	info@purpurwolle.de	www.purpurwolle.de	040 4904579				
	Hanau	Wollparadies	Bangerthstr. 2	63450	info@wollparadies-Hanau@web.de	www.wollparadies-hanau.de	06181 5072732				
	Hannover	Wollkultur	Salstr. 81	30171	info@wollkultur.de	www.wollkultur.de	0511 3009622				
	Heppenheim	Alpaka	Markstr. 18	64646	hennes-schaab@web.de	www.alpaka-online.de	06252 25887				
	Hochstadt	Lämma Wolle	Kellerstr. 35	35315	info@lamma-wolle.de		09564 800120				
	Hofheim	Clothild Wollwerk	Hauptstr. 29	65719	clothild.wollwerk@t-online.de		06192 6827937				
	Holzgerlingen	Handmade	Tübinger Str. 31	71088	handmade@t-online.de		07031 2044732				
	Hoyerhagen	Waltraud Elsner	Hauptstr. 44	27318	blumenstube-hoyerhagen@gmx.de		04251 93477				
	Karlsruhe	Senci	Amalienstr. 81	76133	info@turmwaren-senci.de	http://naehzentrum-senci.de/	0721 25033				
	Kassel	Fil Garn Wolle	Friedrich-Ebert-Str. 147	34119	info@fil-garn-wolle.de	www.fil-garn-wolle.de	0561 710929				
	Kiel	Dörte Dietrich	Damaschkeweg 50a	24113	info@wollwerkstatt-kiel.de	www.wollwerkstatt-kiel.de	0431 2405493				
	Kirchheim	Beggs	Schuhstr. 5	73230			07021 145271				
	Ladenburg	Zierstich	Hauptstr. 48	68526	meinzierstichladen@kabelbw.de		06203 9270957				
	Langenau	Wolle & Mehr	Bahnhofstr. 3	89129	wollelangenau@aol.com		07345 5371933				
	Laupheim	Hobbykunst	Mittelstr. 36	88471	mail@hobbykunst-laupheim.de		07392 9674934				
	Leutkirch	Brigitta Schwarz-Frehner	Markstr. 30	88299			07561 7963				
	Lindau	Ernstädchen	Gothestr. 27	4981	info@ernslaedchen.de	www.ernslaedchen.de	08382 75072				
	Lüneburg	stricx	Reicherbachstr. 2	11335	stricx@stricx.de	www.stricx.com	04131 6030731				
	Mainz	Wollzeit Wolle in Mainz	Flststr. 2	55166	stricx@t-online.de		06131 347796				
	Marburg	Wolle-Lädchen Marburg	Frauenbergstr. 13	35039	wolle-laedchen@t-online.de		06421 34230				
	München	Die Mercerie	Nymphenburger Str. 96	80636	info@diemercerie.de	www.diemercerie.de	089 12003316				
	München	Wolle und Schönes	Wasserburger Landstraße 250	81827	wolleundschoenes@t-online.de	www.wolleundschoenes.de	0894 309534				
	Nürnberg	Tolle Wolle	Weinmarkt 10	90403	mail@tollewolle.de	www.tollewolle.de	0911 209497				
	Nürnberg	Katharina Stumpf	Zerzabelshofer Hauptstr. 4	90480			0911 4645566				
	Offenbach	Maschenwahn	Taunustr. 1	63065	maschenwahn@posteo.de		069 82720353				
	Oldenburg	Die Strickadel	Lindenalle 56	26122			0441 39021818				
	Osnabrück	Woll-Perle	Hakenstr. 3	49074			0541 258561				
	Paderborn	handewurk	Rathausplatz 5	33098			0651 87691571				
	Pirmasens	Wollkörbchen Hügel	Turolerstraße 51	66954			06331 84333				
	Ratingen	Wollkörbchen	Turmstr. 30	40878			02103 553797				
	Reutlingen	Wolle und Mehr	Metzgerstr. 64	72764			07121 310488				
	Rheinberg	Handarbeit	Kamper Strasse 37	47495			02843 959435				
	Salzhausen	Wollart Ole Rudat	Hauptstr. 8	21376	info@wollart.de	www.wollart.de	04172 969123				
	Schorndorf	Isy's Kreativinsel	Gottlieb-Daimler-Straße 32	73614	info@kreativinsel-schorndorf.de		07181 480917-0				

County	Town / City	Stockist	Address	Postcode	Email	Website	Telephone	Yarn	Fabric	Online	Instore
	Schwandorf	Wollwerkstatt	Pfleghofstufen 2	92421	wollwerkstatt@wolle-kreatives.de		09431 7547845	•			•
	Siegen	Stecknadel	Rathausser. 2	57078	creativ@stecknadel.info	http://www.stecknadel.info	02718 9002667	•			•
	Soest	Der Faden	Potsdamer Platz 1	59494			02921 3192277	•			•
	Solingen	Wollfühloase Koch	Ohligser Markt 9	42697			0212 66884	•			•
	Stadtlohn	**FLAGSHIP Wolle und Design**	**Benzstrasse 1**	**48703**	**info@wolleunddesign.de**	**www.wolleunddesign.de**	**02563 98208**	•	•		•
	Steinhude	Schönwerk	Vor dem Tore 1	31515	info@schoenwerk-steinhude.de	www.schoenwerk-steinhude.de	05033 9965071	•			•
	Sulzbach a.d.Murr	Flour-Bretschneider Schettler	Haller Str. 1	71560	m.schetter-flour@vonhand.info	www.vorhand.info	07193 6492	•			•
	Ulm	**FLAGSHIP Wolle & Ideen**	**Kornhausgasse 6**	**89073**	**Heike@Redlinghaus.de**	**www.wolleundideen.de**	**0731 619491**	•	•		•
	Ulm	Rockn Woll	Söflingerstr. 214	89077	rocknwolldesign@aol.com	https://www.rocknwoll-shop.com/	731388203	•		•	•
	Winsen/ Aller	Rumpelkammer	Celler Str. 11	29308	schroeter-winsenaller@t-online.de		0514 35336	•			
			GREECE								
	Sofia	*MEZ Crafts Bulgaria EOOD (Distributor)*	*7 Magnaurska Shkola Str., BG-1784*		*office.bg@mezcrafts.com*	*www.mezcrafts.com*	*+359 2 439 24 24*	•	•		
			HOLLAND								
	Wilnis	*Brouwer & Zn B.V (Distributor)*	*Oudhuijzerweg 69,*	*3648 AB,*	*info@gbrouwer.nl*		*0031 (0) 297-281 557*	•			•
	Alblasserdam	Koperdraadje	Scheldeplein 15	2953 EV	info@koperdraadje.nl	www.koperdraadje.nl		•			
	Ambt Delden	Het Haakwinkeltje	Werninksweg 2	7495 TA	info@hethaakwinkeltje.nl	www.hethaakwinkeltje.nl	074 3765195	•			•
	Amsterdam	**FLAGSHIP de Afstap (Lonnie Bussink)**	**Oude Leliestraat 12**	**1015 AW**	**info@afstap.nl**	**www.afstap.nl**	**020-6231445**	•			•
	Arnemuiden	Atelier Jaffari	Markt 1	4341 EG	jaffari@zeelandnet.nl	www.jaffari.nl	0118 604031	•			•
	Barneveld	Woolfactory	Jan van Schaffelaarstraat 15	3771 BR	info@woolfactory.nl	www.woolfactory.nl	06-20321327	•			•
	Bergen	Finlandia	Kleine Dorpsstraat 26	1861 KN	info@finlandia.nl	www.finlandiaimport.nl	0725 894642	•			•
	Den Ham	De Wolboutique	Dorpstraat 44	7683BK	info@dewolboutique.nl	www.dewolboutique.nl	0546-672271				•
	Driebergen	Trollenwol	Traay 7	3971 GB	info@trollenwol.nl	www.trollenwol.nl	0343-750700	•			•
	Eindhoven	Breimode Brigitte	Ouverture 212	5629 PX	info@brigitte-handwerken.nl	www.brigitte-handwerken.nl	040-2435576	•			•
	Etten-Leur	De Wolboetiek	Bisschopsmolenstraat 169	4876 AL		www.wolboetiek.nl	076-5022597	•			•
	Haarlem	WOL!	Barrevoetestraat 9	2011 WN	barte892@planet.nl	www.wol-online.nl	063 1780100	•			•
	Heerlen	Ut Bolke	Benzenraderweg 92	6417 SV	info@utbolke.nl	www.utbolke.nl	045 /571 64 51	•			•
	Huizen	De Pauw	Voorbaan 25	1271RR	info@handwerkzaakdepauw.nl	www.handwerkzaakdepauw.nl	035 525 1212	•			•
	Joure	Ajoure	Pastorielaan 2	8501 EZ	info@ajoure.nl	www.ajoure.nl	051/3413344	•			•
	Kampen	Pingouin wol & handwerken	Oudestraat 20	8261 CP	pingouinkampen@uwnet.nl		038-3322811	•			•
	Koewacht	Wolboerderij Blij Bezuiden	Het Zand 61	4576 CB	info@wolboerderij.nl	www.wolboerderij.nl	114361402	•			•
	Leiden	Ribbels	Pieterskerk-Choorsteeg 18	2311 TR	annelies.danton@ribbels.nl	www.ribbels.nl	071 5133126	•			•
	Oldenzaal	Lohuis	Steenstraat 26	7571 BK	t.lohuis@planet.nl	www.lohuis-tijhuis.nl	05415-12626	•	•		•
	Rijssen	Het Wolhuis	Haarstraat 148	7462 AV	info@hetwolhuis.nl	www.hetwolhuis.nl	0031 548 78 52 75	•			•
	Sittard	Wollstreet	Rijksweg Noord 61	6131 CJ	info@wollstreet.nl	www.wollstreet.nl	0464-586330	•			•
	Utrecht	Modilaine	Lijnmarkt 22	3511 KH	info@modilaine.nl	www.modilaine.nl	030-2328911	•			•
	Voorburg	Wollig	Herenstraat 95	2271 CC	info@wollig-online.nl	www.wollig-online.nl		•			
	Workum	It Nifelhoekje	it Sud 81	8711CT	info@itnifelhoekje.nl	www.itnifelhoekje.nl	0515 542501	•			•
	Zaandam	Zaans Geluk	Kleine tocht 7L	1507 CB	info@zaansgeluk.nl	www.zaansgeluk.nl	075-6124024	•			•
	Zuidlaren	Ryahuis	Telefoonstraat 26	9471 EN	info@ryahuis.nl	www.ryahuis.nl	050-4092618	•			•
			HONG KONG								
GERMANY	*Herbolzheim*	*MEZ GmbH (Distributor)*	*Haupstrasse 78*	*79336*	*endverbraucherservice@mezcrafts.com*	*www.mezcrafts.com*	*+49 (0) 7643 33 30 288*	•	•		
			HUNGARY								
Pest	Budapest	Gombolyda Fonalbolt	József körút 15.	1085	info@gombolyda.hu	www.gombolyda.hu	06-1-404-5990	•		•	•
Hajdú-Bihar	Debrecen	Gombolyda Fonalbolt	Miklós utca 16.	4225	info@gombolyda.hu	www.gombolyda.hu	06-52-954-561		•		• •
Pest	Budapest	Kriza Marketing & Design Kft.	Aradi Vertanuk u. 23.	1213	info@kezimunkazokboltja.hu	www.kezimunkazokboltja.hu		•		•	
			ICELAND								
	Rødovre	*Carl J. Permin A/S (Distributor)*	*Egegårdsvej 28*	*2610*	*permin@permin.dk*	*www.permin.dk*	*45 36 36 89 89*	•			•
	Reykjavik	Storkurinn	Síðumúli 20	0101	storkurinn@storkurinn.is	nytt.storkurinn.is	354 551 8258	•			•
			ITALY								
MI	*MILANO*	*Mez Cucirini (Distributor)*	*Via Milanese 20, Sesto San Giovanni*	*20099*	*servizio.clienti@mezcrafts.com*	*www.mezcucirini.it*	*0039 0264109080*	•			•
AN	SENIGALLIA	GIRALDI MERCERIE	CSO 2 GIUGNO 80	60019			+39 07163831	•			•
AR	SAN GIOVANNI VALDARNO	AGO E SVAGO DI REDAELLI SIMONETTA	VIA PIAVE 58	52027	simonettaredaelli@live.it		+39 0555275984	•			•
AT	ASTI	LA BOTTEGA DI EVELINA	VIA GIOVANNI GIOBERT 62	14100	ducatipaso@yahoo.it		+39 0141595579	•			•
BA	BARI	CREATTIVA SRL DI MANCINO SECCIA	VIA PASUBIO 43	70125	creattiva.srl@gmail.com		+39 0809678609	•			•
BG	SUISIO	GOGIANDO di A. B.	PIAZZA MARTIRI DI VIA FANI 1/B	24050	gogiando@gogiando.com		+39 3662704081	•			•
BG	BERGAMO	SAVOIR FAIRE di SECOMANDI UGO	VIA CORRIDONI 28/E	24124	ambra.lupini@alice.it		+39 3358075069	•	•		•
BL	TAIBoN AGORDINO	EL GEM DA TIZIANA di DAI PRA	VIA COMEDON 15	32027	elgem.tiziana@libero.it		+39 043765259	•			•
BL	BELLUNO	GOMITOLO D'ORO DI ZAMPIERI RENATA	VIA 30 APRILE 1	32100			+39 0437940516	•			•
BL	CORTINA D'AMPEZZO	LA COOPERATIVA DI CORTINA S.C.	CORSO ITALIA 40	32043	info@coopcortina.com	www.coopcortina.com	+39 0436861245	•			•
BO	S.GIOVANNI IN PERSICETO	AGOFILO di FRASCARI CLAUDIO	VIA MODENA 40	40017	claudio.frascari@agofilo.com	www.agofilo.com	+39 051 822002	•			•
BO	BOLOGNA	ATELIER DELLA LANA DI NINETTA	VIA RIALTO 19/C	40124	nbadile@gmail.com	www.atelierdellalana.it/	+39 051238268	•			•
BO	BOLOGNA	CASA DELLA LANA	VIA AUGUSTO RIGHI 19	40126	monica@cinius.com		+39 051227731	•			•
BO	SAN LAZZARO DI SAVENA	CUCILANDIA BOLOGNA	VIA CARLO JUSSI 71	40068	info@cucilandiabologna.it	www.cucilandiabologna.it	+39 0516271610	•			•
BO	IMOLA	DRITTO FILO DI BARBIERI STEFANIA E PRESTA ILARIA S	VIA PISACANE 43	40026	ilaria.presta71@gmail.com			•			•
BO	CREVALCORE	FILIVARI LA BOTTEGA DEL FILO	VIA MATTEOTTI 247	40014	filivari.bottegadelfilo@gmail.com		+39 3311881062	•			•
BO	BOLOGNA	IL MONDO DI ALICE di EMANUELA BONOR	VIA CASTIGLIONE 58/A	40124	ilmondodialicesnc@libero.it		+39 051744835	•			•
BO	CASTEL SAN PIETRO	MOLINARI DI RAGGI ROBERTA & C. SNC	VIA MATTEOTTI 116	40024	raggiroberta64@gmail.com		+39 051 6958688	•			•
BR	BRINDISI	ARTEMAGLIA DI D'ADDARIO ANTONELLA	VIA APPIA 136	72100	artemaglia@alice.it	www.artemagliacreazioni.it	+39 346 3025490	•			•
BS	DESENZANO DEL GARDA	AMARENGO SRL	VIA BRESCIA 56	25015	amarengo2015@gmail.com		+39 3806371589	•			•
BS	CHIARI	CASA DEL TENDAGGIO	VIA S.MARTINO DELLA BATTAGLIA 13	25032	alessia.vago@alice.it	www.casadeltendaggiomorsia.com	+39 030712022	•			•
BS	CASTENEDOLO	CDB MERCERIE di CASAROTTI A.	VIA BRESCIA 65/67 c/o CITYPER	25014	info@casadelbottone.com		+39 030 2131204	•			•
BS	PROVAGLIO D'ISEO	L'AGORAIO	VIA FIUME 8	25050	info@agoraio.it	www.agoraio.it	+39 0305057946	•			•
BS	BRESCIA	LE FORBICI D'ORO S.R.L.	VIA DELLE BATTAGLIE 8	25122	leforbicidoro@gmail.com		+39 03044203	•			•
BS	BRESCIA	LILLA E LAVANDA DI BONETTI	VIA CAVOUR 28	25122	lillaelavanda@libero.it		+39 3892854758	•			•
BS	MONTICHIARI	SOTTOPUNTO di PIRAS ILARIA	VIA CESARE BATTISTI 8	25018	sottopunto.ilaria@hotmail.it	www.sottopunto.altervista.org	+39 3401578197	•			•
BZ	MERANO	AMALALANA di ISOARDI PAOLA	VIA PORTICI 170	39012	paolaisoardi@gmail.com	www.amalalana.it	+39 3393377936	•			•
CN	BRA	ATTISANIVITTORIA	VIA PIUMATTI 76	12042			+39 017244769	•			•
CN	BORGO SAN DALMAZZO	BRICIOLE DI FANTASIA	VIA LOVERA 31	12011	patdif@libero.it		+39 3495315516	•			•
CO	SORICO	BLANCHE	VIA BOSCHETTO 45	22010	info@blanche-atelier.com		+39 335 6219732	•			•
CR	CREMONA	GOMITOLI di MANGIAROTTI MONICA	CORSO MATTEOTTI 90	26100	monimoni64@gmail.com	gomitolicremona.altervista.org	+39 338 2802699	•			•
CT	MISTERBIANCO	SCUDERI ROSALINDA	VIA DEIVESPRI 236	95045	info@perfilopersegno.it	www.perfilopersegno.it	+39 347 5539876	•			•
FC	CESENA	JOLLY CASA DI DEGLI ANGELI SILVIA	FIORENZUOLA 193	47023	jolly_casa@libero.it	www.jollycasahobbistica.it	+39 0547303026	•			•
FC	CESENA	L'AGO E IL DITALE DI CANTONI LUGHI	VIA STRINATI 6	47521	manuela.cantonilughi@alice.it	www.lagoeilditale.it	+39 0547610296	•			•
FC	FORLI'	PUNTI E SPILLI di MORELLI	PIAZZETTA DELLA GRATA 1	47121	info@puntiespilli.it	www.puntiespilli.it	+39 3667200509	•			•
FI	FIRENZE	LA MERCERIA DEL 900 DI RUSSI STEFAN	VIA DEL POLLAIOLO 108 ROSSO	50142	lamerceriadel900@gmail.com		+39 339 5315731	•			•
FI	TAVARNUZZE	PUNTO SU PUNTO DI MANCINI MARTINA E MANCINI AMMA S	VIA MONTEBUONI 194	50029	info@puntosupunto.it		+39 3409387371	•			•
GE	GENOVA	FONTE DELLA LANA	GALATA 27 R	16121	rita.rollino@gmail.com		+39 010562594	•			•
GE	GENOVA	IL SALOTTO DELLA MADDA SNC DI CINZIA NIVES DE BONI	VIA DELLA MADDALENA 28/30 R	16124	nivesdb@libero.it		+39 010 2091782	•			•
GE	GENOVA	TASSAROLO ANGELA	VIA GIANELLI 91 R	16166	mariangelapontenani@gmail.com		+39 0103725221	•			•
GE	RONCO SCRIVIA	ZIG ZAG DI BARBARINO GIULIA CRISTINA	VIA ROMA 57	16019	zigzag1963@libero.it		+39 3405249077	•			•
GR	GROSSETO	CASA DEL BOTTONE SNC ELLI SANTINI	VIA PAGLIALUNGA 8	58100	mariapiasantini@virgilio.it		+39 056 423971	•			•
IM	DIANO MARINA	BOTTERO MAURA	CORSO ROMA 153	18013	botteromaura@gmail.com		+39 0183 498671	•			•
IS	ISERNIA	BRUSCO ROSARIA	CORSO GARIBALDI 195	86170			+39 086550648	•			•
LE	TRICASE	ANTICA MERCERIA SAS DI CITO IMMACOLATA & C.	VIA L. CADORNA 127	73039	antica-merceria@libero.it		+39 0833543011	•			•
LE	CUTROFIANO	GATTAMATTA SRL	VIA VINCENZO COLI 25	73020	gattamattamaglie@alice.it		+39 0836427805	•			•
LE	CASARANO	IL FILO DI MARIANNA DI PRETE MARIANNA	CORSO XX SETTEMBRE 133	73042	mariannaprete@libero.it		+39 3336784948	•			•
LE	CARMIANO	LA MATASSA DI BENEGIAMO MARIA	VIA REGINA ELENA N.3	73041	mariaritabenegiamo@libero.it		+39 3297859440	•			•
LE	TREPUZZI	PEZZUTO MARIA ANGELA	VIA MONTALE 1	73019	mary1288@live.it		+39 3404957321	•			•
LI	COLLESALVETTI	LA MIA IMPRONTA DI STEFANIA SOZZI	VIA ROMA 236	57014	stefania.sozzi@gmail.com		+39 3476970362	•			•
MI	MILANO	DO KNIT SRL	VIA MOSCATI 20-ANG.VIA CANONICA	20154	do-knit@libero.it	www.do-knit.it	+39 3391242881	•			•
LO	S.ANGELO LODIGIANO	LA BOTTEGA DELLO SCAMPOLO	VIA CESARE BATTISTI 8	26866	Elena.dioli@yahoo.it		+39 037192584	•			•
LO	LODI	LA VIA LATTEA SRL	CORSO ARCHINTI 33	26900	info@penelopeknit.it		+39 3925670758	•			•
LT	CISTERNA DI LATINA	CREIAMO INSIEME	VIA LEONARDO DA VINCI 35	04012	lucidiantonella@virgilio.it		+39 347 8608525	•			•
LU	LUCCA	L'ARCOLAIO DI PASQUINELLI E RAGONE	PIAZZA CITTADELLA 11	55100			+39 0583580248	•			•
LU	PIETRASANTA	LE COSE DI STEFANIA DI VEZZONI STEFANIA	VIA DEL MARZOCCO 128	55045	info@lecosedistefania.it	www.lecosedistefania.it	+39 0584793647	•			•
MB	SEREGNO	I FILATI INCANTATI di ALTOMONTE FRA	VIA MEDICI DA SEREGNO 14	20831	afrancesca590@gmail.com		+39 3381842937	•			•
MC	MACERATA	MENICHELLI - RAMBOZZI DI L.B. & C.	PIAZZA C. BATTISTI 14	62100	merceriamenichelli@libero.it		+39 0733232628	•			•
MI	VIMERCATE	IL BOTTONE di FENAROLI MARIA TERESA	VIA DE CASTILLIA 14	20059	mt.fenaroli@gmail.com		+39 039660890	•			•
MI	MILANO	PLANA MERCERIA	VIA PLANA 43	20155	merceriaplana@gmail.com		+39 02 33002241	•			•
MI	MILANO	STIM ITALIA SRL	VIA TROYA 7	20144	info@stim-italia.com	www.stim-italia.com	+39 3929236898	•			•
MI	MILANO	TRICOTS DI GUIRTI CHIARA	PIAZZA SIENA 8	20146	chiarastella.guirti@fastwebnet.it	www.tricots.it	+39 024075777	•			•
MN	MANTOVA	IL FILO DI USVARDI FRANCA	VIA ALDO MORO 10	46100	usvardifranca@mantovamail.it		+39 0376321637	•			•
MN	CASTIGLIONE DELLE STIVIERE	PUNTI & SPUNTI di MENTA E. e A. SNC	VIA MAZZINI 14	46043	elena.menta@libero.it		+39 340 2978508	•	•		•
MO	MODENA	DRITTO E ROVESCIO	LARGO S. FRANCESCO 144	41121	tizianasoncini@tiscali.it		+39 059 4555316	•			•
MO	FORMIGINE DI MODENA	ZA-MA S.N.C.	VIA DON MINZONI 1/B	41043	marisazampieri@hotmail.it		+39 059 571364	•			•
NA	NAPOLI	CUCISHOP DI PAOLA DORA	GALLERIA VANVITELLI 13 VOMERO	80129	info@cucishop.it	www.cucishop.it	+39 0815584007	•			•
PD	PADOVA	BIASIOLI DONATELLA	GALLERIA S. CARLO 10	35133			+39 049600498	•			•
PD	NOVENTA PADOVANA	CELIN MARILENA "PRIMO LABORATORI	VIA VALMARANA 49/C	35027	primo.laboratorio@libero.it		+39 0498959126	•	•		•
PD	PADOVA	LANE NUOVE DI BARCELLAN MARINA	VIA BARBARIGO 6	35141	barcellan.marina@libero.it		+39 3477109016	•			•
PG	SPOLETO	CIMARELLI AGOSTINA	VIA PASQUALE LAURETI 15	06049			+39 074349450	•			•
PG	CASTIGLIONE DEL LAGO	LANDI SIMONETTA	VIA SESTINO 12 -LOC.BADIACCIA	06061	lslucianosimonetta@gmail.com		+39 0758230220	•			•
PG	TODI	PAZZAGLIA ELISABETTA	VIA S.AGOSTINO 5	06059	gervasi_alessandro@alice.it		+39 0758942580	•			•
PI	PISA	CASA DELLA MERCERIA DI TARABELLA MARZIA	VIA D'AZEGLIO 15	56100	marziatarabella@alice.it		+39 3355956139	•			•
PO	PRATO	PERLE DI ALESSANDRA GHERI	VIA F. FERRUCCI 339/3	59100	perle.ale@libero.it	www.merceriaperle.it	+39 0574575144	•			•
PR	PARMA	DALL'ARGINE - dett	PIAZZA GHIAIA 5	43100	info@dallargine.it		+39 0521607989	•			•
PT	PISTOIA	BORSELLI FILATI	VIA CAN BIANCO 9	51100	nestbor61@gmail.com		+39 0573 26101	•			•
PV	PAVIA	BOUTIQUE LANA CIOTTI DONATELLA	VIA MASCHERONI 18	27100			+39 038223675	•			•
PZ	LAURIA SUPERIORE	L'ALBERO DELLE IDEE S.R.L. ARTIGIANTATO E DESIGN	VIA ROCCO SCOTELLARO 139	85044	marialongo70@gmail.com		+39 3293933769	•			•
RA	FAENZA	IL GOMITOLO DIETRO L'ANGOLO	VIA TORRICELLI 23/A	48018	elisaemiliani@ymail.com	www.ilgomitolodietrolangolo.com	+39 328 6693475	•			•
RA	LUGO DI ROMAGNA	SCARDOVI SNC - SCARDOVI STEFANO & C	VIA MENTANA 71	48022	info@scardovi.com		+39 054526997	•			•
RE	SCANDIANO	IL FILO DI ARIANNA DI GRISENDI ROBE	VIA GARIBALDI 9/C	42019			+39 0522984736	•			•
RE	MONTECCHIO EMILIA	MONTEPIETRA MERCERIA	PIAZZALE CAVOUR 3	42027	merceria_montepietra@libero.it	www.merceriamontepietra.it	+39 0522865658	•	•		•
RM	ROMA	CA.FI.LAN S.R.L.	VIA U. BIANCAMANO 7	00185	info@cafilan.com	www.lanaefilati.com	+39 067000503	•			•
RM	ROMA	CAPUANI MARIANTONIETTA	PIAZZA DELLA TORRETTA 22	00186	mc.capuani@gmail.com		+39 06 6871215	•			•
RM	ROMA	CIOTTI BARBARA	VIA DELLO STATUTO 70	00185	barbaraciotti@inwind.it	www.centrocucitocreativo.com	+39 064872814	•			•
RM	GUIDONIA	CREANDO CON AZZURRA DI AZZURRA MARINO	VIA DEI GIRASOLI 45	00012	info@creandoconazzurra.com	www.creandoconazzurra.com	+39 0774304006	•			•
RM	ROMA	ELLA SAS DI CASPONI MIRELLA	VIA VINCENZO TIERI 215	00123	ella_arte@hotmail.com		+39 0630894351	•			•
RM	ROMA	GENOVESI MIRELLA	L.GO S. EUFRASIA PETTETIER 13	00151	cgenovesi@toy-roma.net		+39 06-58232305	•			•
RM	ROMA	GOMITOLANDO S.R.L.	VIA IGNAZIO GIORGI, 42/44	00162	info@gomitolando.it	www.gomitolando.it	+39 06 45428653	•			•
RM	ROMA	IL TRIANGOLO DI NUNZIATA CRISTINA	VIA DEGLI ORAFI 79	00133	merceriailtriangolo@gmail.com		+39 062023299	•			•
RM	ROMA	LA CARTARECCIA SRLS	VIA DOMENICO PURIFICATO 170	00125	info@lacartareccia.com	www.lacartareccia.com	+39 0652351018	•			•
RM	FIUMICINO	L'ANGOLO DELLE IDEE DI TIZIANA GIAMBARTOLOMEI &C S	VIA TRINCEA DELLE FRASCHE 168/172	00054	s.angolodelleidee@gmail.com		+39 06 65024516	•	•		•
RM	MONTEROTONDO	PERFETT'ARMONIA SNC DI TIZIANA SANTINI E C	VIA EDMONDO RIVA 17	00015	perfettarmonia@gmail.com		+39 0662286823	•			•
RM	ROMA	TUTTO CASA SNC	VIA DI CASALOTTI 103	00166	lorenzodigianni@yahoo.it		+39 0661550920	•			•
RN	RIMINI	BENVENUTI MERC.ADRIATICA	VIA CLEMENTINI 31	47921	mail.signorile@gmail.com		+39 0541 29400	•			•
RO	OCCHIOBELLO LOCALITA' S.MARIA MADDALENA	MONIA FILATI di MONIA COLOGNESI	VIA ERIDANIA 243	45030	monia.colognesi@gmail.com		+39 3921650412	•			•
SI	SARTEANO	IL MONDO DI FRANCESCA DI FRANCESCA GIULIACCI	P.ZZA BARGAGLI 16	53047			+39 347 905 4544	•			•
SI	SIENA	RAFFAELLA di RAFFAELLA CHELLINI	VIA CAMOLLIA 148	53100	studioguerrini@infinito.it		+39 057741161	•			•
SI	POGGIBONSI	SUL FILO DI LANA SNC	VIA SENESE 85	53036		www.sulfilodilana.it	+39 0577 982110	•			•
SP	LA SPEZIA	CERRETTI E C. SNC	CORSO CAVOUR 178	19121	info@cerrettisnc.com	www.cerrettisnc.com	+39 0187735108	•	•		•
SV	CAIRO MONTENOTTE	BRUZZONE P&C SAS	VIA ROMA 91	17014	patriziabruzzone@gmail.com		+39 019503664	•			•
SV	ALBISOLA SUPERIORE	MERCERIA E BIANCHERIA DEL CORSO DI GIANNELLI ANTON	CORSO FERRARI 121	17011	merceriadelcorso@libero.it		+39 0197700510	•			•
TA	MANDURIA	ANRY TUTTO CREA DI DISTRATIS ANTONIO	VIA BELL'ACQUA 3	74024	valeriodistratis@hotmail.it		+39 3391291430	•			•
TA	MARTINA FRANCA	PRETTY MODA DI LEO MARIA	VIA ELIO VITTORINI, 70-72	74015	mariaitleo@alice.it		+39 328 7158227	•			•
TE	GIULIANOVA LIDO	CHIOVI CLAUDIO	VIA NAZARIO SAURO 78	64021			+39 0858004668	•			•
TN	ROVERETO	INCANTESIMO di STEFANO GIOS	VIA RIALTO 58 / 1	38068	incantesimosg@teletu.it		+39 0464 435776	•			•
TO	LEINI'	FILOFILA' di QUARANTOTTO FABIO	VIALE EUROPA 38/B	10040	fabio.filofila@gmail.com		+39 011276 2097	•			•
TO	PINEROLO	FILOSOFIA DI ANTONELLA MELONI	VIA BUNIVA 23	10064	antonella.meloni@gmail.com		+39 3406491860	•			•
TO	TORINO	LA COMPAGNIA DEL COTONE DI DANIELA BASSO & C.	VIA MAZZINI 44	10123	lacompagniadelcotone@tiscali.it		+39 0118178381	•	•		•
TO	IVREA	MERCERIA CRISTINA DIVAIO CRISTINA	VIA CIRCONVALLAZIONE 34	10015	vaiocri@hotmail.it		+39 340 4760973	•			•
TO	TORINO	WOOL CROSSING di GIUDICE FEDERICA	VIA BOCCACCIO 58	10132	federica@woolcrossing.it	woolcrossing.it	+39 3482905189	•			•
TS	TRIESTE	FONDA SILVA SAS	VIA DELLE TORRI 2	34122	roberta.zu.ars@gmail.com		+39 040771717	•			•
TV	VEDELAGO	BARICHELLO SAS DI BARICHELLO PRIMO	VIA VICENZA 20	31050	barichellosas@tiscali.it	www.bottegabarichello.com	+39 0423 700167	•			•
TV	TREVISO	LA MERCERIA PREZZEMOLO	VIA CAMPANA 9	31100	eugenia.dapolito@alice.it		+39 0422 412898	•			•
UD	UDINE	ELISA CESSELLI DI FOI CATERINA	VIA SAVORGNANA 18	33100	caterina.foi@libero.itc		+39 0432 295633	•			•
VI	SAN GIUSEPPE CASSOLA	SIMONCELLO PATRICK	VIA ROSSINI 3	36022				•			•
VR	VERONA Loc. PARONA	FALCETTO S.N.C. DI RIGHETTI LAURA E	VIA DEGLI ARUSNATI 3	37025	info@falcetto.it		+39 045941091	•	•		•
CA	CAGLIARI	PAOLO MELONI SRL	VICO III SANT AVENDRACE 5	9122	paolomeloni@paolomeloni.it	www.paolomeloni.it	+39 070288863	•			
VE	PORTOGRUARO	LANE E FILATI GRAZIELLA	VIA MAZZINI 9	30026			+39 042174808	•			
TV	GODEGA DI S. URBANO	LUISETTA MERCERIA SAS di ULIVATI MARIA	VIA S.URBANO 71	31010	info@luisettamercerie.it	www.luisettamercerie.it	+39 0438430095	•			
PD	ESTE	FANIN LUCIA "NONSOLOMERCERIE"	VIA G. MARCONI 15	35042	lucia@nonsolomercerie.com	www.nonsolomercerie.com	+39 3924340248	•			
VE	VENEZIA	PERTILE MARIANNA MACRIPE	CANNAREGIO 2629	30121	nanni.mp@libero.it		+39 041 8228247	•			
BZ	PRATO ALLO STELVIO	BERGER GERDA	VIA PRINCIPALE 83	39026	unikatbyg.berger@gmail.com		+39 3471747558	•			
TN	BREGUZZO	VIOLET di FERRARI FULGIDA	VIA ROMA 51	38081	fulgida.ferrari@hotmail.it		+39 3338610671	•			
VI	ARZIGNANO	BEVILACQUA LANE SRL	VIA DELL'INDUSTRIA 41	36071	info@bevilacqualanesrl.it	www.bevilacqualanesrl.it	+39 0444 671460	•			
BZ	LANA	ANIMA SNC	VIA GRIES 14	39011	info@anima-lana.it		+39 0473562191		•		
CN	GHIGO IVANA	CARRU'	P.ZZA DANTE 14	12061			+39 017375429	•			
TO	CESANA TORINESE	BLANCHET GIUSEPPINA	VIA ROMA 46	10054	blanchetgiuseppina@gmail.com		+39 012289437	•			
CS	MORMANNO	PAPPATERRA LEONTINA	VIA ROMA 65	87026	nunzia78@hotmail.com		+39 3290913982		•		
PR	PARMA	NON SOLO LANA SAS di CAGGIATI CATIA	STRADA NINO BIXIO 15	43100			+39 3343011306		•		
VI	BASSANO DEL GRAPPA	F.LLI CAMPAGNOLO di CAMPAGNOLO	PIAZZA GARIBALDI 28	36061	campagnolo@tintes.it		+39 0424521732		•		
LU	LUCCA	LOVILANE di CECCHINI PAOLO	VIA FILLUNGO 160	55100			+39 0583467042		•		

County	Town / City	Stockist	Address	Postcode	Email	Website	Telephone	Yarn	Fabric	Online	Instore
BO	CASALECCHIO DI RENO	BARBIERI SERGIO snc	VIA PASCOLI 3	40033	basergio@alice.it		+39 051572162		•		
NU	BUDONI	DARIMAN di VENTRONI ANGELO	VIA PIEMONTE SNC	8020	dh.coseecasa@yahoo.it		+39 0784842015		•		
CS	CASTROVILLARI	MODA MERCERIA di SANCINETO	VIA POLLINO 92 B	87012	modamerceria@gmail.com		+39 0981480406		•		
UD	CERVIGNANO DEL FRIULI	MODAMAGLIA di PERIC MARTA	VIA XXIV MAGGIO 19/1	33052	martaperic72@gmail.com		+39 043132753		•		
BO	BOLOGNA	IL FILARINO di ROTINO LORENZA	VIA MURRI 88/A	40135	info@ilfilarino.it		+39 3393110527		•		
BO	BAZZANO VALSAMOGGIA	MACRAME' 23 di FABBRI ISABELLA	VIA MATTEOTTI 9	40053	info@macrame23.it		+39 3487366385		•		
VR	MONTECCHIA DI CROSARA	BOTEGA PAGANI	VIA CADUTI DEL LAVORO	37030	botegapagani@email.it		+39 3774423419		•		
ME	S.LUCIA DEL MELA	DONATO CATENA	VIA SAN SEBASTIANO 13	98046			+39 3337830675		•		
VR	LUGAGNANO	FAST RICAMI SRL	VIA VENETO 3	37060	info@fastricami.it		+39 0458680344		•		
AO	AOSTA	GROS CIDAC SRL	VIA PARAVERA 4	11100	centralino@groscidac.it		+39 0165237611		•		
GO	GORIZIA	BONI MERCERIE di GIANI ORNELLA	VIA GARIBALDI 9/C	34170	groroberta@libero.it		+39 0481537532		•		
GR	FOLLONICA	OFFICINA DEL CUCITO di BALANESCU	VIA C. COLOMBO, 4	58022	officinadelcucitofollonica@gmail.com		+39 3472257662		•		
BZ	BRUNICO	HOTEL TEXTIL SRL	VIA BRUNICO, 18/A	39030	gattereri@hotex.it		+39 0474479170		•		
RN	SANTARCANGELO DI ROMAGNA	MERCERIA IL GOMITOLO DI DE IESO	VIA ANDREA COSTA 135/B	47822	elena.deieso@studio.unibo.it		+39 3395850728		•		
MI	MILANO	PUNTO DOPO PUNTO di A. GUELI E FIGLI	VIA ETTORE PONTI 21	20143	puntodopopunto@outlook.it		+39 0289125636		•		
MI	MILANO	FLE' R di FRANCESCA FUMAGALLI	VIALE SAN MICHELE DEL CARSO 10	20144	francesca.fumagalli1@gmail.com		+39 3355333653		•		
PG	SPOLETO	MERCERIA AUGUSTA DI SANTINI SERENA	VIA PASQUALE LAURETI 15	6049	serena-91@libero.it		+39 3292598929		•		
JAPAN											
Chiyoda-ku	Tokyo	Daidoh International Ltd.	Sotokanda 3-chome, PUPPY Div. / 1-16	101-8619			0081-3-3257-7135	•			•
Hiroshima	Hiroshima	Puppy Hiroshima	8-16 kamihacchoubori, nakaku	730-0012			81-082-222-0537	•			•
Hukuoka	Kitakyusyu	Izutsuya Department Store	2-4 igashiko, Kokurakitaku	803-0802			81-093-522-2729	•			•
Hyogo	Kobe	Union Wool	1-30-22 Kitanagasadori, Chuouku	650-0012	union@smile.ocn.ne.jp		81-078-331-8854	•			•
Osaka	Osaka	Hankyu Department Store	8-7 kakudacho, Kitaku	530-8350			81-06-6313-8938	•			•
Osaka	Osaka	Masuzakiya	4-5-4 Kawaramachi, Chuouku	541-0048			81-06-6222-1110	•			•
Osaka	Osaka	Room Amie	3-11-8-109Yamate-cho, Suita-city	564-0073	info@roomamie.jp	http://roomamie.jp	81-06-6821-3717	•			•
Tokyo	Tokyo	Mitsubaya	1-1-1 Minamiaoyama, Minatoku	107-0062			81-03-3404-1677	•			•
Tokyo	Tokyo	Mitsukoshi Department Store	Hobby & Craft Salon 8F Mitsukoshi New Bild., 1-4-1 Nihonbashi Chuouku	103-8001			81-03-3273-6500	•			•
Tokyo	Tokyo	Puppy Shimokitazawa	2-26-4 Kitazawa, Setagayaku	155-0031			81-03-3468-0581	•			•
Tokyo	Tokyo	Seibu Department Store	100 idee 7F Seibu Ikebukuro, 1-28-1 Minami-Ikebukuro Toshima-ku				81-03-3983-5433	•			•
KOREA											
Seoul	***Jongno-Gu***	***My Knit Studio (Distributor)***	***3F, 144 Gwanhun-Dong***	***110-300***	***myknit@mykint.com***	***www.myknit.com***	***82-2-722-0006***	•			•
Seoul	Jongno-Gu	Danju	1F, 65-4 Samcheong-Ro	110-200	jade@danju.co.kr	www.danju.co.kr	82-2-720-1127	•			•
Seoul	Seongbuk-gu	KNITCAFE, Co, Ltd	503, Bansuk Tower	110-2829			10 9975 0659	★			
LATVIA											
	Jūrmala	latvian Crafts	12-2, Jurģu street	LV-2011	vjelkins@latviancrafts.lv	www.latviancrafts.lv	37126326825	•	•	•	
LEBANON											
	Beirut	***y.knot (Distributor)***	***Saifi Village, Mkhalissiya Street 162***		***y.knot@cyberia.net.lb***		***(961) 1 992211***	•			•
LITHUANIA											
	Vilnius	***MEZ Crafts Lithuania UAB (Distributor)***	***A. Juozapaviciaus str. 6/2,***	***LT 09310***	***info.lt@mezcrafts.com***	***www.mezcrafts.lt***	***0037052072002***				
	Kaunas	kaSiulai.lt	Parduotuve "Siulai", Savanoriu pr. 192C	LT44151	parduotuve@kasiulai.lt	www.kasiulai.lt	0037068227187	•	•	•	•
	Kaunas	Karaliska Vilna	Vilniaus g. 39-1b, Kaunas	LT44288	karaliskavilna@gmail.com	www.karaliskavilna.com	0037069966699	•		•	•
	Kaunas	Siūlo galas	Kestucio str. 80-9	LT44297	info@siulogalas.lt	www.siulogalas.lt	00370 682 47 334	•		•	
	Siauliai	Casa Lana Siūlų namai, A. Mažeikio įmonė	Vilniaus g. 255	LT76010	g_mazze@yahoo.com		0037068502795	•			•
	Vilnius	kaSiulai.lt	Ladygos g. 5, Zukausko g. 36	LT08235	parduotuve@kasiulai.lt	www.kasiulai.lt	0037068231492	•	•	•	•
	Vilnius	Mezgimo zona	Pylimo g. 38D/1 - 2, Vilnius	LT01136	info@mezgimozona.lt	www.mezgimozona.lt	00370 676 43668	•	•		•
	Siauliai	Siuludama	Svedės g. 41, Ginkūnų km.	LT-81491	info@siuludama.lt	www.siuludama.lt	37067338583	•		•	
	Klaipeda	Auksaranke	Leliju g. 4, Kiskenu k., Klaipedos raj.	LT92490	info@auksaranke.net	www.auksaranke.net	0037060377511	•		•	
LUXEMBOURG											
GERMANY	***Herbolzheim***	***MEZ GmbH (Distributor)***	***Haupstrasse 78***	***79336***	***endverbraucherservice@mezcrafts.com***	***www.mezcrafts.com***	***+49 (0) 7643 33 30 288***	•	•		
	Foetz	Veritas	Rue du Brill 18-22, commerce 2	3898	aankoopcreatief@veritas.be	www.veritas.eu	00352 265 517 33	•		•	•
MEXICO											
Mexico	***Santa Catarina, NL***	***Estambres Crochet SA de CV (Distributor)***	***Calle 1° de Mayo # 230 Interior 8, Col. Trabajadores***	***64650***	***abremer@redmundial.com.mx***		***+52 (81) 8335-3870***	•			•
Mexico	Mexico City	Crochet Pedregal	Plaza Santa Teresa, Periferico Sur	4020			+52 (55) 5652-0694	•			•
Mexico	Mexico City	Crochet Masaryk	Pasaje Polanco, Masaryk	360			+52 (55) 5280-5385	•			•
Mexico	Monterrey	Crochet Cumbres	Plaza Milenium, Paseo de los Leones	2968			+52 (81) 1167-0992	•			•
Mexico	Monterrey	Crochet Valle	Plaza Las Palmas, Gomez Morin	911-7			+52 (81) 8335-2980	•			
Mexico	Mexico City	Crochet Insurgentes	Parroquia # 179 L-216	03100			+52 (55) 5627-8397	•			•
Mexico	Mexico City	Crochet Santa Fe	Ave.Vasco de Quiroga # 3800 L-510	05109			+52 (55) 2167-4266	•			•
Mexico	Mexico City	Crochet Lomas Verdes	Av. Colina de la Paz # 25 Local 210	53120			+52 (55) 5374-3167	•			•
Mexico	Mexico City	Crochet Lindavista	Rio Bamba # 589 Local 237	07760			+52 (55) 5586-1743	•			•
Mexico	Mexico City	Crochet Interlomas	Av. Magnocentro # 26 L-104	52760			+52 (55) 5247-7187	•			•
Mexico	Mexico City	Crochet Atizapan	Av. Dr. Jimenez Cantú S/N Mz1 Lt1 Local 25	52930			+52 (55) 1668-9175	•			•
Mexico	Monterrey	Crochet Paseo La Fe	Av. Miguel Alemán No. 200 Local B-08	66473			+52 (81) 2169-2267	•			•
Mexico	Monterrey	Crochet Pueblo Serena	Carretera Nacional 500 Local D-123	64989			+52 (81) 2126-3800	•			•
Mexico	Guadalajara	Crochet Guadalupe	Av. Guadalupe # 4797 Local 1B	45030			+52 (33) 3125-1243	•			•
Mexico	Guadalajara	Crochet Unicenter	Real Acueducto # 125 Local 19	45119			+52 (33) 3611-0403	•			•
Mexico	Aguascalientes	Crochet Aguascalientes	Centro Comercial Punto 45, Local 113	20116			+52 (449) 688-4339	•			•
Mexico	San Luis Potosi	Crochet San Luis Potosi	Ave. Sierra Leona No. 360 Local 111	78214			+52 (444) 841-5121	•			•
Mexico	Morelia	Crochet Paseo Altozano	Ave. Montaña Monarca Norte # 1000 1N-60	58350			+52 (443) 204-1670	•			•
Mexico	Metepec	Crochet Metepec	Av. Leona Vicario # 501 Local 12	52541			+52 (722) 232-7098	•			•
Mexico	Puebla	Crochet Puebla	Av. Zavaleta # 313-A Local 9	72000			+52 (222) 555-7172	•			•
Mexico	Leon	Crochet Leon	Av. Paseo del Moral # 1030 Local 16C	37180			+52 (477) 717-1080	•			•
Mexico	Queretaro	Crochet Queretaro	Blvd. Bernardo Quintana # 4607 -Local 13	76160			+52 (442) 543-0020	•			•
Mexico	Cancun	Crochet Puerto Cancun	Centro Comercial Marina Town Center, Local B-06	77500			+52 (998) 313-3094	•			•
NEW ZEALAND											
Auckland		Alterknitives	PO Box 47961				(64 9) 376 0337	•			•
Aukland	Devonport	Wild and Woolly Yarns	10 Victoria Road		wildandwoollyyarns@gmail.com	www.wildandwoollyyarns@gmail.com	09 445 3255	•			•
Christchurch		Knit World	189 Peterborough St				03 379 2300	•			•
Nelson		Creations Unlimited	118 Hardy Street		creations@jasnelson.co.nz		03 548 4297	•			•
Northland	Kaiwaka	The Apple Basket	1914 State Highway 1		applebasketquilts@xtra.co.nz		09 4312 443	•			•
Northland	Warkworth	Robyn Egge Yarns	15 Elizabeth Street	910	info@robyneggeyarns.co.nz		09 425 7246	•			•
Northland		Twinset and Pearls	Elizabeth Street		twinsetandpearls@clear.net.nz		09 425 7246	•			•
Taupo		Fabryx	Unit 5a, 29 Totara Street				07 376 7494	•			•
Tauranga		Tauranga Knitting Centre	8/152 11th Avenue		tgaknitcentre@hotmail.com		07 571 8892	•			•
Wellington	Cuba Mall	Knit World	Shop 210b, Left Bank				04 385 1918	•			•
		Knit World Mail Order	PO Box 30 645		info@knitting.co.nz,	www.knitworldstudio.co.nz	04 586 4530	•		•	
NORWAY											
	Rødovre	***Carl J. Permin A/S (Distributor)***	***Selma Ellefsensvei 6***	***2610***	***permin@permin.dk***	***www.permin.dk***	***45 36 36 89 89***	•			•
	Åsgårdstrand	Leo Design	Grey Vedels gate 46	3167	leoellen@online.no		33082779	•			•
	Årnes	Garnbutikken	Jernbanegt. 18D	2150	amarito@online.no		63 90 20 78	•			•
	Bergen	Norwegian Spirit	Seiersbjerget 4	5022	anne@norwegian-spirit.com	www.norwegian-spirit.com	48123799	•			•
	Brumunddal	Morgrethe	Nygata 11	2380	grethe@morgrethe.no		48 09 50 22	•			•
	Bærums Verk	Strikkeverket AS	Verksgata 14	1353	tove@strikkeverket.no		91 38 90 29	•			•
	Drammen	Ulla Garn & Broderi	Sankt Olavsgate 2	3018	butikk@ullgarn.no	www.ullagarn.no	32 89 00 58	•			•
	Drøbak	PROJO AS	Oslovegan 96	1443	post@projo.no		64 98 90 80	•			•
	HØNEFOSS	STRIKKEGRY AS	STORGT. 1	3510	gry@strikkegry.no		99259708	•			•
	Kongsberg	Pinnsvin Design	Kirkegt. 7	3616	strikkestua@online.no		32731899	•			•
	Laksevåg	Pinsvin Design	Lyngboveien 160	5164	kontakt@pinnsvinsdesign.no	www.pinnsvindesign.no	92370912	•			•
	Oslo	Nøstet Mitt	Storo Senter	485	henille@gmail.no		48 06 66 63	•			•
	Oslo	Nye Sømsenteret A/S	Akersgt. 8	158	oslo@somsenteret.no		22 41 35 69	•			•
	Oslo	Saturnia Garn AS	Ekebergveien 228C	1162	line@saturniagarn.no	www.saturniagarn.no	0047 40 41 26 16	•			•
	Sandvika	Stoffhjørnet	Engervannsveien 39	1337	maia__55@hotmail.com		40241556	•			•
	SANNIDAL	STRIKK INNOM!	Kjølebrøndsveien 9	3766	POST@STRIKKINNOM.NO		93061060	•			•
	Stord	Kvist og Kvast A/S	Borggata 20	5411			92858797	•			•
	Tromsø	Bundingen	Heiløvn 4	9015	bundingen@bundingen.no		95835525	•			•
POLAND											
	Brzoza	Motkolandia	Brzozowa 5	86-061	sklep@motkolandia.pl	www.motkolandia.pl	48605288117	•		•	
	Kraków	ART-BIJOU	os. Krakowiaków 5/31	31-962	kontakt@art-bijou.com	www.art-bijou.com	48602316541	•		•	
PORTUGAL											
Portugal	***Gaia***	***Mez Crafts Portugal, Lda (Distributor)***	***Av. Vasco da Gama, 774***	***4431-059 V.N,***	***sales.iberia@mezcrafts.com***		***223770700***	•			•
Portugal	Funchal	Eduardo G. Luiz & Fº (Coats & Clark agent in Madeira)	Av. De Zarco, 22, Cx. Postal 155	9002			291201990	•			•
Portugal	Ponta Delgada	Eduardo J. Moura (Coats & Clark agent in Azores)	R. Arcanjo Lar, Cave. Apartado 182	9500			296284341	•			•
Portugal	Laranjeiro	ARCO-IRIS A METRO	Alameda Guerra Junqueiro 34A	2810-072	info@arcoirisametro.com		912 215 330	•			•
Portugal	Lisboa	AT HOME HOBBY	Rua das Picoas, nº 10 C	1050-173	kiang@athome.com.pt		213543723	•			•
Portugal	Lisboa	AURI	Rua Oliveira Martins 10E	1000-123	loja.auri.lisboa@gmail.com		961201042	•			•
Portugal	Lisboa	DOTQUILTS	Estrada de Benfica,521 B	1500-085	dotquilts@gmail.com		213627173	•			•
Portugal	Lisboa	EL CORTE INGLÉS LISBOA	Av. António Augusto de Aguiar 31	1069-413			213711700	•			•
Portugal	Lisboa	PRAKRIAR.	Praça São João de Bosco Nº1 A	1350-299	prakriar@sapo.pt		263469410	•			•
Portugal	Mafra	TRICOT- LAS	R 1º De Dezembro N9 LJ 2	2640-454	tricot-las@sapo.pt						
Portugal	Moscavide	BOTONIA	R.Artur Ferreira da Silva ,32	1885-010	botonia.mfatima@gmail.com		219433219	•			•
Portugal	Parede	MALHAS E CIA	Av. da República, nº 1144 Lj 1	2775-386	loja.malhas.cia@gmail.com		214581078	•			•
Portugal	Porto	OVELHA NEGRA	Rua da Conceição, 100	4050-214	info@ovelha-negra.com	www.ovelha-negra.com	220935847	•		•	•
Portugal	Sertã	TEXTILAR	Av.Gonçalo Rodrig.Caldeira,nº31	6100-732	anaingres@textilar.pt		274600213	•			•
Portugal	Vila Nova de Gaia	EL CORTE INGLÉS GAIA	Av. da República 1435	4415-687			223781400	•			•
RUSSIA											
	Moscow	**FLAGSHIP Family Hobby** (Distributor) ROWAN FLAGSHIP	**Zelenograd, Haus, 1505, Ramu III**	**124683**	**ty@fhobby.ru**		**007 (499) 2703247**	•	•		•
Moscow	Zelenograd	YA SAMA	Haus 1505, office III	124683	tv@fhobby.ru		007 (499) 270-32-47	•			•
Moscow		YA SAMA - PRYAZA	Pyatnitskoye shosse, 36/1		tv@fhobby.ru		007 (495) 754-67-93	•			•
Moscow	Zelenograd	YA SAMA	Central'nyj prospekt, 401		tv@fhobby.ru		007 (499) 762-36-31	•			•
Moscow	Zelenograd	YA SAMA	Privokzal'naya ploshhad', 1/4		tv@fhobby.ru		007 (499) 738-61-31	•			•
Moscow	Reutov	YA SAMA	shopping center "Reutov Park", 45, 4th floor, Nosovikhiskoye shosse, 45, 4th floor		tv@fhobby.ru		007 (499) 995-17-06	•			•
	Moscow	Cityarn	Shopping Center "Roll Holl" office 312a, Holodilny per., 3	115191	info@cityarn.ru		007 (495) 933-87-98	•			•
	Moscow	ili-ili	Territory of design plant "Flakon", ul. Bolshaya Nododmitrovskaya 36/4, строение 2	127015	welcome@ili-ili.net		007 (495) 969-71-12	•			•
	Kaliningrad	Klubok	ul. Teatralnaya 21	236006			007 (911) 464-60-54	•			•
	Vladivostok	Mir pryazi	ul. Semenovskaya, 10	690091			007 (4232) 22-06-40	•			•
Moscow region	Korolyov	ili-ili	Shopping mall "Sigma", 3-rd floor, ul.Kalinina 6B	141070			007 (985) 385-36-36	•			•
	Irkutsk	Tanza knit	per. Kooperativnyiy 2	664011	tanza-knit@mail.ru		007 (3952) 72-13-02	•			•
	Moscow	Motochki	ul. 3 ya Tverskaya Yamskaya 11	125047			007 (495) 766-57-17	•			•
	Moscow	Triskeli	Shopping mall "Ostankino Krasniy", 2nd floor, pav. Ж 24 25 26 27, ul. 1 ya Ostankinskaya 53	129515	triskeli@triskeli.ru		007 (495) 926-88-64	•			•
	Moscow	Triskeli	ul. Prospekt Mira 91 hous. 3	129085	triskeli@triskeli.ru		007 (926) 779-96-70	•			•
	Novokuznetsk	Uzelok	ul. Metallurgov 15	654079			007 (905) 961-58-19	•			•
	Moscow	Elite Style	Shopping mall "UniverCity", 1-st floor, pav. 37, Jawaharlal Nehru Sq. 1	119311	zakaz@elstl.ru		007 (926) 106 67-75	•			•
Moscow region	Dzerzhinskij	Ruchnye shtuchki	ul. Lesnaya 17a	140093			007 (903) 155 56-07	•			•
Moscow region	Shhelkovo	Premiere	Shopping mall "Premiere", ul.Tsentralnaya 17	141108			007 (496) 250 95-05	•			•
	Saint Petersburg	**FLAGSHIP Magia pryazi** ROWAN FLAGSHIP	**ul. Komsomola 51**	**195009**	**magiap@mail.ru**		**007 (812) 541**	•			•
	Saint Petersburg	**FLAGSHIP Magia pryazi** ROWAN FLAGSHIP	**pr t Kolomyazhskiy 15, hous. 2**	**197348**	**magiap@mail.ru**		**007 (812) 921**	•			•
	Saint Petersburg	Kardigan	Shopping mall "Kosmos", pav. 242	196211			007 (931) 291 32-93	•			•
	Angarsk	Tanza knit	Shopping mall "Barguzin", 2-nd floor pav. 61, ul. Tipanova 27/39	665816	tanza knit@mail.ru		007 (902) 542 66-05	•			•
	Voronezh		ul. Tsyurupyi 36	394036			007 (473) 228 78-30	•			•
	Kasan	Pryazha ot Alyony	ul. Ostrovskogo 1/6	420111			007 (917) 865 27-44	•			•
	Krasnodar	Rukodelie	ul. Gorkogo 119	350000			007 (918) 251 52-54	•			•
	Krasnoyarsk	Izumrudnyiy gorod	Shopping mall "Izumrudnyiy gorod", ul. Televizornaya 1	660028			007 (908) 011 97-63	•			•
	Mahachkala		ul. Yaragskogo 60	367015			007 (903) 423 81-23	•			•
	Novj Urengoj	Dom knigi	"Dom knigi", ul. Molodezhnaya 3	629306			007 (3494) 94 75-78	•			•
	Orsk	MIX	"MIX" shop, ul. Prospekt Mira 15	462419			007 (3537) 317-073	•			•
	Severodvinsk	Raduga	"Raduga" department store, ul. Sovetskaya 56	164501			007 (911) 599 73-84	•			•
	Temryuk	Dekor	ul.Lenina 40	353500			007 (861) 485 45-54	•			•
	Ussurijsk	Farvater	Shopping mall "Farvater", 3-rd floor, ul. Chicherina 68	692500			007 (924) 261 90-08	•			•
	Zhukovskij	Pryazha v Zhukovskom	"Pryazha v Zhukovskom", ul.bazhenova 11, supermarket spar, 2 floor				007 (917) 580-83-18	•			•
	Dubna	Klubochek	Salon rukodeliya "Klubochek"				007 (916) 302-42-96	•			•
	Novokuznetsk	Domashnee rukodelie	Magazin "Domashnee rukodelie"		domashnee-rukodelie@yandex.ru		007 (3843)74-76-83	•			•
	Moscow	Damskoe rukodelie	Damskoe rukodelie, ul. Rozhdestvenka, 5/7, str 2				007 (499) 714-22-66	•			•
	Sergiev Posad	Metelica	Shopping Center "Trikotazhka", store "Metelica", Pozharnyj pereulok				007 (903) 101-03-89	•			•
	Arhangelsk		Novgorodskij prospekt 153	163061			007 (960) 012-99-32	•			•
	Ekaterinburg	Masterskaya vyazaniya	ul.vajnera 19, "Masterskaya vyazaniya", butik 311				007 (343) 287-87-83	•			•
	Habarovsk	Pryazha dlya vas	ul.pushkina 54, "Pryazha dlya vas"				007 (914) 547-71-12	•			•
	Moscow	Mir pryazhi	32-j km.mkad, shopping center "Shelkovyj put"				007 (915) 407-57-37	•			•
SLOVAKIA											
	Bratislava	MEZ Crafts Slovakia, s.r.o. (distributor)	s.r.o. Seberíniho 1	821 03	info@mezcrafts-sk.sk	www.mezcrafts-sk.sk	(421) 2 3230 3119	•	•		
SOUTH AFRICA											
South Africa	***Johannesburg***	***Arthur Bales Ltd (Distributor)***	***62 Fourth Avenue, Linden***	***2195***	***info@arthurbales.co.za***	***www.arthurbales.co.za***	***(27) 118 882 401***	•			
SPAIN											
Alicante	L'ALBIR	Locas por la lana	JOAQUIN TURINA, 4	03581	KRISTIN@LOCASPORLALANA.COM		629 287 641	•			•
Bizkaia	***GERNIKA***	***TXOKOPUNTO***	***BARRENKALEA, 9***	***48300***	***natalia.canivell@gmail.com***		***946028334***	•			•
Alicante	ELCHE	Las Tijeras Mágicas	CALLE CAPITAN ANTONI MENA, 150	03201	info@lastijerasmagicas.com	lastijerasmagicas.com	966 656 452	•			•
Gipuzkoa	SAN SEBASTIAN	Casa de Labores - Eskulanen Etxea	ELKANO, 5	20004	eskulanenetxea@gmail.com		943420205	•			•
barcelona	BARCELONA	Fil&Tropia	TORRENT DE L'OLLA, 23 BOTIGA	08012	ADMIN@FILANDTROPIA.COM		610716746	•			•

County	Town / City	Stockist	Address	Postcode	Email	Website	Telephone	Yarn	Fabric	Online	Instore
Bizkaia	BILBAO	El Punto Bobo	ALAMEDA URKIJO, 20	48008	dams@elpuntobobo.com		946855612	•			•
madrid	POZUELO DE ALARCON	El mundo de Marieta	AVDA DE EUROPA, 18	28224	elmundodemarieta@yahoo.es		911731900	•			•
madrid	MADRID	Mamamadejas	C/ MONASTERIO DE OSERIA, 9	28049	info@mamamadejas.com		696412761 91	•			•
barcelona	BARCELONA	El Club de la Aguja	Via Augusta, 100	08006	cristina@clubdelaaguja.com		934143815	•			•
valencia	VALENCIA	Derecho y Reves	MUSICO PADILLA 4	46005	asuncionchaves@gmail.com		618778072	•			•
barcelona	BARCELONA	Oyambre	ROGER DE LLURIA 92	08009	info@oyambreonline.com		934872672	•	•		•
madrid	MADRID	Lanas Madrid	CALLE RODRIGUEZ SANPEDRO, 20	28015	info@lanasmadrid.com		915 438 549	•			•
barcelona	SANT CUGAT DEL VALLES	Llanes del Mon	C/ ENRIC GRANADOS Nº15	08172	llanesdelmon@gmail.com		935 878 110	•			•
madrid	MADRID	El Corte Ingles Campo Naciones	AVDA DE LOS ANDES, 50	28042			913248800 - 2380	•			•
toledo	ILLESCAS	La Rosa de Plata	C/ FRANCISCO GUZMAN, 28	45200	FLORPIQUERAS@HOTMAIL.ES		925 532 287	•		•	•
valencia	VALENCIA	La tia Pepa	C/ Felix Pizcueta 23 bj Izq	46004	latiapepa@latiapepa.es		963 510 199	•			•
A Coruña	A CORUÑA	Picknits	online store	15011	veronicaoliveros@gmail.com		607 402 528	•		•	•
valladolid	VALLADOLID	Mi Marinita	C/ NUÑEZ DE ARCE, 14 BAJO	47002	luz@mimarinita.com		637 536 191	•			•
zaragoza	ZARAGOZA	Telas de Luna	C/ GIL DE JASA Nº 12 LOCAL	50006	info@telasdeluna.com		976 229 130	•			•
barcelona	BARCELONA	Traça	C/ MAJOR DE SARRIA, 150 BOTIGA	08017			626 082 117	•			•
madrid	MAJADAHONDA - MADRID	MERCERIA BOTONES	C/ IGLESIA, Nº8	28220	elclubdelabores@gmail.com		916 384 051	•			•
barcelona	BARCELONA	Milana Bonita	CAMP 87	08022			670 294 671	•			•
albacete	ALBACETE	Tejeadictos	PEDRO COCA, 7 DERECHA	02006	pilarcallejasg@gmail.com		667 338 270	•	•		•
la Rioja	LOGROÑO (LA RIOJA)	Al Solecito	DOCTORES CASTROVIEJO, 42	26003	alsolecito@alsolecito.com		679812463	•			•
Tarragona	REUS	Fet amb	AMARGURA Nº 11	43201			670930258	•			•
Malaga	MALAGA	LAS 13 MADEJAS	CALLE PANADEROS, 4	29001	las13madejas@gmail.com		952650337	•			•
murcia	MURCIA	Labores y por qué no	C/ DE LA AURORA 10	30001	laboresyporqueno@gmail.com		968201645	•			•
madrid	LAS ROZAS	La Tertulia del Patch	C/ PRAGA Nº 15	28232	fouparlabores@gmail.com		917104258	•			•
A Coruña	SANTIAGO DE COMPOSTELA	Bolillos	RUA NOVA, Nº40	15705			981-589-776	•			•
barcelona	BARCELONA	El Almacén de las Lanas	PROVIDENCIA,130-132	08024	lanasrodriguez@gmail.com		661 741 261	•			•
madrid	MADRID	El Punto Madrid	MELENDEZ VALDES, 68	28015	elpunto@elpuntomadrid.com		651922777	•			•
Alava	VITORIA	Log Cabin	SAN ANTONIO, 28 BJS B-2	01005	logcabin.vitoria@gmail.com		945 142 430	•			•
Alicante	ELCHE	Fenosan	REINA VICTORIA, 51 1	03201	fenosan@gmail.com		965 448 231	•			•
Gipuzkoa	EIBAR	ARTILE	BIDEBARRIETA, 18	20600	isabelartile@gmail.com		943 207 227	•			•
navarra	PAMPLONA	La chica de las lanas	POZOBLANCO, 17	31001	lachicadelaslanas@hotmail.com		948 221 684	•			
valencia	VALENCIA	Adeor Lanas	CUENCA, 38	46007			963 853 398	•		•	•
madrid	MADRID	La perla	BATALLA DEL SALADO, 19	28045	mluisa1@hotmail.com		915 279 301	•			•
madrid	MADRID	El Club de Labores	INFANTA MARIA TERESA, 11	28016	cmessat@gmail.com		913 441 068	•			•
barcelona	BADALONA	Mohair	MARIA CRISTINA, 11	08910	montsemohair@gmail.com		625 138 345	•			•
baleares	PALMA DE MALLORCA	El Corte Inglés Avenidas	ALEXANDRE ROSELLO	07002			971 770177	•			•
barcelona	BARCELONA	El Corte Inglés Diagonal	EUROPA, S/N	08028			93 3667100	•			•
murcia	MURCIA	El Corte Inglés Murcia	AVDA.DE LA LIBERTAD, 1	30009			968 298050	•			
valencia	VALENCIA	El Corte Inglés Sorolla	COLON, 27	46004			96 3159500	•		•	
valencia	VALENCIA	El Corte Inglés Nuevo Centro	MENENDEZ PIDAL, 15 EDF A	46009			96 3175700	•			•
Bizkaia	BILBAO	El Corte Inglés Gran Via	GRANVIA, 9	48001			944253500	•			•
zaragoza	ZARAGOZA	El Corte Inglés P. Sagasta	Pº SAGASTA, 3	50008			976 211121	•			•
A Coruña	LA CORUÑA	El Corte Inglés Ramon y Cajal	RAMON Y CAJAL, S/N	15006			981 189400	•			•
madrid	MADRID	El Corte Inglés Callao	PLAZA DE CALLAO, 2	28013			91 3798000	•			•
madrid	MADRID	El Corte Inglés Goya	GOYA, 76	28009			914329300	•			•
madrid	MADRID	El Corte Inglés Princesa	PRINCESA, 56	28008			914546000	•			•
madrid	MADRID	El Corte Inglés Castellana	RAIMUNDO F.VILLAVERDE, 79	28003			91 4188800	•			•
madrid	POZUELO ALARCON-MADRID-	El Corte Inglés Pozuelo	CT.CORUÑA 12,500 CERRO GAMOS	28223			91 7089200	•			•
madrid	MADRID	El Corte Inglés Sanchinarro	MARGARITA PARMA, 1	28050			650 708881	•			•
Sevilla	SEVILLA	El Corte Inglés Duque	PZA.DUQUE DE LA VICTORIA 10	41006			954-222-991	•			•
sevilla	SEVILLA	El Corte Inglés Nervión	LUIS MONTOTO, 122-128	41006			954 571440	•			•
Gran Canaria	LAS PALMAS DE GRAN CANARIA	El Corte Inglés Mesa López	MESA LOPEZ, 18 S12 D18	35007			928263000	•			•
canarias	LAS PALMAS DE GRAN CANARIA	El Corte Inglés Siete Palmas	AV.SIETE PALMAS	35018			928423000	•			•
tenerife	SANTA CRUZ DE TENERIFE	El Corte Inglés Tenerife	AVDA. TRES DE MAYO 7	38003			922849400	•			•
valladolid	VALLADOLID	Mi Marinita	C/ NUÑEZ DE ARCE, 14 BAJO	47002	luzmarina@hotmail.com		637 536 191	•		•	•
Alava	VITORIA	Log Cabin	PL DEL CARMEN/MANUEL IRADIER	1005	logcabin.vitoria@gmail.com		945142430	•	•		•
zaragoza	ZARAGOZA	El Corte Inglés P. Sagasta	Pº SAGASTA, 3	50008			976 211121	•			•
zaragoza	ZARAGOZA	Entre algodones	C/ SAN MIGUEL, 29 bjo DERECHA	50001	entrealgodonesther@gmail.com		669974949	•			•
zaragoza	ZARAGOZA	Telas de Luna	C/ GIL DE JASA Nº 12 LOCAL	50006	info@telasdeluna.com		976 229 130	•	•	•	•
valladolid	VALLADOLID	Tira del Ovillos	online store	47170		ww.tiradelovillo.com	686 361 083		•		
VALENCIA	VALENCIA	Lanas Tatino	Avª MALVARROSA, 116	46011	ampariguesmc@hotmail.es		961 477 669	•			•
VALENCIA	VALENCIA	Derecho y Revés	MUSICO PADILLA 4	46005	asuncionchaves@gmail.com		618778072	•			•
VALLADOLID	VALLADOLID	Mi Marinita	C/ NUÑEZ DE ARCE, 14 BAJO	47002	luzmarina@hotmail.com	www.mimarinita.com	637 536 191	•		•	•
				SWEDEN							
	Rødovre	***Carl J. Permin A/S (Distributor)***	***Skaraborgsvägen 35C, 3tr***	***50 630***	***permin@permin.dk***	***www.permin.dk***	***45 36 36 89 89***	•			•
	Åhus	PP CO i Åhus	Gamla Skeppsbron 10	296 31	kristina@ppco.se		044-240521	•			
	ÅMÅL	Widedals Interiør AB	Mellanbrogatan 6	66231	info@widedals.se		0532-10156	•			•
	Borås	Stickat och Klart EF	Hallbergsgatan 2	503 30	kristina.karlson@hotmail.com		(033) 10 32 38	•			•
	Göteborg	Lizbettan AB/Tummelisa Garn	N. Gubberogatan 8	416 63	musiklisbeth@gmail.com		031-252813	•			•
	Göteborg	Marita Rolin Design	Skiljemyntsgatan 18 A	41480	info@maritarolin.se		0707-528210	•			•
	GRÆSTORP	Garn & Mera	Tengene plan 10	46792	info@garnomera.se		731598577	•			•
	Helsingborg	Tant Thea AB	Södra Storgatan 14	252 23	info@tantthea.se		42135153	•			•
	HØRBY	Garnverandan	Gamla Torg 5	24231	info@garnverandan.se		0415-311300	•			•
	LIDKÖPING	HEMSLÖJDEN I LIDKÖPING	Sunnersberg Solbacken 1	531 98	info@hemslojden.se		0510 22635	•			
	Lund	SLANDAN I LUND AB	Lilla Fiskaregatan 1	222 22	slandan@telia.com	www.slandaninlund.se	046 128077	•			
	Malmö	Rætstickan	Regementsgatan 84	217 51	fagelfenix2@gmail.com		040-269446	•			•
	Stockholm	Wincent Garn	Norrtullsgatan 27	113 27	wincent@gmail.com	www.wincentgarner.se	(08) 33 70 60	•			•
	Sundsvall	GARNKORGEN HANDARBETEN	Klackvägen 17	856 53	info@garnkorgen.se	www.garnkorgen.se	(060) 124 501	•			•
	Täby	Trasselgarn & Broderi	Stationsvägen 16	187 30	info@trassel.se	www.trassel.se	(08) 638 00 59	•			
	Uppsala	Yll & Tyll	Bredgrænd 7C	753 00	info@yllotyll.com		018-105190	•			•
	Värnamo	C-Knit	Malmstensgatan 16A	331 31	info@c-knit.com	www.c-knit.com	703131949	•			•
	Vellinge	Vellinge Garnhörna	Östergatan 4	235 33	info@garnhornan.com		040-42 44 05	•			
				SWITZERLAND							
	Zürich	***MEZ Crafts Switzerland GmbH (Distributor)***	***c/o Puplicitas AG, Mürtenstrasse 39***	***8048***		***www.mezcrafts.com***		•			•
	Aarberg	Wolle Aarberg	Ursula Kaiser, Lyssstrasse 1	3270	ursula-kaiser@bluewin.ch		032 392 41 41	•			•
	Appenzell	Wollelade	Weissbadstrasse 7	9050	info@wollelade.ch		071 7871116	•			•
	Basel	Zum Roten Faden	Steinenring 41	4051			079 919 71 87	•			•
	Bern	WollWirrWare	Wylestrasse 53	3014	info@wollwirrware.ch	www.wollwirrware.ch	031332 06 33	•			•
	Biel	Tasche & Masche	Schmiedengasse 13	2502	tasche@tascheundmasche.ch		032 322 26 12	•			•
	Buchs	Wollig-Anstalt	Grünaustr. 17	9470	info@wollig.ch	www.wollig.ch	081 756 36 19	•			
	Chur	AHA-Mode	Kreuzgasse 1	7000	info@aha-mode.ch		081 650 25 30	•	•		
	Chur	Wundertrüggli	Reichsgasse 52	7000	wutru@sunrise.ch		081 416 21 00	•			
	Duebendorf	Sarah Gaffuri	Oberdorfstrasse 12	8600	info@mondolana.ch			•			
	Frick	Ain's Yarn Design	Hauptstr. 66	5070	ain@ains-yarndesign.ch		062-8716588	•			
	Fislisbach	Lana Versum	Badenerstraße 15	5442	info@lanaversum.ch		056 470 90 00	•			•
	Flawil	WOLLA-FADÄ	Schweissbrunnstrasse 1	9230	info@wollae-fadae.ch	www.wollae-fadae.ch	071 393 11 03	•			•
	Geneve	Elna SA Centre Balexert	Avenue Louis-Casaï 27	1209			022 796 00 51	•			•
	Heiden	Naraki	Poststrasse 18	9410	be.gantenbein@bluewin.ch	www.naraki.ch	071 888 06 10	•			•
	Hölstein	Wullestübli Hölstein	Haupstraße 19	4434	huber.dora@bluewin.ch		061 951 19 53	•			•
	Lausanne	Boutique Tricot-Thé	Av. d'Echallens 4a	1004	info@tricot-the.ch		021 62 51 81 0	•			•
	Luzern	Naturel	Habsburgerstr. 33	6003			041 210 65 41	•			
	Luzern	Strickwelt GmbH	Langensandstrasse 23	6005	monika.meyer@strickwelt.ch	www.strickwelt.ch	041 361 65 65	•			•
	Maienfeld	Bacchini	Schellenbergstraße 8	7304	ambubac@bluewin.ch		078 853 31 88	•			•
	Martigny	Le Monde des Laines	rue du Grand-Verger 11	1920	info@lemondedeslaines.ch	www.lemondedeslaines.ch	027 722 10 35	•			
	Münchenstein	Wulle Atelier Müchenstein	Verena Tschanz, Hauptstrasse 35	4142	info@wulleatelier.ch	www.wulleatelier.ch	079 652 52 61	•			•
	Muri	Stoff-und Wullehuesli	H. Keller, Marktstr. 17	5630	wullehuesli@bluewin.ch		056 664 41 20	•			•
	Nidau	Atelier 25	Hauptstrasse 25	2560	mail@atelier25.ch	www.atelier25.ch	079 392 43 34	•			•
	Orbe	Il était une fois	Rue des Terreaux 19	1350	iletaitunefois19€gmail.com		024 441 24 19	•			•
	Richterswil	Rosa Träume	Poststrasse 21	8805	rosa.traeume@bluewin.ch	www.rosa-traeume.ch	079 883 17 77	•			•
	Romanshorn	Strick-IN	Aleestrasse 44	8590			071 463 68 18	•			•
	St. Gallen	Boutique Tonja Mode mit Wolle	Vadianstrasse 22	9000	britta.nydegger@sunrise.ch		071 223 12 71	•			•
	Steffisburg	Silvia Heller	Oberdorfstrasse 31a	3612	info@strickbar.ch		079 219 67 54	•			•
	Steffisburg	Hinkel Pinkel Folmer Winkel	M. Folmer, Thunstr. 57	3612	mfolmer@bluewin.ch		033/437 08 80	•			•
	Sursee	strick-art	Mühleplatz 2	6210	strick-art@gmx.ch		041 921 66 31	•			•
	Teufen	Presto-Lana	Alte Haslenstrasse 5	9053	info@presto-lana.ch		071 3336565	•			•
	Thun	we love wool	Obere Hauptgasse 25	3600	charlotteschmid@gmx.ch		033 222 54 46	•			•
	Uster	Fallmasche GmbH	Poststrasse 6	8610	info@fallmasche.ch		044 942 38 58	•			•
	Visp	Web and Wollstube	Hildegard Margelist, Kantonsstr. 14	3930	web-wollstube@bluewin.ch		027 946 47 06	•			•
	Weinfelden	Wollring	Rathausstrasse 14	8570			071 622 19 27	•			•
	Zürich	Hand-Art	Neumarkt 10	8001	guldenschuh@tuttolana.ch		044 55757	•			•
	Zürich	Vilfil	Kreuzstrasse 39, Beim Kreuzplatz	8032	office@vilfil.com	www.vilfil.com	044 3839903	•			•
				THE FAROE ISLANDS							
	Klaksvik	Búnin	Nolsgarpálsgøta 18	700	bunin2010@hotmail.com		298 455210	•			•
				USA							
North Carolina	***Hickory***	***Sirdar USA Inc (Distributor)***	***406 20th Street SE***	***28602***	***sirdarusa@sirdar.co.uk***	***www.sirdar.co.uk***	***001 828 404 3705***	•			•
Alabama	Birmingham	In the Making	4232 Dolly Ridge Road	35243	orders@shopinthemaking.com	www.shopinthemaking.com	(205) 298 1309	•			•
Alaska	Anchorage	Southside Knitting Nook	12201 Industry Way Unit 3	99515	deeknit12201@gmail.com		(907) 317 0484	•			•
Arkansas	Rogers	Mockingbird Moon	315 N. Second	72756	mockingbirdmoon@gmail.com		(473) 202 5640	•			•
California	Albany	Avenue Yarn	1325 Solano Avenue	94706	karen@avenueyarn.com	www.avenueyarn.com	510-526-9276	•			
California	Chico	HeartStrings Yarn Studio	1909 Esplanade	95926	joanne@heartstringsyarn.com	www.heartstringsyarn.com	530-894-1434	•			
California	Danville	A Yarn Less Raveled	730 Camino Ramon	94526	info@ayarnlessraveled.com	www.ayarnlessraveled.com	(925) 263 2661	•			•
California	Encinitas	Common Threads	191 North El Camino Real	92024	invoice@fiberartshop.com	www.fiberartshop.com	(760) 436 6119	•			•
California	Eureka	Yarn	518 Russ Street	95501	sunshineyarn@gmail.com		(707) 443 9276	•			•
California	Fair Oaks	Babetta's Yarn & Gifts	4400 San Juan Ave	95628	info@babettasyarnandgifts.com	www.babettasyarnandgifts.com	916-965-6043	•			
California	Fresno	Janna's Needle Art	1085 Herndon	93710	jannasneedleart@att.net		559-227-6333	•			
California	Fort Bragg	Navarro River Knits	169 Boatyard Drive	75437	yarn@mcn.org		707-964-9665	•			
California	Healdsburg	Purls of Joy	461 Healdsburg Avenue	95448	rosanne@purlsofjoy.com	www.purlsofjoy.com	707-433-5697	•			
California	Little River	Mendocino Yarns	7901 N. Highway One	95456	yarnshop@mcn.org		(707) 937 0921	•			•
California	**Los Altos**	**FLAGSHIP Uncommon Threads**	**293 State Street**	**94022**	**info@uncommonthreadsyarn.com**	**www.uncommonthreadsyarn.com**	**650-941-1815**	•			•
California	Napa	Yarns on First	1305 First Street	94559	contact@yarnsonfirst.com	www.yarnsonfirst.com	(707) 257 1363	•			•
California	Oakland	Piedmont Yarn & Apparel	4171 Piedomnt Avenue	94611	info@piedmontyarn.com		(510) 595 9595	•			•
California	Pacifica	The Royal Bee Yarn Company	90 Eureka Square	94044	kelleycorten@gmail.com		650-219-6287	•			
California	Pacific Grove	Monarch Knitting	529 Central Ave	93950	ann@monarchknitting.com	www.monarchknittingcom	(831) 647 9276	•			•
California	Petaluma	Knitterly	1 14th Street	94952	knitterly@comast.net	www.knitterly.net	(707) 762-9276	•			
California	Placerville	Lofty Lou's Yarn Shop	263 Main Street	95667		www.loftylouknit.us	530-642-2270	•			
California	**Redondo Beach**	**FLAGSHIP L'Antelier Inc.**	**1722 S Catalina Ave**	**90277**	**kddamskey@gmail.com**		**(310) 540 4440**	•			•
California	Sacramento	Rumpelstiltskin	1021 R Strret	95811	rumpel@yarnyarnyarn.com		(916) 442 9225	•			•
California	San Anselmo	Atelier Marin Inc	217 San Anselmo Ave	94960	ateliermarin@gmail.com		(415) 256 9618	•			•
California	San Francisco	Atelier Yarns	1945 Divisadero Street	94115	atelieryarns@gmail.com		(415) 771 1550	•			•
California	San Francisco	Imagiknit	3897 18th Street	94114	info@imagiknit.com	www.imagiknit.com	415-621-6642	•			•
California	San Rafael	Dharma Trading Company	1604 Fourth Street	94901	store@dharmatrading.com		(415) 456 1211	•			•
California	Santa Cruz	The Swift Stitch	402 Ingalls St. #12	95060	info@theswiftstitch.com	www.theswiftstitch.com	(831) 427 9276	•			•
California	Santa Cruz	Yarn Shop Santa Cruz	765 Cedar Street Suite 103	95060	corymeyers@mac.com		(831) 515 7966	•			•
California	Santa Rosa	Cast Away	100 4th Street	95401	justine@castawayandfolk.com	www.castawayandfolk.com	(707) 546 9276	•			•
California	Studio City	La Knitterie Parisienne	12642 Ventura Boulevard	91604	info@laknitterieparisienne.com	www.laknitterieparisienne.com	(818) 766 1515	•			•
California	Tarzana	Zoe's Knit Studio	18596 Ventura Boulevard	91356	info@zoesknitstudio.com		(818) 881 9637	•			•
California	Truckee	Atelier Trukee	10130 Donner Pass Road	96161	info@ateliertruckee.com	www.ateliertruckee.com	530-582-5500	•			
California	Ukiah	Heidi's Yarn Haven	180 South School Street	95482	hyhyarn@pacific.net		(707) 462 0544	•			•
California	Ventura	Anacapa Fine Yarns	4572 Telephone Rd #909	93003	lois@anacafineyarns.com		(805) 654 9500	•			•
California	Winters	Cloth Carousel	14 Main Street	95694	adina@clothcarousel.com	www.clothcarousel.com	530-794-6114	•			
Colorado	Colorado Springs	Ewe and Me…	1045 K Garden of the Gods Road	80907	debbiegray@eweandmeyarnbou.comcastbiz.net		(719) 203 5240	•			•
Colorado	Denver	Lamb Shoppe	3512 E 12th Ave	80206	info@thelambeshoppe.com	www.thelambshoppe.com	(303) 322-2223	•			•
Colorado	**Fort Collins**	**FLAGSHIP Lambspun of Colorado**	**1101 E Lincoln Ave**	**80524**	**staff@lambspun.com**	**www.lambspun.com**	**(800) 558 5262**	•			•
Colorado	Fort Collins	My Sister Knits	1408 West Moutain Ave	80521	julie@mysisterknits	www.mysisterknits.com	(970) 407-1461	•			•
Colorado	Frisco	Knititation	107 S. 6th Avenue	80443	kistelaine@gmail.com	www.knititation.com	719-839-5817	•			
Colorado	Lafayette	Mew Mew's Yarn Shop	2770 Dagny Way, #108	80026	sue@mewmewsyarnshop.com	www.mewmewsyarnshop.com	303-665-5591	•			
Colorado	Steamboat Springs	Sew Steamboat	929 Lincoln Ave	80477	info@sewsteamboat.com	www.sewsteamboat.com	970-879-3222	•			
California	Centennial	Colorful Yarns	2001 East Easter Ave #101	80122	colorfulyarns@gmail.com	www.colorfulyarns.com	(303) 798 2299	•			•
Connecticut	Granby	Marji's Yarncrafts	381 Salmon Brook Street	06035	marjisyarn@sbcglobal.net		(860) 653 9700	•			•
Connecticut	Ridgefield	Nancy O	23 Catoonah Street	06877	nancyo.nancyo@gmail.com		(203) 431 2266	•			•
Connecticut	New Haven	Knit New Haven	26 Whitney Avenue	06510	knitnewhaven@att.net		(203) 777 5648	•			•
Connecticut	Glastonbury	Village Wool	2279 Main Street	06033	marion@villagewoolyarnshop.com		(860) 633 0898	•			•
Connecticut	Westport	Westport Yarns	582 Post Road East	06880	beth@westportyarns.com		(203) 454 4300	•			•
Connecticut	Woodbridge	The Yarn Barn	1666 Litchfield Turnpike	06525	yarnbarn@optonline.net		(203) 389-5117	•			•
Delaware	Bethany Beach	Sea Needles	780 Garfield Parkway	19930	gb@seaneedles.com		(302) 539 0574	•			•
Delaware	Newark	Stitches with Style	16-E Polly Drummond	19711	knitsws@comcast.net		(302) 453 8130	•			•
District of Columbia	Washington	Looped Yarn Works	1732 Connecticut Avenue NW, #200	20009	web@loopedyarnworks.com	www.loopedyarnsworks.com	202-714-5667	•			•
Florida	Hollywood	Raging Wool	1850 NW 122nd Terrace	33026	Alice@raginwoolshop.com		(954) 385 0861	•			•
Florida	Lake Worth	Just Imaginknit	6663-B Lake Worth Road	33467	justimaginknit@comcast.net		(561) 433 3444	•			•
Florida	Lady Lake	The Yarn Lady	304 Oak Street	32159	theyarnlady@comcast.net		(352) 775 7779	•			•
Florida	Miami	The Kniting Garden	1923 Ponce de lEon Blvd	33134	info@theknittinggarden.org		(305) 774 1060	•			•
Florida	Naples	Knitting with Nancy	3804 Tamiami Trail East	34112	knittingwithnancy@comcast.ent		(239) 7938141	•			•
Florida	Tampa	Roxy's Yarns	3347 South Westshore Blvd	33629	bnjventures@verizon.net		(813) 839 7699	•			•
Georgia	Atlanta	Yarning For Ewe	3220 Cobb Parkway Suite 102	30339	yarningforewe@gmail.com		(678) 909 4963	•			•

County	Town / City	Stockist	Address	Postcode	Email	Website	Telephone	Yarn	Fabric	Online	Instore
Georgia	Clarksville	Bumbleberry LLC	1345 Washington Street	30523	bumbleberry@windstream.net		(706) 754 0462	•		•	
Georgia	Roswell	Cast On Cottage	Coleman Village, 860 Marietta Hwy	30075	info@castoncattage.com	www.castoncottage.com	(770) 998-3483	•		•	
Georgia	Saint Simons Island	The Stichery of St Simons	3411 Frederica Road	31552	ulladesigns@gmail.com		(912) 638 3401	•		•	
Georgia	Savannah	The Frayed Knot LLC	6 West State Street	31401	thefrayedknotsav@yahoo.com		(912) 233 1240	•		•	
Georgia	Savannah	Unwind LLC	7710 Waters Avenue	31406	to.unwind@yahoo.com		(912) 303 3970	•		•	
Gerorgia	Woodstock	The Whole Nine Yarns	8826 Main Street	30188	info@thewholenineyarns.com		(678) 494 5242	•		•	
Illinois	Bloomington	Le Mouton Rouge Knittery	1206 Towanda Ave	61701	kelly@lmtknittery.com	www.lmtknittery.com	309-319-7692	•			
Illinois	Chicago	Yarnify	47 West Polk Street Suite G2B	60605	barbaraofyarnify@gmail.com		(312) 583 9276	•		•	
Illinois	Downers Grove	Knitche	5221 Main Street	60515	kathy@knitche.com		(630) 652 5648	•		•	
Illinois	Evanston	Close Knit	1630 Orrington Avenue	60201	closeknit@sbcglobal.net		(847) 328 6760	•		•	
Illinois	Forest Park	Knit Nirvana	7453 W Madison	60130	sue@knitnirvana.com	www.knitnirvana.com	708-771-5232	•		•	
Illinois	Galena	Fiber Wild	304 South Main Street	61036	amy@fiberwild.com	www.fiberwild.com	815-777-3550	•		•	
Illinois	Herrin	The Yarn Shoppe	105 N 16th Street	62948	herrinyarnshoppe@gmail.com		(618) 988 9276	•		•	
Illinois	Saint Charles	Wool And Company	107 West Main Street	60174	team@woolandcompany.com	www.woolandcompany.com	630-444-0480	•			
Illinois	Marengo	The Fold	3316 Millstream Road	60152	thefold@mc.net		815-568-5730	•			
Illinois	**Northbrook**	**FLAGSHIP Three Bags Full Knitting**	**1927 Cherry Lane**	**60062**	**knittingstudio@aol.com**		**847-291-9933**	•			
Indiana	Fort Wayne	Knitting Off Broadway	1309 Broadway	46802	yarn@knittingoffbroadway.com	www.knittingoffbroadway.com	280-422-9276	•		•	
Indiana	Indianapolis	Broad Ripple Knits	6510 N. Cornell Avenue	46220	www.broadrippleknits.com		317-255-0540	•		•	
Indiana	Indianapolis	Mass Avenue Knit Shop	862 Virginia Avenue	46203	massaveknitship@ameritech.net	www.massaveknitshoponline.com	317-638-1833	•			
Indiana	Valparaiso	Sheep's Clothing Knitting	60 West Lincolnway	46383	paula@knitdoctor.com		219 462 1700	•		•	
Indiana	Zionsville	Village Yarn Company	209 South Main Street	46077	maryvaughn@villageyarncompany.com	www.villageyarncompany.com	(317) 873 0004	•		•	
Iowa	Ankeny	Knitting Next Door	704 SW 3rd Street	50023	knittingnextdoor@yahoo.com	www.knittingnextdoor.com	(515) 963 0396	•		•	
Iowa	Iowa City	The Knitting Shoppe	2141 Muscatine Avenue	52240	theknittingshoppe@etherbiz.net	www.theknittingshoppeic.com	(319) 337 4920	•		•	
Iowa	West Des Moines	Yarn Junction Company	132 5th Street	50265	yarnjunction@gmail.com	www.yarnjunction.com	(515) 277 2770	•		•	
Kansas	Lawrence	The Yarn Barn	930 Mass Ave. 930 Massachussetts Street	66044	info@yarnbarn-ks.com	www.yarnbarn-ks.com	(800) 468-0035	•		•	
Kentucky	Lexington	Magpie Yarn	513 East High Street	40502	magpieyarn@windstream.net		(859) 455 7437	•		•	
Louisiana	Baton Rouge	Knits By Nana	7612 Old Hammnd Hwy	70809	missy@knitsbynana.com		(225) 216 9460	•		•	
Maine	Bath	Halcyon Yarn	12 School Street	04530	purchasing@halcyonyarn.com		(207) 442 7909	•		•	
Maine	Belfast	Heavenly Socks Yarn	82 Main Street	04915	hsy@myfairpoint.net		(207) 338 8388	•		•	
Maine	Camden	The Cashmere Goat	20 Bayview Street	04843	info@thecashmeregoatknit.com		(207) 236 7236	•		•	
Maine	**Freeport**	**FLAGSHIP Grace Robinson & Co**	**208 US Rte 1, Ste 1**	**04032**	**grandco@gwi.net**	**www.yarnandneedlepoint.com**	**(207) 865-6110**	•		•	
Maine	Glenburn	Essentially Felt Studio	865 Pushaw Road	04401	sandy@essentiallyfelt.com		(207) 942 0365	•		•	
Maine	Portland	KnitWit	247A Congress Street	04101	yarnbrain@gmail.com		(207) 774 6444	•		•	
Maryland	Annapolis	Knits and Pieces	626 Admiral Dr Suite E	21401		www.knitsandpiecesannapolis.com	(410) 216-2897	•			
Maryland	**Annapolis**	**FLAGSHIP Woolwinders**	**709 Skippers Lane**	**21401**	**info@woolwinders.com**		**(240) 632 9276**	•		•	
Maryland	Annapolis	Yarn Basket	53 Maryland Avenue	21401	yarnbasketmaryland@gmail.com		(410) 295 7000	•		•	
Maryland	Baltimore	Woolworks	6117 Falls Rd	21209	info@worksbalt.com	www.woolworksbalt.com	(410) 377-2060	•		•	
Maryland	Bethesda	Second Story Knits	4706 Bethesda Ave	20814	biz@secondstoryknits.com	www.secondstoryknits.com	301 652-8688	•		•	
Maryland	Catonsville	Cloverhill Yarn Shop	77 Mellor Ave	21228	temptingewe@cloverhillyarn.com	www.cloverhillyarn.com	(410) 788 7262	•		•	
Maryland	Chesapeake City	Vulcan's Rest Fibers	2728 Augustine Herman Hwy	21915		www.vulcansrest.com	(410) 885-2890				
Maryland	Columbia	All About Yarn	8970 MD-108	21045		www.allaboutyarn.com	(410) 992-5648				
Maryland	**Rockville**	**FLAGSHIP Woolwinders**	**404 King Farm Blvd**	**20850**	**info@woolwinders.com**	**www.woolwinders.com**	**240-632-9276**	•			
Massachusetts	Beverly	Yarns in the Farms	641 Hale Street	01915	info@yarnsinthefarms.com	www.yarnsinthefarms.com	(978) 927 2108	•		•	
Massachusetts	Boston	Newbury Yarns	2 Milk Street	02108	knitting@newburyyarns.com	www.newburyyarns.com	(617) 572 3733	•		•	
Massachusetts	Brookline	Uncommon Yarn	PO Box 1899	02446	uncommonyarn@gmail.com		(857) 352 4281	•			
Massachusetts	**Burlington**	**FLAGSHIP Another Yarn**	**15 Cambridge Street**	**01803**	**distrib@anotheryarn.com**	**www.anotheryarn.com**	**781 570 2134**	•		•	
Massachusetts	Dennis	Yarn Hound	620 Rt. 6A	02638	yarnhound@comcast.net		508 385 6951	•		•	
Massachusetts	Dorchester	Stitch Horse	846 Dorchester Ave	02125	info@stitchhousedorchester.com	www.stitchhousedorchester.com	(617) 265 8013	•		•	
Massachusetts	Hingham	Yarns in the Square	400 Lincoln Street Unit #2	02043	info@yarnsinthesquare.com	www.yarnsinthesquare.com	(781) 749 2280	•		•	
Massachusetts	Lenox	Colorful Stitches	48 Main Street / Rear	02140	bonnie@colorfulstitches.com	www.colorfulstitches.com	(413) 637 8206	•		•	
Massachusetts	Mendon	Yarn Garden	3 Maple Street	01756	cheryl.leider@gmail.com		(617) 599 6922	•		•	
Massachusetts	Natick	Fabric Place Basement	321 Speen Street	01760	peter@fabricplacebasement.com		(508) 655 2000	•		•	
Massachusetts	Natick	Iron Horse	3 Pond Street	01760	ironhorsefiberart@gmail.com		(508) 647 4722	•		•	
Massachusetts	Natick	Amazing Threads	3 Pond Street	1760	ironhorsefiberart@gmail.com		(508) 647 4722	•		•	
Massachusetts	Needham	Black Sheep Knitting Co.	1500 Highland Ave	02492	nancy.shulman@blacksheepknitting.com		(781) 444 0694	•			
Massachusetts	Northbourgh	Craftworks	243 West Main Street	01532	craftworks.coop@gmail.com		(508) 393 9435	•		•	
Massachusetts	**Northampton**	**FLAGSHIP Webs**	**75 Service Center Road**	**01060**	**customerservice@yarn.com**	**www.yarn.com**	**(413)584-2225**	•		•	
Massachusetts	Plainville	In the Loop	60 Man Mar #3	02762	intheloop@comcast.net		(774) 847 7977				
Massachusetts	Salem	Circle of Stitches	66 Wharf Street	01970	info@circleofstitches		(978) 745 9276	•		•	
Massachusetts	Williamstown	The Spin-Off Yarn Shop	130 Water Street	01267	beth@spinoffyarnshop.com	www.spinoffyarnshop.com	(413) 344 6257	•		•	
Michigan	East Lansing	Woven Art Inc.	325B Groove Street	48823	wovenartshop@gmail.com		(517) 203 4467	•		•	
Michigan	East Tawas	Tawas Bay Yarn Co. Inc.	1820 East US-23	48730	misso@att.net		(989) 362 4463	•		•	
Michigan	Grand Blanc	Beyond The Rain Forest	12830 South Saginaw	48439	slord41496@aol.com		(810) 953 0089	•		•	
Michigan	Grandville	Threadbender	5570 Wilson Avenue SW	49418	threadbenderinc@msn.com		616-531-6641	•			
Michigan	Grosse Pointe	Knotted Needle	20229 Mack Avenue	48236	knottedneedle@gmail.com		(313) 886 2828	•		•	
Michigan	Macomb	Crafty Lady Trio	15401 Hall Road	48044	contact.us@craftyladytrio.com	www.craftyladiotrio.com	(586) 566 8008	•		•	
Michigan	Harrison Township	City Knits	26050 Crocker Blvd	48045	admin@cityknits.com	www.cityknits.com	586-469-9665	•			
Michigan	Holland	Garenhuis Yarn Studio	27 W 9th Street	48423	Yarn@garenhuis.com	www.garenhuis.com	616-294-3492	•			
Michigan	Holland	Lizzie Ann's Wool Co.	54 E. 8TH Street	49423	llzgraff@aol.com		616 392-2035	•		•	
Michigan	**Ludington**	**FLAGSHIP Nautical Yarn**	**108 South Rath Avenue**	**49431**	**info@nauticalyarn.com**	**www.nauticalyarn.com**	**231-845-9868**	•			
Michigan	Port Huron	Mary Maxim	2001 Holland Avenue	48060	barb@marymaxim.com	www.marymaxim.com	810-987-2000	•			
Michigan	Royal Oak	Ewe-Nique Knits	515 South Lafayette Avenue	48067	amy@ewe-niqueknits.com	www.ewe-niqueknits.com	(248) 584 3001	•		•	
Michigan	Traverse City	Lost Art Yarn Shoppe	741 Woodmere Avenue	49686	gerhilduhl@centurytel.net		(231) 941 1263	•		•	
Minnesota	Coon Rapids	All About Yarn	455 99th Ave NW # 180	55433	info@allaboutyarn.com	www.allaboutyarn.biz	763-785-4900	•			
Minnesota	Duluth	Yarn Harbor Inc	4629 East Superior Street	55804	yarnharbor@yahoo.com		(218) 724 6432	•		•	
Minnesota	Lakeville	Unwind Yarn Shop	10460-170th Street West	55044	unwindyarnshopmn@gmail.com		(952) 303 6617	•		•	
Minnesota	**Maple Grove**	**FLAGSHIP Amazing Threads**	**11262 86th Avenue North**	**55369**	**info@amazing-threads.com**	**www.amazing-threads.com**	**763-391-7700**	•	•	•	
Minnesota	Mendota Heights	3 Kitten Needle Arts	750 Main Street Suite 112	55118	laura@3kittensneedlesarts.com		(651) 457 4969	•		•	
Minnesota	Minneapolis	Linden Yarn & Textiles	5814 Excellsior Boulevard	55416	chrisknits@lindenyarn.com	www.lindenyarn.com	(952) 303 3895	•			
Minnesota	Minneapolis	Depth of Field	409 Cedar Ave South	55454	dfyarn@gmail.com	www.depthoffieldyarn.com	(612) 340-0529	•			
Minnesota	Northfield	Northfield Yarn	314 Division Street South	55057	info@northfieldyarn.com	www.northfieldyarn.com	(507) 645-1330	•			
Minnesota	Saint Cloud	Bonnie's Spinning Wheel	16 21st Avenue SO	56301	bonnies@integra.net		(320) 253 2426	•		•	
Minnesota	St Paul	The Yarnery	840 Grand Ave	55105	yarnery@gmail.com	www.yarnery.com	(651) 222-5793	•		•	
Minnesota	Still Water	Darn Knit Anyway	423 South Main Street	55082	aimee@darnknitanyway.com		(651) 342 1386	•		•	
Minnesota	**White Bear Lake**	**FLAGSHIP A Sheepy Yarn Shoppe, Inc.**	**2185 3rd Street**	**55110**	**info@sheepyyarn.com**	**www. sheepyyarn.com**	**651 426-5463**	•		•	
Minnesota	Winona	Yarnology LLC	65 E 3rd Street	55987	info@yarnologymn.com		(507) 474 9444	•		•	
Minnesota	Woodbury	Knitting From The Heart	1785 Radio Drive	55125	heartknits@comcast.net	www.heartknits.com	651.702.0880	•			
Minnesota	Moorhead	Prairie Fiber Arts Center	127 4th Street South	56560	prairiefiberarts@outlook.com	www.prairiefiberarts.com	(218) 284-0004	•			
Missouri	Independence	Angelika's Yarn Store	500 Dodgion Street	64050	angelikas@yarn-store.com		(816) 461 5505	•		•	
Missouri	St. Louis	Knitorious	3268 Watson Road	63139	sandy@knitorious.com	www.knitorious.com	314-646-8276	•			
Montana	**Billings**	**FLAGSHIP Yarn Bar**	**1940 Grand Ave**	**59102**	**yarnbarmt@gmail.com**		**406-534-4032**	•			•
Montana	Eureka	The Woolery Mammoth LLC	576 US Highway 93 North	59917	woolerymammoth@gmail.com		(406) 297 7403	•		•	
Montana	Hamilton	The Yarn Center	110 Pinckney	59840	threeyorkiesyarn@aol.com		(406) 363 1400	•		•	
Montana	Missoula	Joseph's Coat Yarn	115 South 3rd St West	59801	josephscoatyarn@gmail.com		(406) 549 1419	•		•	
Nebraska	**Lincoln**	**FLAGSHIP Knit Paper Scissors**	**6701 Vanderslice Circle**	**68516**	**knitandpaperandscissors@gmail.com**	**www.knit-paper-scissors.com**	**(402) 429 8029**	•		•	
Nebraska	Omaha	Personal Threads Boutique	8600 Cass Street	68114	sales@personalthreads.com	www.personalthreads.com	402 391-7733	•		•	
Nevada	Reno	Yarn Refuge	20 Saint Lawrence Ave	89698	pam@yarnrefuge.com	www.yarnrefuge.com	707-384-1600	•			
Nevada	**Reno**	**FLAGSHIP Jimmy Beans Wool**	**4850 Joule Street Suite A1**	**89502**	**support@jimmybeanswool.com**	**www.jimmybeanswool.com**	**(775) 827-9276**	•		•	
New Hampshire	Concord	The Elegant Ewe	75 South Main Street Unit #3	03301	info@elegantewe.com		(603) 226 0066	•		•	
New Hampshire	Dover	Spinning Yarns	511 Central Avenue	03820	info@spinningyarnsnh.com		(603) 740 6476	•			
New Hampshire	Harrisville	Harrisville Designs Inc	4 Mill Alley	03450	hdretail@harrisville.com		(603) 827 3333	•			
New Jersey	Madison	The Blue Purl	60 Main Street	07940	thebluepurl@gmail.com		(973) 377 5648	•		•	
New Jersey	Hazlet	Moore Yarn LLC	1366 Route 36	07730	mitzy@mooreyarn.com		(732) 847 3665	•		•	
New Jersey	Hillsborough	The Yarn Attic	5 Layton Court	08844	rhonda@theyarnattic.com		(908) 864 5311	•		•	
New Jersey	Montclair	Yarnia	282 N Mountain Ave	07043	amanda@shoopyarnia.com	www.shopyarnia.com	862-368-1715	•			
New Jersey	Mount Holly	Woolbearers LLC	90 High Street	08060	woolbearers@verizon.net		(609) 914 0003	•		•	
New Jersey	Princeton	Pins And Needles	8 Chambers Street	08542	pinsandneedlesinfo@gmail.com		(609) 921 9075	•		•	
New Jersey	Teaneck	Yarndezvous	495 Cedar Lane	07666	lori@yarndezvous.com	www.yarndezvous.com	201-357-4710	•			
New Mexico	Albuquerque	The Yarn Store at Nob Hill	120 Amherst Drive NE	87106	teresa@theyarnstoreatnobhill.com		(505) 717 1535	•		•	
New York	Barrytown	Fabulous Yarn	117 Barrytown Road	12507	fabulousyarn@gmail.com		(917) 226 5074	•		•	
New York	Brooklyn	M & M Yarn Connection	1766-46th Street	11204	em1766@gmail.com		(718) 436 5262	•		•	
New York	Canton	The Celtic Knot Textiles	17 Main Street	13617	theceltic knot@hotmail.com		(315) 714 3206	•		•	
New York	Farmingdale	Infinite Yarns Inc.	34 Hemstead Turnpike 3B	11735	annes@infiniteyarns.com	www.infiniteyarns.com	(516) 293-0010	•			
New York	Ithaca	Homespun Boutique	314 East State Street	14850			(607) 277 0954	•		•	
New York	**Jamesville**	**FLAGSHIP Yarn Cupboard**	**6487 East Seneca Turnpike**	**13078**	**info@yarncupboard.com**		**(315) 399 5148**	•		•	
New York	Kauneonga Lake	Knit One Needlepoint Too	140 Lake Street	12749	k1n2@aol.com		(845) 583 5648	•		•	
New York	New York	Annie & Company Needlepoint	1763 2nd Avenue	10128	annies knitting@gmail.com		(212) 360-7266				
New York	New York	Knitty City	208 West 79th Street	10024	pearl@knittycitynyc.com		(212) 787-5896				
New York	**New York**	**FLAGSHIP String**	**144 E 74th Street**	**10021**	**info@stringyarns.com**	**www.stringyarns.com**	**212-288-9276**	•	•	•	
New York	Nyack	Knitting Nation	30 North Broadway	10960	knittingnation@gmail.com		(845) 348 0100	•		•	
New York	Sayville	Rumpelstiltskin	22 Main Street	11782	milton2@optonline.net		(631)750-1790	•		•	
New York	Staten Island	The Naked Sheep Inc.	4038 Victory Boulevard	10309	tracygliaos@me.com		(718) 477-9276				
North Carolina	Apex	Downtown Knits	12 North Salem	27502	info@downtownknits.com		(919) 249 5638	•		•	
North Carolina	Franklin	Silver Threads & Golden Needle	41 East Main Street	28734	franklinncyarn@yahoo.com		(828) 349 0515	•		•	
North Carolina	Nags Head	Yarn and More	4104 S Virginia Dare Trail #21	27959	deanna@yarnandmoreinc.com		(252) 715 2244	•		•	
North Carolina	**Raleigh**	**FLAGSHIP Great Yarns**	**1208 Ridge Rd**	**27607**	**PJWhartman@yahoo.com**	**www.greatyarns.net**	**919-271-1699**	•		•	•
North Carolina	Swansboro	The Salty Sheep Yarn Shop	101-4 Church Street	28584	thesaltysheep@gmail.com		(910) 325 0018	•		•	
North Carolina	Winston Salem	Knit One Smock Too	4003-A Country Club Road	27104	knitonesmocktoo@gmail.com		(336) 765 9099	•		•	
Ohio	Cincinnati	Hank Yarn LLC	2651 Observatory Avenue, Suite 101	45208	hankyarn@me.com	www.hankyarn.com	513 386-9869	•		•	
Ohio	Cincinnati	Keepsake/Patternworks	10151 Carver Road Suite 200	45242	lynne.lounsbury@fwcommunity		(603) 253 8148	•		•	
Ohio	Cincinnati	Silk Road Textile	6106 Hamilton Avenue	45224	silkroadcincy@gmail.com		(513) 541-3700				
Ohio	Cleveland	Fine Points Inc.	12620 Larchmere Boulevard	44120	liz@finepoints.com		(216) 229-6644				
Ohio	Dayton	Fiberworks LLC	1350 A North Fairfield Road	45432	fiberworksdayton@att.net		(937) 429-9276				
Ohio	Dayton	Strings Attached Yarns	225 North Main Street	45402	kristen@stringsattachedyarns.com		(937) 221 9585	•		•	
Ohio	Dublin	Knitting Temptations	35 South High Street	43017	knit2temptations@gmail.com		(614) 734 0618	•		•	
Ohio	Hamilton	Lambikins Hideaway	217 South B Street	45013	nora@lambikinshideaway.com		(513) 895-5648				
Ohio	Lakewood	River Colors Studio	1387 Sloane Avenue	44107	orders@rivercolors.com		(216) 228 9276	•		•	
Ohio	Mason	Main Street Yarns	126 West Main Street	45040	liseporter@ymail.com		(513) 204 0078	•		•	
Ohio	Perrysburg	Yarn Cravin' LLC	146 East Second Street	43551	yarncravin@bex.net		(419) 872-9276				
Ohio	Springboro	Wooly Bully Yarn Company	1355 Main Street	45066	woolybullyyarnco@aol.com		(937) 748 1002	•		•	
Oregon	**Ashland**	**FLAGSHIP The Web-Sters**	**11 North Main St**	**97520**	**info@yarnatwebsters.com**	**www.yarnatwebsters.com**	**(800) 482-9801**	•		•	
Oregon	Bandon	The Wool Company	990 2nd Street SE	97411	woolco@mycomspan.com		(541) 347 3912	•		•	
Oregon	**Beaverton**	**FLAGSHIP For Yarns Sake**	**11767 SW Beaverton**	**97005**	**anne@foryarnssake.com**	**www.foryarnssake.com**	**(503)469-9500**	•		•	
Oregon	Eugene	The Knit Shop	2811 Oak Street	97405	jean@knit-shop.com		(541) 434 0430	•		•	
Oregon	Hillsboro	Black Sheep at Orenco	6154 NE Brighton Street	97209	tina@blacksheepatorenco.com		(971) 732 5391	•		•	
Oregon	Hood River	Knot Another Hat	16 Oak Street, Suite 202	97031	customerservice@knotanotherhat.com		541-308-0002	•		•	
Oregon	McMinnville	Oregon Knitting Company LLC	448 NE 3rd St.	07128	oregonknittingco@gmail.com		(971) 261 9608	•		•	
Oregon	Portland	Dublin Bay Knitting Co.	1227 NW 11th Avenue	97209	info@dublinbay.net		(503) 223 3229	•		•	
Oregon	**Portland**	**FLAGSHIP Northwest Wools**	**3524 SW Troy**	**97219**			**(503) 244-5024**	•		•	
Oregon	Roseburg	Knotty Lady Yarns, LLC	642 SE Jackson Street	97470	knottyladyyarns@yahoo.com	knottyladyyarns@yahoo.com	541-673-2199	•			
Pennsylvania	Bethlehem	The Knitters Edge	1601 West Broad Street	18018	unwind@theknittersedge.com		(610) 419 9276	•		•	
Pennsylvania	Bridgeville	Kid Ewe Knot, Inc.	429 Washington Avenue, Suite 4	15017	owner@kideweknot.com		(412) 257-2557				
Pennsylvania	Doylestown	Forever Yarn	15 W. Oakland Ave	18901	foreveryarn@yahoo.com		(215) 348 5648	•		•	
Pennsylvania	Emmaus	Conversational Threads Inc	6 South 4th Street	18049	cfitzpa289@aol.com		(610) 421 8889	•		•	
Pennsylvania	Ligonier	Bo Peep Fine Yarn	221 West Main Street	15658	michelleg411@hotmail.com		(724) 238 4040	•		•	
Pennsylvania	Lititz	Ewebiquitous LLC	39 East Main Street	17543	ewebiquitous@yahoo.com		(717) 568 8890	•		•	
Pennsylvania	New Holland	The Speckled Sheep	423 Diem Woods Drive	17557	info@thespeckledsheep.com		(717) 435 8359	•		•	
Pennsylvania	Newtown Square	Slip Knot	3715 West Chester Pike	19073	info@slipknotknit.com		(610) 359 9070	•		•	
Pennsylvania	Phoenixville	Purls of Wisdom	2208 Kimberton Road	19460	purlsofwisdompa@gmail.com		(610) 933 5010	•		•	
Pennsylvania	**Pittsburgh**	**FLAGSHIP Dyed In The Wool**	**3458 Babcock Boulevard**	**15237**	**dyedinthewool@msn.com**		**(412) 364-0310**				
Pennsylvania	Pittsburgh	Knit One	2721 Murray Avenue	15217	lknoopvery@gmail.com		(412) 421 6666	•		•	
Pennsylvania	Sewickley	Sewickley Yarns	435 Beaver Street	15143	sewickleyyarns@gmail.com		(412) 741 8894	•		•	
Rhode Island	**Barrington**	**FLAGSHIP Knit One Quilt Too LLC**	**10 Anoka**	**02806**	**info@knitonequilttoo.com**		**(410) 337 5578**	•		•	
South Carolina	Beaufort	Coastal Knitting LLC	900 Port Republic	29902	judyalgar@yahoo.com		(843) 470 0148	•		•	
South Dakota	Sioux Falls	Athena Fibers	3915 S. Hawthorne	57105	athenafibers@gmail.com	www.athenafibers.com	(605) 271 0741	•		•	
Tennessee	Brentwood	Bliss Yarns	127 Franklin Road	37027	info@blissyarns.com	www.blissyarns.com	615-370-8717	•			
Tennessee	Knoxville	Loopville	5204 Kingston Pike	37919	jinka@loopvilleyarn.com		(865) 584 9772	•		•	
Texas	Austin	Red Beauty Textiles	PO Box 153216	78715	redbeautytextiles@gmail.com		(512) 900 1092	•		•	
Texas	Austin	Yarnbow	1310 Ranch Road 620 South, Suite B202	78734	mail@yarnbow.com	www.yarnbow.com	512-777-1703	•		•	
Texas	Comfort	The Tinsmith's Wife	405 7th Street	78013	tinsmithwife@hctc.net		(830) 995 5539	•		•	
Texas	Dallas	Holley's Yarn Shoppe	5211 Forest Lane, Suite 115	75244	info@holleysyarn.com	www.holleysyarn.com	972-503-5648	•		•	

County	Town / City	Stockist	Address	Postcode	Email	Website	Telephone	Yarn	Fabric	Online	Instore
Texas	Dripping Springs	The Sated Sheep LLC	100 Commons Road Suite 5	78620	thesatedsheep@gmail.com		(512) 858 2053	•			•
Texas	Fort Worth	West 7th Wool	3612 West 7th	76107	info@west7thwool.com		(817) 731 5044	•			•
Texas	Houston	Nimblefingers	12456 Memorial Drive	77024	nimblefingerstx@gmail.com		(713) 722 7244	•			•
Texas	Novasota	WC Mercantile	201 East Washington Avenue	77868	info@wcmercantile.com		(936) 825 3378	•			•
Utah	Ogden	The Needlepoint Joint LLC	241 Historic 25th Street	84401	npj@xmission.com		(801) 394 4355	•			•
Utah	Provo	Wasatch and Wool Yarns	1635 West Redstone Ctr Drive	84098	wasatchandwool@outlook.com		(435) 901 0525	•			•
Utah	Provo	Harmony LLC	315 East Center Street	84606	lauratharmon@gmail.com		(801) 615 0268	•			•
Vermont	Chester	Six Loose Ladies Yarn	287 Main Street	5143	sixlooseladies@gmail.com		(802) 875 7373	•			•
Vermont	Norwich	Northern Lights Yarn Shop	289 Main Street	5055	nnys2000@aol.com		(802) 649 2000	•			•
Vermont	Woodstock	Whippletree Yarn Shop	7 Central Street	5091	whippletreeyarnshop@gmail.com		(802) 457 1325	•			•
Virginia	Fredericksburg	Hidden Purls	PO Box 142	22404	shop@hiddenpurls.com		(800) 285 1605	•			•
Virginia	**Fredericksburg**	**FLAGSHIP Untangled Purls LLC**	**2561 Cowan Blvd.**	**22401**	**untangledpurls@gmail.com**	**www.untangledpurls.com**	**540-479-8382**	•			
Virginia	Haymarket	Needles in the Haymarket	15125 Washington Street	20169	needlesinthehaymarket@gmail.com		(703) 659 1062	•			•
Virginia	Henrico	Knitting B LLC	8801 Three Chopt Rd	23229	info@knittingb.com		(804) 484 6005	•			•
Virginia	North Chesterfield	Got Yarn	723 Boulder Springs Drive	23225	yarnie@gotyarn.com		(804) 300 1155	•			•
Virginia	Occoquan	Yarn Cloud	204 Washington St	22125	Robyn@YarnCloud.com	www.yarncloud.com	(571) 408-4236				
Virginia	Yorktown	Coordinated Colors	4320 George Washington Memorial Hwy	23692		www.coordinatedcolors.com	(757) 874-3939				
Virginia	Middleburg	Hunt Country Yarns	PO Box 1206	20118	hcy@skeins.com		(540) 253 9990	•			
Virginia	Midlothian	Dances With Wool	1229 Sycamore Square	23113	shop@danceswithwoolrva.com		(804) 690 2978	•			•
Washington	**Bainbridge Island**	**FLAGSHIP Churchmouse Yarn and Teas**	**118 Madrone Lane**	**98110**	**info@churchmouseyarns.com**	**www.churchmouseyarns.com**	**704-373-7442**	•		•	•
Washington	Burien	Town Square Fabric & Yarn	445 S.W 152nd Street #100	98166	cnouits@hotmail.com		(206) 246 9276	•			•
Washington	Carnation	Tolt Yarn And Wool LLC	PO Box 33	98014	kimberley@toltyarnandwool.com		(425) 333 4066	•			
Washington	Issaquah	The Nifty Knitter	317 NW Gilman Boulevard	98027	theniftyknittershop@gmail.com		(319) 512 9834	•			•
Washington	**Kennewick**	**FLAGSHIP Sheep's Clothing**	**3311 West Clearwater Ave B120**	**99336**	**latisha@aknottyhabit.com**		**(509) 734 2484**	•			•
Washington	Mount Vernon	Wildfibers	706 South First St	98273	sparker@wildfibers.net		360-336-5202	•			•
Washington	Olympia	Canvas Works	525 Columbia Street SW	98501	canvasworks@aol.com		(360) 352 4481	•			•
Washington	Renton	Knittery	601 S Grady Way	98057	gramywin1@hotmail.com		(425) 228 4694	•			•
Washington	Seattle	Acorn Street Shop	2818 NE 55th Street	98105	shop@acornstreet.com		(206) 525 1726	•			•
Washington	Seattle	The Fiber Gallery	8212 Greenwood Avenue North	98103	megan@fibergallery.com		(206) 706 4197	•			•
Washington	Seattle	The Tea Cozy Yarn Shop	5816 24th Avenue	98107	jean@teacozyyarn.com		(206) 783 3322	•			•
Washington	Seattle	The Weaving Works Inc.	6514 Roosevelt Way NE	98115	info@weavingworks.com		(206) 524 1221	•			•
Washington	Seattle	Tricoter	3121 E. Madison Street	98112	tricoter@tricoter.com		(206) 328 6506	•			•
Washington	Vancouver	Blizzard Yarn and Fiber	6924 NE Fourth Plain Blvd	98661	irina@blizzardyarnandfiber.com		(360) 991 5350	•			•
Wisconsin	Appleton	Iris Fine Yarns	132 E.Wisconsin Ave	54911	info@irisfineyarns.com	www.irisfineyarns.com	(920) 954 9001	•			•
Wisconsin	Bayfield	Brown Stone Centre	121 Rittenhouse Avenue	54814	brownstonecentre@gmail.com		(715) 779 3400	•			•
Wisconsin	Brookfield	Cream City Yarn	15565 W. North Avenue	53005	info@creamcityyarn.com	www.creamcityyarn.com	262 923-7014	•			•
Wisconsin	Delafield	Knitch	608 Milwaukee Street	53018	Knitch@knitch.net		262-646-9392	•			•
Wisconsin	Edina	Harriet & Alice	3922 West 50th Street	55424	kate@harrietandalice.com	www.harrietandalice.com	952-500-9724	•			
Wisconsin	Green Bay	Silver Thimble Quilt & Yarn	2475 University Avenue	54302	silverthimble@tds.net		(920) 468 1495	•			•
Wisconsin	Kenosha	Fiddlehead Yarns	7511-26th Ave	53142		www.fiddleheadyarns.com	262-925-6487	•			
Wisconsin	Madison	The Knitting Tree	2636 Monroe Street	53711	knittingtree@yahoo.com	www.knittingtree.com	608-238-0121	•			•
Wisconsin	Milwaukee	Knitting Knook LLC	6858 North Santa Monica Blvd	53217	knittingknook@me.com		(414) 540 4080	•			•
Wisconsin	Milwaukee	Fiberwood Studio	2709 N 92nd Street	53222	info@fiberwoodstudio.com	www.fiberwoodstudio.com	414-302-1849	•			
Wisconsin	Saint Germain	Just Yarnin LLC	446C Hwy 70 East	54558	justyarnin@gmail.com		(715) 479 9276	•			•
Wisconsin	Sheboygan	The Lost Sheep	808 Pennsylvania Ave	53081	pam@lostsheepyarnshop.com	www.lostsheepyarnshop.com	(920) 453-0316	•			
Wisconsin	Sturgeon Bay	Spin of Door County	108 South Madison Ave	54235	Spin@att.net	www.spinofdoorcounty.com	(920) 746 7746	•			•
Wisconsin	Verona	The Sow's Ear	125 South Main Street	53593	sylvie@knitandsip.com		(608) 848 2755	•			•
		Got Yarn			yarn4u@gmail.com	www.gotyarn.com	804-300-1155	•			
UNITED KINGDOM											
West Yorkshire	*Huddersfield*	*MEZ Crafts UK Ltd. (Distributor)*	*Unit 17F, Brooke's Mill, Armitage Bridge,*	*HD4 7NR*		*www.mezcrafts.com*	*01484 950630*	•	•	•	
Aberdeenshire	Aberdeen	Baa	43 Evan Street, Stonehaven	AB39 2ET	hello@baawool.co.uk	www.baawool.co.uk	01569 668 298	•		•	•
Aberdeenshire	Aberdeen	John Lewis	George Street	AB9 1BT		www.johnlewis.com	01224 625000	•	•		•
Aberdeenshire	Aberdeen	Wool for Ewe	83-85 Rosemount Place	AB25 2YE	info@woolforewe.co.uk	www.woolforewe.com	01224 643738	•			•
Aberdeenshire	Fraserburgh	Mary Bobbins	31 Commerce Street, Fraserburgh	AB43 9AQ		www.marybobbinsshop.co.uk	01346 510 784	•			•
Aberdeenshire	Banchory	Meg's Attic	70 High Street, Banchory	AB31 5SS		www.megsattic.co.uk		•			
Avon	Bristol	John Lewis	Cribbs Causeway	BS12 5TP		www.johnlewis.com	0117 959 1100	•	•		•
Bedfordshire	Leighton Buzzard	The Spotted Sheep	1 - 4 Peacock Mews	LU7 1JH		www.thespottedsheep.co.uk	01525 376456	•			•
Berkshire	Reading	John Lewis	Broad Street	RG7 4AH		www.johnlewis.com	01189 575955	•	•		•
Berkshire	Windsor	C & H Fabrics concession in Daniel	121-125 Peascod st	SL4 1Dp	windsor@candhfabrics.co.uk	www.candh.co.uk	01753 856315	•		•	•
Berkshire	Wokingham	Stitchery Do	31/35 Denmark Street	RG40 2AY	dreelanm@googlemail.com	www.stitcherydo.co.uk	01189 770 181	•	•		•
Buckinghamshire		Elliquilt				http://stores.ebay.co.uk/fabricologist			•		•
Buckinghamshire	Milton Keynes	Threads and Patches	15 Watling Street, Fenny Stratford	MK2 2BU	threadsandpatches@gmail.com	www.threadsandpatches.co.uk	01908 649687		•	•	•
Buckinghamshire	Marlow	Lady Sew and Sew	Institute Rd	SL7 1BN	info@ladysewandsew.co.uk		01628 890532	•			•
Buckinghamshire	Milton Keynes	John Lewis	Central Milton Keynes	MK1 1NN		www.johnlewis.com	01908 679171	•	•		•
Cambridgeshire	Barton	Backstitch	Burwash Manor Barns, New Road	CB23 7EY				•			•
Cambridgeshire	Cambridge	John Lewis	10 Downing Street	CB2 3DS		www.johnlewis.com	01223 361292	•	•		•
Cambridgeshire	Cambridge	The Sheep Shop	72 Beche Road	CB5 8HU	sarah@sheepshopcambridge.co.uk	www.sheepshopcambridge.co.uk	01223 311 268	•			•
Cambridgeshire	Peterborough	John Lewis	Queensgate Centre	PE1 1NL		www.johnlewis.com	01733 344644	•	•		•
Cambridgeshire	Kimbolton	Purlwise	21a High Street	PE28 OHB	jacqui@purlwise.co.uk		01480 861 727				•
Cambridgeshire	Ely	Sew Much To Do	7 High Street Passage, Ely	CB7 4NB		www.sewmuchtodo.co.uk		•			•
Cambridgeshire	Wisbech	Button Up and Stitch	5 Market Street	PE13 1EX	buttonupandstitch@hotmail.com		01945 580463		•		•
Carmarthenshire	Whitland	Colourways	Market Street	SA34 0AJ	shop@colourway.co.uk	www.colourway.co.uk	01994 241333				•
Carmarthenshire		Esgair Fibres						•			•
Ceredigion	Lampeter	Calico Kate	36 High Street	SA48 7BB	kate@calicokate.co.uk	www.calicokate.co.uk	01570 422866		•	•	•
Ceredigion	Aberystwyth	Clare Wools	13 Great Darkgate Street	SY23 1DE	cynthia@clarewools.co.uk	www.clarewools.co.uk	01970 617786	•			•
Cheshire	Cheadle	John Lewis	Wilmslow Road	SK9 3RN		www.johnlewis.com	0161 491 4914	•	•		•
Cheshire	Marple	Sew-In of Marple	46 Market Street, Marple	SK6 7AD		www.myknittingyarnandwool.co.uk	0161 427 2529	•		•	•
Cheshire	Nantwich	Stitch	3 Mill Street	CW5 5ST	nfo@StitchNantwich.co.uk		01270 625318	•	•		•
Cheshire	**Warrington**	**FLAGSHIP Black Sheep Wools**	**Glaziers Lane, Culcheth**	**WA3 4AQ**	**orders@blacksheepwools.com**	**www.blacksheepwools.com**	**01925 764231**	•	•	•	•
Clackmannanshire	Alloa	Wee County Yarns			clare@wee-county-yarns.co.uk	www.wee-county-yarns.co.uk	01259 759000	•		•	•
Conwy	Abergele	Snowdonia Wools	2 Pen Y Bont House	LL22 7HA	glenys@snowdoniawool.co.uk		1745823835	•			•
Conwy	Llanrwst	Ar-y-Gweill	24 Station Road	LL26 0EP	arygweill@aol.com		01492 641149	•	•		•
Cornwall	Bude	Coastal Yarns	The Old Forge , Lower Wharf, Cornwall	EX23 8LG	info@coastalyarns.co.uk	www.coastalyarns.co.uk	01288 350304	•			•
Cornwall	Truro	Truro Fabrics	Telegraph House, Calenick Street	TR1 2SF	info@trurofabrics.co.uk	www.trurofabrics.com	01872 222130	•	•		•
Cornwall	Penzance	Harbour Crystals and Wools	25 Causewayhead	TR18 2SP	helen@harbour-wools.co.uk	www.harbour-wools.co.uk	01736 874455	•			•
Cornwall	Launceston	Cowslip Workshops	Newhouse Farm, St Stephens	PL15 8JX	info@cowslipworkshops.co.uk	www.cowslipworkshops.co.uk	01566 772654		•	•	
Cumbria	Carlisle	Superior Sewing Centre	14 Rosemary Lane	CA3 8PW	sales@sewingknitting.co.uk	www.sewingknitting.co.uk	01228 599 880	•			
Cumbria	Ulverston	Loopy	51 Market Street, Ulverston			www.loopywool.co.uk	01229 480080	•			•
Derbyshire	Buxton	Sew-In of Buxton	1 Spring Gardens	SK17 6BJ		www.myknittingyarnandwool.co.uk	01298 26636	•		•	•
Devon	Bovey Tracy	Spin A Yarn	26 Fore Street	TQ13 9AD	info@spinayarndevon.co.uk	www.spinayarndevon.co.uk	01626 836203	•			•
Devon	Modbury	Hulu	Sentinel House, Poundwell	PL21 0XX	sales@hulucraft.co.uk	www.hulucrafts.co.uk	01548 831911	•		•	•
Devon	Dartington	The Wool Merchant	The Shops at Dartington, Shinners Bridge	TQ9 6TQ	info@thewoolmerchant.co.uk	www.thewoolmerchant.co.uk	01884 243569	•			•
Devon	Totnes	Creative Crafts & Needlework	18 High Street	TQ9 5RY	naomi_mason@hotmail.com	www.creative-crafts-needlework.co.uk	01803 866002	•			•
Devon	Exeter	Exeter Sewing Machine Company	7 Heavitree Road, Exeter	EX1 2LD	info@exetersewing.co.uk	www.exetersewing.co.uk	01392 275660	•	•		•
Devon	Paignton	Knitting Solutions	13 Seaway	TQ3 2NX	beads@beadsolutions.co.uk	www.knittingwoolsolutions.co.uk	01803 552072	•		•	•
Devon	Tavistock	Knitting Korner	Pepper Street	PL19 OBD	knittingkorner@hotmail.co.uk	www.knittingkorner.co.uk	01822 617410	•		•	•
Devon	Tiverton	Tiverton Bead and Wool Shop	5 William Street	EX16 6BJ	info@beadandwoolshop.co.uk	www.beadandwoolshop.co.uk	07525 233996	•		•	•
Dorset	Bournemouth	Carly's Crafts	1a Cardigan Road, Bournemouth	BH9 1BJ	michelek1964@hotmail.com	carlyscrafts.org.uk	01202 512106	•			•
Dorset	Ferndown	Golden Hands	150 Station Road, West Moors	BH22 0JB	suey141@hotmail.co.uk	www.goldenhandswestmoors.co.uk	01202 639360	•		•	•
Dorset	Christchurch	The Crafty Knitter	103 Bargates, Christchurch	BH23 1QQ	jo@thecraftyknitter.co.uk	www.thecraftyknitter.co.uk	01202 474449	•			•
Dorset	Blandford Forum	Knitwits	15 East Street	DT11 7DU	judith.evans7@btinternet.com		01258 488542	•			•
Dumfries & Galloway	Castle Douglas	Art 2 Go	130-132 King Street	DG7 1LU	sarah@outbackyarns.co.uk	www.outbackyarns.com	01556 504900	•	•	•	•
Edinburgh	Edinburgh	John Lewis	St James Centre	EH1 3SP		www.johnlewis.com	0131 556 9121	•	•		•
Lanarkshire	Biggar	Biggar Stitches	81 High Street	ML12 6DL	kim@biggarstitches.com	www.biggarstitches.com	01899 220837	•	•	•	•
Lothian	**Edinburgh**	**FLAGSHIP McAree Bros**	**19 Howe Street**	**EH3 6TE**	**sales@mcadirect.com**	**www.mcadirect.com**	**0131 558 1747**	•	•	•	•
Lothian	Edinburgh	Edinburgh Patchwork	4 Belleyue Street	EH7 4BY	edinburghpatchwork@gmail.com	www.edinburghpatchwork.com	0131 538 5030		•		•
Lothian	Edinburgh	My Bear Paw	50 Lochrin Buildings	EH3 9ND	hello@mybearpaw.co.uk	www.mybearpaw.co.uk	0131 228 6377		•	•	•
Lothian	Edinburgh	Fabric Focus	131 East Claremont Street	EH7 4JA	fabricfocus@outlook.com	www.fabricfocus.co.uk	0131 558 3888		•		•
East Sussex	Brighton	C & H Fabrics	179 Western Road,	BN1 2BA		www.candh.co.uk	01273 321959	•	•		•
East Sussex	Eastbourne	C & H Fabrics	82/86 Terminus Road	BN21 3LX		www.candh.co.uk	01323 410428	•			•
East Yorks	Driffield	C Foster & Son	Little Houndales Knits, Little Houndale Farm	YO25 4LF	kath@littlehoundalesknits.com		01377 255093				•
Essex	Baintree	Sconch	Blake House Craft Centre, Blake End near Baintree	CM776RA	sales@sconch.com	www.sconch.com	01376 743123	•		•	•
Essex	Billericay	Craft Arena	Studios 48-50, Barleylands Craft Village, Barleylands Road,	CM11 2UD		www.craftarena.co.uk	01268 523780	•		•	•
Essex	Burnham-on-Crouch	Creative Lady	1 High Street	CM0 8AG	creativelady70@yahoo.co.uk	www.creativelady.co.uk	01621 928225		•		•
Essex	Blake End, Rayne	And Sew On Fabrics	Unit 12 Blake House Craft Centre	CM77 6SH	info@andsewonfabrics.com	www.andsewonfabrics.com	01376 346 532		•	•	•
Fife	Dunfermline	Sew Yarn Crafty	61 High Street	KY12 7DL	shop@sewyarncrafty.co.uk	www.sewyarncrafty.co.uk	01383 621 894	•		•	•
Fife	Pittenweem	The Woolly Brew	39 High Street	KY10 2PG		www.thewoollybrew.co.uk	01333 312042	•		•	•
Flintshire	Mold	Yarn O'clock	2 Earl Road, Mold	CH7 1AJ	yarnoclock@gmail.com	www.yarnoclock.co.uk	01352 218082	•			•
Flintshire	Mostyn	Abakhan	Coast Road	CH8 9DX			01745 562 100	•			•
	Altrincham	Abakhan	112 George Street	WA14 1RF			0161 928 2178	•			•
Glamorgan	Cardiff	John Lewis	The Hayes	CF10 1EG		www.johnlewis.com	029 2053 6000	•	•		•
Glamorgan	Penarth	Yarn & Yarns	22 Cornerswell Road	CF64 2UZ	yarnnyarns@yahoo.com	https://yarnnyarns.wordpress.com	02920 712097	•			•
Glamorgan	Swansea	Swansea Bay Yarns	88, St Helens Avenue	SA1 4NN	info@swanseabayyarns.co.uk	www.swanseabayyarns.co.uk	01792 469171	•			•
Gloucestershire	Stroud	Haberdashery Twist	28 High Street	GL5 1AJ			01453 297639	•	•		•
Gloucestershire	Cainscross	In Stitches	22 Westward Road	GL5 4JQ		www.institchesshop.co.uk	01453 764887	•			•
Greater Manchester	Manchester	John Lewis	Peel Avenue, The Trafford Centre	M17 8JL		www.johnlewis.com	0161 491 4040	•			•
Greater Manchester	Cheadle	Sew-in of Cheadle	43 Wilmslow Road	SK8 1DR		www.myknittingyarnandwool.co.uk	0161 376 8643				
Gwynedd	Dolegllau	Knit One…	Maes Gwyn	LL40 1RB	angharad.murgatroyd@gmail.com	knitonedolgellau.com	01341 422194	•			•
Hampshire	Basingstoke	Pack Lane Wool Shop	171 Pack Lane, Kempshott	RG22 5HN	enquiries@packlanewool.co.uk	www.packlanewool.co.uk	01256 462590	•	•		•
Hampshire	Rowlands Castle	Handmade Studios	4 The Green	PO9 6BN	info@handmadestudios.org	www.handmadestudios.org	02392 412901	•	•		•
Hampshire	Southampton	John Lewis	West Quay Shopping Centre	SO15 1GY		www.johnlewis.com	0238 021 6400	•	•		•
Hampshire	Winchester	C & H Fabrics	8 High St	SO23 9JX		www.candh.co.uk	01962 843355	•	•		•
Hampshire	Liss	Liss Wools	38-40 Station Road	GU33 7DP	jacquiekennedy6@gmail.com	www.lisswools.co.uk	01730 893941	•			
Hertfordshire	Watford	John Lewis	The Harlequin, High St	WD2 8HL		www.johnlewis.com	01923 244266	•			•
Hertfordshire	Welwyn Garden City	John Lewis	Bridge Road	AL8 6TP		www.johnlewis.com	01707 323456	•	•		•
Hertfordshire	Buntingford	Crafty Angel	Unit 2b, Hyde Hall Farm, Sandon, Buntingford	SG9 0RU	info@craftyangel.co.uk	www.craftyangel.co.uk	01763 271 991	•	•	•	•
Hertfordshire	Ware	Crates of Wool	8a East Street	SG12 9HJ	brigid@cratesofwool.co.uk	www.cratesofwool.co.uk	01920 463436	•			•
Isle of Wight	Shanklin	Strictly Knitting	61 Regent Street	PO37 7AE	shop@strictlyknitting.co.uk	www.strictlyknitting.co.uk	01983 716252	•		•	•
Jersey	St Helier	Rachel's Textiles Studio	47 La Colomberie	JE2 4QA	rachel@rachelstextilesstudio.com	www.rachelstextilesstudio.com	01534 878877		•		•
Jersey	St Helier	Treadles	1 Hue Street	JE2 3RE	treadles@gmail.com		01534 280044	•	•		•
Kent	Broadstairs	C Wools	17 High Street	CT10 1LP	info@cwool.co.uk		01843 862848	•			•
Kent	Canterbury	C & H Fabrics	20-21 St Margarets St	CT1 2TH		www.candh.co.uk	01227 459760	•	•		•
Kent	Greenhithe	John Lewis	Bluewater	DA9 9SA		www.johnlewis.com	01322 624123	•	•		•
Kent	**Tenterden**	**FLAGSHIP Hoop**	**92 High Street**	**TN30 6JB**	**vanessa@hoopandloop.co.uk**		**1580388011**	•			•
Kent	Tunbridge Wells	C & H Fabrics	113/115 Mount Pleasant	TN1 1QS		www.candh.co.uk	01892 522618	•	•		•
Kent	Broadstairs	Chang Crafted	27 Station rd	CT7 9DB	changcrafted@outlook.com	www.changcrafted.co.uk	01843 210105	•			•
Kent	New Romney	Stitch N B…. In time	16 High st	TN28 8BY	sabine.winter@btinternet.com	www..knit1drop1.co.uk	07958 427853	•			•
Kinross-Shire	Kinross	Skeins and Bobbins	120 High Street, Kinross	KY13 8DA	skeinsandbobbins@outlook.com		01577 208 107	•			•
Lanarkshire	Glasgow	John Lewis	Buchanan Galleries	G4 0BZ		www.johnlewis.com	0141 353 6677	•	•		•
Leicestershire	Leicester	John Lewis	2 Bath House Lane, Highcross	LE1 4SA		www.johnlewis.com	0116 242 5777	•	•		•
Leicestershire	Leicester	Knit One	11 Pocklingtons Walk	LE1 6BU		www.knitone.uk.com	0116 254 0650	•		•	•
Lincolnshire	Cleethorpes	A Good Yarn	53 Cambridge Street	DN35 8HD	kate@agoodyarn.co.uk	www.agoodyarn.co.uk	01472 508707	•			•
Lincolnshire	Louth	M&G Designs	14 Eastgate	LN11 9NE	mandgneedleworkdesigns@btconnect.com	www.mandgdesignsneedlecraft.co.uk	1507604923	•	•		•
Lincolnshire	**Stamford**	**FLAGSHIP Ewe Wool Shop**	**4 Stamford Walk**	**PE9 2JE**	**i_love_ewe@ymail.com**	**www.i-love-ewe.com**	**01780 763838**	•			•
London	**Central London**	**FLAGSHIP John Lewis**	**300 Oxford Street**	**W1C 1DX**		www.johnlewis.com	**020 7629 7711**	•	•		•
London	**Central London**	**FLAGSHIP Liberty**	**Regent St**	**W1B 5AH**			**020 7734 1234**	•			•
London	Central London	Peter Jones	Sloane Square	SW1W 8EL			0207 881 6364	•			•
London	Crouch End	Nest	102 Weston Park	N8 9PP	info@handmadenest.co.uk	www.handmadenest.co.uk	2083408852	•			•
London	Herne Hill	Sharp Works	220 Railton Road	SE24 0JD	mail@sharpworks.co.uk	www.sharpworks.co.uk	2077387668	•			•
London	London	Fringe	108 Alexandra Park Road	N10 2AE	admin@fringe108.london	http://fringe108.london/	0208 8839478	•			•
London	London	Stitch Up Sewing Ltd	130 Arthur Road, Wimbledon	SW19 5PN	sandiebon@btinternet.com		0208 9446488	•			•
London	North London	John Lewis	Brent Cross Shopping Centre	NW4 3FL		www.johnlewis.com	020 8202 6535	•			•
London	Stratford	John Lewis	101 The Arcade, Montfichet Road	E20 1EL		www.johnlewis.com	020 8532 3500	•	•		•
London	London	Wild and Woolly	116 Lower Clapton Road	E5 OQX	wildandwoolly@gn.apc.org	www.wildandwoolyshop.co.uk	02089855231	•			•
London	East Dulwich	Really Maria	15 Lordship Lane	SE22 8EW	maria@sammur.com	www.reallymaria.com	020 3581 0909	•	•		•
London	White City	John Lewis	Westfield London shopping centre, Ariel way	W12 7FU		www.johnlewis.com		•		•	•
Merseyside	Liverpool	John Lewis	70 South John Street	L1 8BJ		www.johnlewis.com	0151 709 7070	•	•		•
Monmouthshire	**Abergavenny**	**FLAGSHIP The Wool Croft**	**9 Cross Street**	**NP7 5EH**	**info@thewoolcroft.co.uk**	**www.thewoolcroft.co.uk**	**01873 851551**	•	•		•
Moray	Elgin	Veronique's	20 Commerce Street	IV30 IBS			01343 547559	•	•		•
Norfolk	Diss	Diss Wool & Craft Shop	2 Cobbs Yard, St Nicholas Street	IP22 4LB	sales@disswoolandcrafts.com	www.disswoolandcrafts.com	01379 650640	•	•		•
Norfolk	Norwich	John Lewis	All Saints Green	NR1 3LX		www.johnlewis.com	01603 660021	•	•		•
Norfolk	**Norwich**	**FLAGSHIP Norfolk Yarn**	**11, Pottergate**	**NR2 1DS**	**norfolk_yarn@yahoo.co.uk**	**www.norfolkyarn.co.uk**	**01603 927034**	•	•	•	•
North Yorkshire	Bedale	New Jersey	38 Market Place	DL8 1EQ			01677 427 746	•			•
North Yorkshire	Clapham	Beckside Yarn & Needlecraft	Church Avenue	LA2 8EA	info@becksideyarns.co.uk	www.becksideyarns.co.uk	01524 251122	•			•
North Yorkshire	Filey	Beachcomber	35 Belle Vue St	YO14 9HU			01723 514434	•			•
North Yorkshire	Harrogate	Fine Fabrics of Harrogate	28 Regent Parade	HG1 5AZ	info@finefabricsofharrogate.co.uk	www.finefabricsofharrogate.co.uk	01423 530409	•	•	•	•

County	Town / City	Stockist	Address	Postcode	Email	Website	Telephone	Yarn	Fabric	Online	Instore
North Yorkshire	Harrogate	The Knitters Yarn		YO32 9AE		www.theknittersyarn.com	01423 816618				
North Yorkshire	York	John Lewis				www.johnlewis.com					
North Yorkshire	North Allerton	Natural Knitter Wool Shop	1a Friarage Street, Northallerton	DL6 1DP			01609 760348				
Northamptonshire	Rushden	Manfield Crafts	24 Griffiths Street	NN10 0RL	enquiries@manfieldcrafts.com		01933 314920				
Northamptonshire	Wellingborough	Jools Wools of Finedon	1a High Street	NN9 5JN	juliebusby14@hotmail.com	www.joolswools.co.uk	01933 680119				
Northern Ireland	Cullybackey	The Glen Gallery	48 Fenagh Road	BT43 5PH			02825 880354				
Northern Ireland	Newtownards	Yarn With Joanne	33 South Street	BT23 6DA	joanne@yarnwithjoanne.com	www.yarnwithjoanne.com	028 9182 9434				
Nottinghamshire	Beeston	Yarn	55 Chilwell Road	NG9 1EN	info@yarn-in-notts.com	www.yarn-in-notts.com	0115 925 3606				
Nottinghamshire	Nottingham	Evented Yarns and Gift Shop	72 Main Street, Long Eaton	NG10 1GW	crafts_united@btinternet.com		0115 972 4965				
Nottinghamshire	Nottingham	John Lewis	Victoria Centre	NG1 3QA		www.johnlewis.com	0115 941 8282				
Nottinghamshire	Mansfield Woodhouse	Sweet Sheep Fine Yarns	118 Hucknall Rd	NG5 1AD	yarnloft@gmail.com		07525 702433				
Oxfordshire	Bicester	Bicester Wools	86 Sheep Street	OX26 6JD	sweetsheep@sky.com	www.bicesterwools.com	01869 253966				
Oxfordshire	Burford	Burford Needlecraft	53 High Street	OX18 4QA	burfordneedlecraft@gmail.com		01993 822316				
Oxfordshire	**Henley on Thames**	**FLAGSHIP Lady Sew and Sew Warehouse** [ROWAN]	**Farm Road**	**RG9 1EJ**	jon@ladysewandsew.co.uk	www.ladysewandsewknits.co.uk	**01491 572528**				
Oxfordshire	**Oxford**	**FLAGSHIP Oxford Yarn Store** [ROWAN]	**3 North Parade Avenue**	**OX2 6LX**	karen@oxfordyarnstore.co.uk	www.oxfordyarnstore.co.uk	**01865 604112**				
Oxfordshire	Oxford	The Fibreworks	10a Middle Row, Chipping Norton	OX7 5NH		www.thefibreworks.com	01608 645070				
Oxfordshire	Oxford	John Lewis	101 The Westgate, Queen st	OX1 1PB		www.johnlewis.com	01865 351310				
Oxfordshire	Witney	Witney Sewing & Knitting Centre	61 High Street	OX28 6JA		www.witney-sewing-knitting.co.uk	01993 702772				
Pembrokeshire	Fishguard	Jane's of Fishguard	14 High Street	SA65 9AR		www.janes-fishguard.co.uk	01348 874443				
Perthshire	**Aberfeldy**	**FLAGSHIP Karelia House** [ROWAN]	**Kenmore Road, Comrie Bridge**	**PH15 2LS**			**01887 822027**				
Perthshire	Perth	Great British Yarns LTD	Lermoos, Duncrievi, Glenfarg, Perth	PH2 9PD	info@greatbritishyarns.co.uk	www.greatbritishyarns.co.uk	01577 830742				
Perthshire	By Blair Atholl	The House of Bruar		PH18 5TW		www.houseofbruar.com	01796 483236				
Perthshire	Perth	The Peacock and the Tortoise	29 George Street	PH1 5LA	thepeacockandthetortoise@gmail.com	www.thepeacockandthetortoise.co.uk	01738 787309				
Scottish Borders	Jedburgh	Stitchin at No 1	32 High Street	TD8 6DG	stitchinatno1@gmail.com		01835 863366				
Scottish Borders	Melrose	The Fabric Shop Melrose	27 High Street	TD6 9PA	melanie@fabricshopmelrose.com	www.fabricshopmelrose.com	01896 823423				
Shropshire	Ludlow	The Wool Shop	13 Broad Street	SY8 1NG	thewoolshop.jean@hotmail.co.uk	www.ludlow-woolshop.co.uk	01584 872586				
Shropshire	Much Wenlock	Ippikin	59 The High Street	TF13 6AE	ippikin@googlemail.com	www.ippikin.co.uk	01952 728871				
Shropshire	Shrewsbury	Felt Sew Wooly	Unit 10, The Mall, Bank Farm Road	SY3 6DU		www.feltsewwooly.co.uk	01743 249504				
Somerset	Bath	wool	19 Old Orchard Street	BA1 1JU	laura@woolbath.co.uk	www.woolbath.co.uk	01225 469144				
Somerset	Frome	Marmalade Yarns	11 Catherine Hill	BA11 1BZ	marmaladeyarns@gmail.com	www.marmaladeyarns.co.uk	01373 473252				
Somerset	Porlock	Jana Henrie	Bridge House, High Street, Exmoor National Park	TA24 8PY	janahenrie@btconnect.com	www.janahenrie.co.uk	01643 862058				
Somerset	Ilminster	The Sewing Corner	18b Silver Street	TA19 0DJ	thesewingcorner26@gmail.com	www.thesewingcorner.co.uk	07581 221228				
Somerset	Weston Super Mare	The Wool Sanctuary	68 Ashcombe Road	BS23 3DX	suziebeans@outlook.com	www.thewoolsanctuary.com	07805 126078				
Somerset	Yeovil	C&H Concession in Beales	23-25 High st	BA20 1RU	yeovil@candhfabrics.co.uk	www.candh.co.uk	07710 70137				
South Yorkshire	Sheffield	John Lewis	Barkers Pool	S1 1EP		www.johnlewis.com	0114 276 8831				
Staffordshire	Leek	Bibelot	7 Sheepmarket	ST13 5HW	hello@bibelot.co.uk	www.bibelot.co.uk	01538 388764				
Staffordshire	Lichfield	The Knitting Corner	Unit 3, Curborough Hall Farm, Watery Lane	WS13 8ES	theknittingcorner@btinternet.com		01543 415833				
Staffordshire	Newcastle under Lyme	K2tog	63 High Street, Wolstanton	ST5 0EB	sales@cucumberpatch.com	www.cucumberpatch.com	01782 577263				
Staffordshire	Barton under Needwood	Zarela	25 Park Road, Barton Under Needwood, Burton Upon Trent	DE13 8DW	sales@zarela.co.uk	www.zarela.co.uk	01283 713742				
Staffordshire	Burton on Trent	Chrissy's Crafts	Craythorne Farm, Craythorne Road, Burton on Trent	DE13 0AZ	thewoolshop@chrissyscrafts.com		01283 532336				
Suffolk	**Bury St Edmonds**	**FLAGSHIP Sew Much To Do** [ROWAN]	**23 Hatter Street, Bury St Edmonds, Suffolk**	**IP33 1NE**		www.sewmuchtodo.co.uk	**01284 755 459**				
Suffolk	Long Melford	The Woolpatch	Aerial House, Hall Road	CO10 9JR	stuart@thewoolpatch.com	www.thewoolpatch.com	01787 313452				
Suffolk	Bredfield	The Knitters Attic			enquiries@theknittersattic.co.uk	www.theknittersattic.co.uk	01394 542 077				
Suffolk	Ipswich	Daisy May Quilting	34 Westland, Martlesham Heath	IP5 3SU	info@daisymay.biz	www.daisymay.biz	01473				
Suffolk	Monks Eleigh	Oliven	Bridge Farm Barns	IP7 7AY	info@oliven.co.uk	www.oliven.co.uk	01449 741530				
Suffolk	Stowmarket	Stitch X Stitch	24 Bury Street	IP14 1HH	hello@stitchxstitch.co.uk	www.stitchxstitch.co.uk	01449 257070				
Surrey	Guildford	C & H Fabrics	7/8 white lion walk, Guildford	GU1 3DN		www.candh.co.uk	01483 301380				
Surrey	Kingston	John Lewis	Wood Street	KT1 1TE		www.johnlewis.com	020 8547 3000				
County Durham	Durham	The Woolly Workshop	Cottage 1, Fowlers Yard, Back Silver Street, Durham	DH1 3RA		www.thewoollyworkshop.co.uk					
Tyne & Wear	Newcastle upon Tyne	John Lewis	Eldon Square	NE99 1AB		www.johnlewis.com	0191 232 5000				
Warwickshire	Warwick	Warwick Wools	17 Market Place	CV34 4S	mail@warwickwools.co.uk	www.warwickwools.co.uk	01926 492853				
West Midlands	Coleshill	Remember When	80 High Street	B46 3AH	info@rememberwhenshop.co.uk	www.rememberwhenshop.co.uk	01675 466418				
West Midlands	Solihull	John Lewis	Touchwood	B90 4SH		www.johnlewis.com	0121 704 1121				
West Midlands	Solihull	Stitch Solihull	Cedar Cottage, Notcutts	B94 4EN	sales@stitchsolihull.com	www.stitchsolihull.com	0121 3146888				
West Sussex	Chichester	C & H Fabrics	33/34 North Street	PO19 1LX		www.candh.co.uk	01243 783300				
West Sussex	Horsham	C & H Fabrics	7 Black Horse Way	RH12 1NP	horsham@candhfabrics.co.uk	www.candh.co.uk	01403 242127				
West Sussex	**Shoreham by Sea**	**FLAGSHIP Shoreham Knitting** [ROWAN]	**19 East Street**	**BN43 5ZE**	sales@englishyarns.co.uk	www.englishyarns.co.uk	**01273 461029**				
West Sussex	Worthing	The Eclectic Maker	13 Station Parade, Tarring Road	BN11 4SS	hello@theeclecticmaker.co.uk	www.theeclecticmaker.co.uk	01903 681000				
West Yorkshire	Brighouse	Baa Baa Brighouse	11 Church Street, Rastrick, Brighouse	HD6 3NF		www.baabaabrighouse.co.uk					
West Yorkshire	Hebden Bridge	Attica	Unit 10E Top Land Country Business Park	HX7 5RW	info@attica-yarns.co.uk	www.attica-yarns.co.uk					
Wiltshire	Bradford on Avon	Nosek's Just Gems	4 Lamb Yard, Kingston Road	BA15 1FG	caron@noseks.co.uk	www.noseksjustgems.com	01225 706222				
Wiltshire	Cricklade	Cricklade Needlecrafts	89a High Street	SN6 6DF	info@crickladecrafts.co.uk	www.crickladecrafts.co.uk	01793 750604				
Wiltshire	Salisbury	Born To Knit	Studio 4, Fisherton Mill, Fisherton Street	SP2 7QY	info@borntoknit.co.uk	www.borntoknit.co.uk	07557 985935				
Wiltshire	Malmesbury	Fabric Shack	Unit 3, Park Road Centre	SN16 0BX	helen@fabricshack.co.uk	www.fabricshack.co.uk	01666 826841				
Wirral	Heswall	Love Stitch	242 Telegraph Rd	CH60 7SG	info@lovestitch.co.uk	www.lovestitch.co.uk	0151 345 6738				
Worcestershire	Broadway	Sew U Knit Crafts	2 Cotswold Court	WR12 7AA	sewuknitcrafts@outlook.com	www.sewuknitcrafts.co.uk	01386 853779				
Worcestershire	Droitwich	Emm's Haberdashery	6-8 High Street	WR9 8EW	sales@loveemms.com	www.loveemms.co.uk	1905778381				
Worcestershire	Worcester	House of Haby	Market Hall, The Shambles	WR1 2RA							
		A Bit Woolly				www.abitwoolly.co.uk					
		Art of Yarn			sales@artofyarn.co.uk	www.artofyarn.co.uk					
		Baa Baa Brighouse			info@baabaabrighouse.co.uk	www.baabaabrighouse.co.uk	01484 722662				
		FLAGSHIP Deramores [ROWAN]				www.deramores.com					
		Hobbycraft				www.hobbycraft.co.uk					
		Jannette's Rare Yarns			jannette@easynet.co.uk	www.jannettesrareyarns.co.uk					
		Knittiss Yarns			sales@knitbissyarns.co.uk	www.knitbissyarns.co.uk					
		Knit UK			knituk@live.co.uk	www.knituk.com					
		FLAGSHIP Laughing Hens [ROWAN]				www.laughinghens.com					
		FLAGSHIP Love Knitting [ROWAN]				www.loveknitting.com					
		Wise Badger Limited			customer.services@wisebadger.com	www.wisebadger.co.uk	01789 773021				
		Once A Sheep			info@onceasheep.co.uk	www.onceasheep.co.uk					
		Poppy's			admin@poppys-holmfirth.com	www.poppys-holmfirth.co.uk	07557 950935				
		Sew At Home			hello@sew-at-home.co.uk	www.sew-at-home.co.uk					
		SMD Knitting			info@knittingwool.com	www.knittingwool.com	0800 622 6225				
		Susie's Craft Basket			susan@artfuldodgers.co.uk	www.artfuldodgers.co.uk	0161 819 9933				
		Sweet Sheep Fine Yarns				www.sweetsheep.co.uk					
		FLAGSHIP Wool Warehouse Direct Ltd [ROWAN]			sales@woolwarehouse.co.uk	www.woolwarehouse.co.uk	**01926 882818**				

GALLERY

Our easy reference guide to the designs featured in this magazine.

. . . .

R O W A N

MODERN HERITAGE

| KIRKIN | AESTER | OWRE | YATLEN | RAKKI | WITTER | PENGA | TOORIE | MAREEL |

Summerlite 4ply & Kidsilk Haze
Sasha Kagan
Pattern 125
Main image 8, 9

Cotton Cashmere
ARNE & CARLOS
Pattern 140
Main image 10, 11

Summerlite DK
Vibe Ulrik
Pattern 139
Main image 12, 13

Kidsilk Haze
Grace Jones
Pattern 116
Main image 14, 15

Kidsilk Haze & Fine Lace
Martin Storey
Pattern 134
Main image 16, 17

Softyak DK
Martin Storey
Pattern 160
Main image 18, 19

Creative Linen
Emma Wright
Pattern 150
Main image 20, 21

Felted Tweed
Martin Storey
Pattern 154
Main image 23, 24, 25

Cotton Cashmere
Sarah Hatton
Pattern 130
Main image 26, 27

PLAIN & SIMPLE

| ELEMENTARY | ESSENTIAL | MINIMAL | RESTORE | RECLAIM | INTRINSIC | PURPOSE | REGAIN | VITAL |

Softyak DK
Martin Storey
Pattern 148
Main image 40, 41

Fine Lace
Lisa Richardson
Pattern 156
Main image 42, 43

Cotton Glacé
Martin Storey
Pattern 122
Main image 44, 45

Cotton Glacé & Kidsilk Haze
Lisa Richardson
Pattern 136
Main image 46, 47

Softyak DK
Martin Storey
Pattern 109
Main image 48, 49

Creative Linen
Lisa Richardson
Pattern 127
Main image 50, 51

Creative Linen
Lisa Richardson
Pattern 118
Main image 52, 53

Kidsilk Haze
Martin Storey
Pattern 161
Main image 54, 55

Fine Lace
Lisa Richardson
Pattern 110
Main image 56, 57

REFLECTIONS

| PIA | RIVERA | FRITZIA | TOREY | CORNELIA | DALI | DADA | KINETIC | PALOMA |

Cotton Cashmere
Martin Storey
Pattern 132
Main image 68, 69, 70

Cotton Cashmere
Quail Studio
Pattern 138
Main image 70, 71

Cotton Cashmere
Martin Storey
Pattern 143
Main image 72, 73

Cotton Cashmere & Kidsilk Haze
Martin Storey
Pattern 163
Main image 74, 75

Kidsilk Haze & Fine Lace
Martin Storey
Pattern 149
Main image 76

Cotton Cashmere
Lisa Richardson
Pattern 153
Main image 77

Cotton Cashmere & Kidsilk Haze
Lisa Richardson
Pattern 142
Main image 78, 79

Cotton Cashmere & Kidsilk Haze
Lisa Richardson
Pattern 126
Main image 79, 80

Fine Lace
Lisa Richardson
Pattern 108
Main image 80, 100, 101

| FONTANA | MONDRIAN | MUCHA | PICASSO | MARISOL | YOKO |

Cotton Cashmere
ARNE & CARLOS
Pattern 159
Main image 90, 91

Fine Lace
Annika Andrea Wolke
Pattern 119
Main image 92, 93

Cotton Cashmere
Galina Caroll
Pattern 115
Main image 94, 95

Cotton Cashmere
Lisa Richardson
Pattern 124
Main image 96

Cotton Cashmere
Lisa Richardson
Pattern 128
Main image 98, 99

Fine Lace
Sharon Miller
Pattern 113
Main image 102, 103